IELTS

PREPARATION AND PRACTICE

Reading & Writing
Academic

SECOND EDITION

BRIDGET AUCOIN | LOUISA CHAWHAN
STEPHANIE HIRAISHI | JANELLE THOLET

CONSULTING EDITOR: WENDY SAHANAYA

OXFORD

OXFORD
UNIVERSITY PRESS

Oxford University Press is a department of the University of Oxford.

It furthers the University's objective of excellence in research, scholarship, and education by publishing worldwide. Oxford is a registered trademark of Oxford University Press in the UK and in certain other countries.

Published in Australia by
Oxford University Press
253 Normanby Road, South Melbourne, Victoria 3205, Australia

© Bridget Aucoin, Louisa Chawhan, Stephanie Hiraishi, Janelle Tholet 2013

The moral rights of the authors have been asserted

First published 1998
Second edition 2013

National Library of Australia Cataloguing-in-Publication data

Aucoin, Bridget, author.
IELTS preparation and practice: reading & writing academic / Bridget Aucoin; Louisa Chawhan; Stephanie Hiraishi; Janelle Tholet; consulting editor: Wendy Sahanaya.

Second edition.

ISBN 978 0 19 552099 6

IELTS preparation and practice.

Includes bibliographical references.

English language—Examinations.
International English Language Testing System.
English language—Examinations, questions, etc.

Chawhan, Louisa, author.
Hiraishi, Stephanie, author.
Tholet, Janelle, author.
Sahanaya, Wendy, editor.

428

Consulting editor Wendy Sahanaya
Edited by Cathryn Game
Cover design by Sardine Design
Text design by Sardine Design
Illustrations by Kerry Cooke, eggplant communications
Typeset by diacriTech, Chennai, India
Printed in China by Golden Cup Printing Co. Ltd

CONTENTS

PART 3 ACADEMIC WRITING TASK 2   228

INTRODUCTION

How to use this book

There are three main parts to this book. The Academic Reading is Part 1 and the Academic Writing is divided into two sections: Part 2 for Task 1 and Part 3 for Task 2. The units and the activities have been numbered separately in each section. Answers for the activities and the practice tests are in the Answer Key at the end of the book.

Part 1: Academic Reading

Part 1 gives you:

- an overview of the test that describes the Academic Reading, the form of the instructions, and the question types. There is then a reading that contains examples of all the different question types found in the IELTS exam.
- a chapter on the skills you will need for success in the IELTS exam.
- the question types in detail. For each question type there is an *Explanation* at the beginning. The purpose of this explanation is to help you understand the purpose of the question type and the appropriate skill for answering the question. After the explanation, there is a *Guided Practice*. Here useful skills and strategies are explained in detail and there are activities for you to practise the skills. Then there is an *Exam-style Practice,* which provides a reading and questions for you to work through as you would for the actual IELTS exam. Follow the instructions for each activity and, when you have finished, check your answers in the Answer Key at the back of the book. Because working fast and efficiently is very important in tests, many exercises have a *Time Target*. The time target gives you a suggested time limit for the activity.
- four practice reading tests and a reading answer sheet, which you may copy.

Parts 2 and 3: Academic Writing

Part 2

- gives you an overview of Task 1.
- takes you through each of the features the examiner uses to mark Task 1: Task achievement, Coherence and cohesion, Lexical resource, and Grammatical range and accuracy. Here useful skills and language will be explained in detail and there are activities for you to practise the skills and the language.
- There are then some Task 1 questions with candidate answers and analysis of those answers. There are also several Task 1 questions for you to practise on.

Part 3

- gives you an overview of Task 2.
- takes you through the process of analysing the task question in order to plan your essay. Useful skills and language for writing an effective Task 2 response will be explained in detail and there are activities for you to practise the skills and the language.
- There are then some Task 2 questions for you to practise writing before you look at the sample answers given in the Appendix.

There are editing checklists for Tasks 1 and 2 that you can copy and use to assess your own writing.

You can do the sections in any sequence you wish, but you will gain most benefit by working through the units before you do any practice tests.

PART 1

ACADEMIC READING

UNIT 1

About the Academic Reading Test

The Reading module consists of three passages with a total of 2150–2750 words to read and a total of 40 questions to answer. You are given 60 minutes to finish the entire module.

Reading (Academic) Test Format

Reading Passage 1:
700–1000-word text
Questions 1–13 (usually)

Reading Passage 2:
700–1000-word text
Questions 14–26 (usually)

Reading Passage 3:
700–1000-word text
Questions 27–40 (usually)

Total time: 60 mins

> **TIP** Remember to write your answers directly onto the answer sheet. No extra time is given to transfer your answers.

The reading passages are on topics of general interest and are taken from books, journals, magazines and newspapers. The content in these passages is appropriate for any undergraduate-level candidate. The passages may be written in narrative, descriptive, discursive or argumentative style and may include a diagram, graph or illustration. The passages tend to increase in difficulty from the first to the last.

> **TIP** Aim to do the first passage as quickly as you can (within 15 minutes or so) so that you have plenty of time left for the second and third passages, which are usually more difficult.

Questions in the IELTS Academic Reading module test different reading abilities and skills. Therefore, they are designed differently and need to be answered in different ways. In the following pages you will learn what these question types are, what skills they aim to assess, and what strategies you can use to answer them with confidence and accuracy.

Activity 1.1: Types of questions

Look at some question types, listed on the left, and think of what each type of question expects you to do to answer it.

Multiple-choice questions	e.g. choose one item as my answer out of the given four or five options
Matching questions	1 _____
Identifying information questions	2 _____
Completion questions	3 _____
Short answer questions	4 _____

Answers to this exercise will vary so you should discuss them with a friend or teacher.

Once you have done Activity 1.2 below, you will be able to check whether you correctly identified the necessary skills. Using the above five basic question types in different ways, IELTS assesses your different reading skills and abilities.

TIP In the IELTS Academic Reading module, each correct answer is worth one mark. Also, a correct answer must have correct spelling and be within the prescribed word limit.

Activity 1.2: Introductory reading

The following reading contains examples of the different question types found in the IELTS exam. Once you have answered the questions, check your answers in the Answer Key in Appendix 1 at the back of the book.

More Water for Western Australia

Industry, Science and Innovation Division of the Western Australian Government Department of Commerce

A

Supplying quality water for a healthy life and a strong community is a major concern for Australia. A lack of rain, warmer conditions, population, agriculture and industry growth put strain on our existing and traditional supplies, especially in Western Australia.

Fortunately, innovative Western Australians manage this global quality water challenge by encouraging open dialogue and undertaking meaningful research to develop infrastructure and technology.

Desalination is just one of the solutions, and in 2006 Western Australia led the way in delivering more water into Perth's public supply system with the opening of Australia's first large-scale seawater desalination plant in Kwinana.

The Perth Seawater Desalination Plant is the Water Corporation's biggest single water source, providing some 17 per cent of Perth's water needs. The state's second plant in the Shire of Harvey is being constructed.

The National Centre of Excellence in Desalination (NCED) at Murdoch University leads and coordinates Australian research into desalination technology. Through the NCED, Australia is building national capacity and capabilities in desalination with a dual focus on breakthrough fundamental and applied research, with a goal to deliver meaningful improvements at a commercial scale.

NCED is currently partnering a project to develop a suitable and sustainable desalination system for providing drinking water in remote areas.

B

A need to supply more freshwater to the remote Tjuntjunjarra community prompted the research by Academic Chair of Energy Studies at Murdoch University Dr Trevor Pryor.

Located 800 kilometres north-east of Kalgoorlie with a population of 120, the community requires more freshwater of a better quality than can be supplied by the current source.

C

An innovative technology by Singapore company memsys clearwater, the thermal vacuum-multi-effect-membrane-distillation (V-MEMD) desalination system, will make the water suitable for use.

V-MEMD combines thermal and membrane technologies, working in a vacuum so that the water boils at much lower temperatures of 50 to 80 degrees Celsius instead of the usual 100 degrees Celsius.

memsys Managing Director Götz Lange said the company had the first small-scale modular thermal separation process.

'We didn't change the thermal technology itself – you can't change physics – we are just the first to put this advanced technology of thermal separation in a very tiny, cheap and reliable modular concept,' he said.

D

However, the next challenge is finding a power source for the system in such a remote area. Dr Pryor and his team aim to overcome the problem of the intermittency of renewable energy resources by developing a cost-effective hybrid solar/waste thermal system.

Dr Trevor Pryor said the 2-year project would explore the use of solar thermal and waste heat to power the V-MEMD.

'This project aims to extract groundwater to supply the Indigenous community's needs through chemical free, sustainable and energy efficient pre-treatment that has been customised to the Tjuntjunjarra water resource,' Dr Pryor said.

The project partners are Murdoch University, University of Technology Sydney, WA Department of Housing, Parsons Brinkerhoff, memsys clearwater, the Institute of Filtration and Techniques of Separation in France, and the Singapore Membrane Technology Centre.

The Department of Commerce provided the National Centre of Excellence in Desalination $3 million to help design, establish and operate a range of testing facilities.

QUESTIONS 1–4

Complete the summary below by choosing the correct word from the box to complete each gap. There are more words than you need.

activities	problems	freshwater	achieve	process	desalination
population	combat	pressure	seawater	agriculture	

Water supplies in Western Australia are under **1** ___Pressure___ as

a result of climate conditions and human **2** ___activities___. One of the

ways to **3** ___combat___ this problem is through the processing of

4 ___desalinatin___ to make it less salty.

QUESTIONS 5–7

Do the following statements reflect the information in the text?
Write:
TRUE *if the statement is true*
FALSE *if the statement is false*
NOT GIVEN *if the statement is not in the text*

5.   The amount of rain Western Australia receives has decreased.

6.   The Kwinana desalination plant does not provide the majority of Perth's water.

7.   The Tjuntjunjarra community currently has no source of fresh water.

QUESTIONS 8–11

*From the following list of headings choose the most suitable heading for sections **A–D**.*
There is one more heading than you need.

HEADINGS

i.   Using existing technology in a new way

ii.   The project

iii.   Getting it off the ground

iv.   Why desalination?

v.   Dealing with Western Australia's conditions

8.   Section **A**

9.   Section **B**

10. Section **C**

11. Section **D**

QUESTIONS 12–13

*Using **NO MORE THAN THREE WORDS** from the reading passage, answer the following questions.*

12. Where is the second desalination plant being built?

13. What do Dr Trevor Pryor and his team plan to extract and treat?

QUESTIONS 14–15

*Complete the sentences below using **NO MORE THAN TWO WORDS** from the reading passage.*

14. The V-MEMD is expected to be powered by a combination of energy from the

     sun and _____.

15. Because the V-MEMD uses a vacuum, water can be boiled at _____.

[continued from previous page]

QUESTION 16

*Choose the appropriate option **A–D** to answer question 16.*

16. What problem associated with renewable energy resources is mentioned in the text?

    a They are too expensive.   **b** They are unproven.

    c They provide power irregularly.   **d** People mistrust them.

QUESTIONS 17–18

Match each person to the information given about them in the text.

GL Götz Lange

TP Trevor Pryor

17. has made existing technology less expensive

18. works at Murdoch University

When you have finished, check your answers in the Answer Key in Appendix 1.

So, how did you do?

It's a good idea to keep a record of your score each time you do a practice reading. It's also a good idea to be strict with yourself about timing. From now on, each reading practice will have a suggested time limit, which you should try to follow.

In the real exam, your score out of 40 will be converted into a band score out of 9. It is impossible to predict how your score will translate into a band score, but to do well in the IELTS test you should be achieving results of at least 65–70 per cent. You may need even higher than this for some university courses.

As well as doing the practice exercises in this book, you should try to read as much as possible. Read in English every day, even if it's only for 10 or 15 minutes. You don't always have to read IELTS-style materials; anything that you read (magazines, newspapers, novels, even comics) will improve your skills and vocabulary. Remember: your brain is a muscle that needs training like any other muscle in your body.

If you would like more information on the reading module, you can visit www.ielts.org.

UNIT 2

The Skills You Need

Scanning

You cannot sit down and read the IELTS test the way you would read a book at home. You have to use a variety of reading skills. The first of these is **scanning**. When you scan, you look for names, numbers or other specific information. Think about the way you usually read a phone book, a timetable, or a price list: when you do this, you are scanning!

Activity 2.1: Scanning

Here is a newspaper article and some questions testing specific details such as names and percentages. Although the article is quite long (almost 1000 words), you should be able to find the information quickly by **scanning** for the specific information only.

The answers to this and all other practice activities can be found in Appendix 1.
Suggested time: as quickly as possible (no more than 5 minutes)

NAMES (of people, places or organisations):

1. Who is the director of CSIRO's Climate Adaptation National Research Flagship?

2. Who is the director of World Wildlife Fund WA?

3. Who is the manager of the Department of Environment and Conservation's biodiversity and climate change unit?

4. Who is the Department of Health's director of Environmental Health?

5. What organisation is David Ness from?

NUMBERS (includes dates and percentages):

1. How much are temperatures in Australia projected to rise by 2030?

2. How much are temperatures in Australia projected to rise by 2070?

3. How many endangered cockatoos died in a heatwave last year?

[continued from previous page]

4.   When are mainland quokkas expected to run out of room?

5.   How many days above 35°C does Western Australia now have annually?

6.   How many are expected by 2070?

7.   How much could wheat production decline by 2030?

8.   How much could it decline by 2050?

How a 2°C rise will change the face of WA

Katherine Fleming

Two degrees. It doesn't sound like much but if – or, as some scientists say, when – WA gets that much warmer it will look different. If temperatures rise and the South West continues to dry, farming belts will likely move south, forests will struggle, some animals will be pushed towards extinction and the weather in Perth and Bunbury could be more like Geraldton's. Temperatures are projected to rise in Australia 0.6–1.5°C by 2030 and 2.2–5°C by 2070 if greenhouse gas emissions continue to grow. But regardless of our actions, a 2°C warming in the long term was already 'locked in', Andrew Ash, director of CSIRO's Climate Adaptation National Research Flagship, said. The United Nations' Inter-governmental Panel on Climate Change's predictions for Australia include more frequent and intense heatwaves and fires, as well as floods, landslides, droughts and storm surges, as well as less snow and frost.

Biodiversity

The triangular area between Shark Bay and Esperance is Australia's only global biodiversity 'hot spot'. It was also 'one of the canaries in the coalmine for climate change', World Wildlife Fund WA director Paul Gamblin said. The IPCC noted: 'Many narrow-ranged endemic species will be vulnerable to extinction with relatively small warning.' A heatwave last year resulted in the mass death of more than 100 endangered Carnaby's cockatoos near Hopetoun. Modelling showed mainland quokkas, which prefer cool, wet conditions, would attempt to move south but run out of room by 2070, under the most extreme temperature scenario. Some species would benefit and others would adapt, Colin Yates, manager of the Department of Environment and Conservation's biodiversity and climate change unit, said. But others could die out and habitat destruction would make it difficult for those that needed to migrate. WA's iconic forests were also vulnerable, Dr Yates said. 'We don't know how quickly those might become under threat,' he said. Marine ecosystems were at imminent risk of the worst spate of extinctions in millions of years from threats including climate change and overfishing, the International Programme on the State of the Ocean reported.

Health

As well as direct physical injuries and fatalities from extreme weather events, hotter and drier conditions could have potentially 'catastrophic consequences' for melanoma rates as people spend more time outdoors, a Department of Health report on global warming says. Scientists say global warming would be felt through an increase in hot days, with days above 35°C projected to increase from 28 to 67 by 2070, if emissions aren't reduced. The most vulnerable to health problems from climate change, including heat-related deaths, include the elderly and young, the disabled, homeless or sick. Jim Dodds, the department's director of environmental health, said it had focused on extreme weather events but was increasingly looking at air quality, including more potential for smog and bushfires. A jump in mosquito numbers after high tides in Peel this year gave a glimpse of potential conditions with higher sea levels. 'Climate change will give us sea level rises and areas will be inundated and some of those will be closer to existing populations than they currently are,' he said. Mr Dodds said water availability and quality were also likely to be a major concern, including use of recycled water and more chance of contamination in stagnant pools or warmer water.

Agriculture

Farming belts in the South West may shift south-west by 30–50 km by 2030 under the worst-case scenarios, according to the Department of Agriculture. While higher carbon dioxide levels could fuel more crop and pasture growth, those benefits would reduce as temperatures continued to rise. Wheat production could decline by 8 per cent by 2030 and 12 per cent by 2050, with similar declines in sheep meat. The department predicted the area where farmers could grow grain crops would contract and there would be fewer sheep in the Wheatbelt. The challenge of more fly strikes and lice and the need to cart and store water would make farming more difficult. In the Kimberley, farmers may need to consider moving into other industries, such as ecotourism and biofuel trees. Dr Ash said there were also opportunities. In the traditionally wet southern part of WA, less rainfall might open up more areas to cropping. About half of the 15 per cent drop in rainfall in the South West since the 1970s has been attributed to climate change.

Planning

Under a 1.1 m sea level rise, between 20,000 and 30,000 WA homes would be at risk of inundation, according to the Federal Department of Climate Change and Energy Efficiency. It would also threaten roads and railways. The Climate Commission recently reported seas were rising more quickly off WA than elsewhere in Australia and a national rise of 0.5–1 m was plausible by 2100. Higher sea levels and storm surges would become a major planning issue, Dr Ash said. 'The immediate prognosis is not too bad but we need to plan in order to not put people in harm's way,' he said. 'Roads or bridges or dams we want to last for 100 years need to be built for tomorrow's climate.' The Town of Cottesloe gave the go-ahead for development of a 100-year plan for the beachfront. The City of South Perth is investigating future flood-prone areas and planning to raise river walls. David Ness, from the National Climate Change Adaptation Research Facility, examined planning for Bunbury, using Geraldton's weather as a guide.

Skimming

The next skill is **skimming**. When you skim, you read quickly to get the main idea. You DON'T read every word. You might read any headings or subheadings, the first sentence, the last sentence and a few key words and phrases. Here's an example of a paragraph:

Art education fluctuates in popularity and presently seems to have sunk into an all-time low, with large numbers of art teachers retraining in other directions or joining Centrelink queues. Many parents believe that art education is a waste of time, and with the problems of unemployment faced by those with Visual Arts degrees, this view is reinforced. In times of economic stability, schools are typically expected to develop individuals and prepare them for life, as intelligent, well-adjusted and thinking people. However, at times of economic stress, education is suddenly expected to change to job preparation. As there's little money to be gained by studying art, many people reason, there is no point in doing it. What is more, those students who wish to continue to university will find themselves severely handicapped if they choose to do TEE Art, as their examination results will automatically be scaled down, resulting in lower aggregates than those of students studying mathematics and sciences. Where university entry levels are important, this becomes a major factor in steering students away from art.

Here's what you might read of the paragraph if you were skimming:

Art education fluctuates in popularity and seems to have reached an all-time low, with large numbers of art teachers retraining in other directions or joining Centrelink queues. Many parents believe … waste of time … times of economic stress … job preparation …
… students … severely handicapped if they choose to do TEE Art …
… results … scaled down … Where university entry levels are important, this becomes a major factor in steering students away from art.

Were you still able to get the main idea? You should have been able to, and by reading 69 words instead of nearly 200, you save yourself time.

Activity 2.2: Skimming

Here are a number of extracts from texts that you will see in full in later chapters. For each, answer the questions by **skimming**. Don't worry about details, and ignore any unfamiliar vocabulary.
    Suggested time: 1 minute per extract

Extract 1

A solution to prevent potential induced degradation, a recently discovered new trend in high voltage solar systems throughout the world, has been researched by SOLON SE's Dr Lars Podlowski and Daniel Hundmaier. In photovoltaic (PV) modules, an initial drop in efficiency is a well-known phenomenon. Known as light induced degradation, it has long been included in the performance guarantees offered by producers in the industry or the calculations of project developers and plant operators. Light induced degradation can cause an approximate 2 per cent decrease in system performance in the first few hours of operation of any new PV installation.

What is the topic of the paragraph?

a   photography

b   solar energy

c   house plants

What is the purpose of the paragraph?

a   to explain a problem

b   to describe a person

c   to give an opinion

Extract 2

Facebook will allow users to block all third parties from accessing their information without their explicit permission. It will also make less information available in its user directory and reduce the number of settings required to make all information private from nearly 50 to less than 15. The back tracking by Internet companies on how they use our private data has demonstrated that they cannot take our trust for granted. If social networking becomes increasingly important to companies such as Google, Apple and Microsoft, they will have to be careful not to violate their users' trust in the future.

What is the topic of this paragraph?

a   The Internet and children

b   The Internet and communication

c   The Internet and privacy

What is the purpose of the paragraph?

a   to give instructions

b   to explain a problem

c   to give an opinion

Extract 3

One of the world's biggest brands has made a lot of money out of youthful rebellion – or, in many cases, nostalgia for it. 'Who doesn't have a little something to rebel against in their life?' Harley-Davidson's global chief marketing officer, Mark Hans-Richer, says about the raw attraction of the big, high-powered

[continued from previous page]

motorcycles. Blame Peter Fonda and the late Dennis Hopper in the 1969 classic film *Easy Rider* for producing instant, iconic images of freedom, rebellion and the desire to push back.

Where would you expect to see this paragraph?

a   in a magazine about business

b   in a magazine about science

c   in a magazine about fashion

Which of these is the paragraph focused on?

a   what people buy

b   where people buy

c   why people buy

TIP   It is unlikely that you will be able to answer questions in the IELTS exam by **just** skimming or scanning. Instead, you should work on combining these skills with reading carefully and critically where necessary.

Vocabulary in context

The next important skill that you need for the IELTS exam is understanding **vocabulary through context**. In the exam you are not allowed to use your dictionary, so when there are words you don't know you either have to ignore them or try to understand their meaning in context. Do you know the meaning of the word below?

affluent

By itself it's hard to guess. Here is the word in a sentence:

Australia is an affluent nation.

Now you know that *affluent* is an adjective that can be used to describe a country, but the precise meaning is still unclear. Here is another sentence providing more context for the word:

Affluent countries like Australia and Canada have a responsibility to help poorer countries.

From this you can guess that *affluent* has a similar meaning to *wealthy*.

Activity 2.3: Understanding vocabulary through context

Look at the word in *italics* in each of the following sentences and decide the part of speech of the word (noun, verb, etc.) and its approximate meaning.

A. *eminent*

She is an *eminent* psychologist who has won a number of awards.

Part of speech: _____

Approximate meaning: _____

B. *exacerbate*

Climate change is likely to *exacerbate* existing flood problems in India and Bangladesh.

Part of speech: _____

Approximate meaning: _____

C. *nocturnal*

Nocturnal animals usually have eyes that are adapted to seeing in the dark.

Part of speech: _____

Approximate meaning: _____

D. *aroma*

Many people think that the *aroma* of coffee is better than the taste.

Part of speech: _____

Approximate meaning: _____

E. *jeopardy*

Hundreds of jobs will be in *jeopardy* if the factory closes.

Part of speech: _____

Approximate meaning: _____

F. *revere*

Many traditional cultures *revere* the elderly for their wisdom and experience.

Part of speech: _____

Approximate meaning: _____

When you have finished, check your answers in the Answer Key in Appendix 1.

The skills you have looked at in this chapter can be used in all IELTS questions. In the next chapters, you will look at specific question types used in the IELTS and how to answer each one.

UNIT 3

Multiple-choice Questions

This unit and the following units deal with the different question types in IELTS.

What do they test?

These questions test your ability to recognise specific points in a passage or to distinguish between what the passage says and what it does not say. In other words, you demonstrate your reading comprehension by indicating what, according to the passage, is correct.

These questions may also test your ability to identify the main idea of a section of a passage or an overall understanding of the entire reading passage.

What do you need to do?

- Note the instructions given with the multiple-choice question, quickly.
- Skim-read the passage to get a general idea of the passage.
- Then read one question at a time and underline the key word(s) in it.
- If you can, guess which part or paragraph in the passage would have the answer.
- Then read all the given answer options carefully and note in what respect they are different. (That should give you a clue as to what type of answer is expected and will make it easier to locate the correct answer in the passage.)
- Choose the correct answer and write the letter A, B, C, or D indicating that option on the Answer Sheet.

> **TIPS** Multiple-choice questions appear in the same order as the information is presented in the text.
>
> Write only one letter in each box on the answer sheet.

Activity 3.1: Guided practice

Read the paragraph below and work out what the main idea is. You may choose one option out of the four given.

> Too much or too little water can have devastating consequences. When rivers burst their banks, or a tsunami hits, the resulting floods can sweep away buildings, crops, cattle, and people. At the other extreme, a temporary shortage of water can kill crops and cattle. During droughts in poorer countries, people die from lack of food and clean water. The extent to which people are affected by flood or drought depends on local climate and the resources available to combat the effects.

The passage is about

A   natural disasters.

B   floods and droughts.

C   how floods and droughts affect life on earth.

D   how flood or drought depends on local climate and resources.

You should have chosen option **C**. Options **A** and **B** are too general, while option **D** is only a detail, not the main idea.

Now, here's a different type of question. Read the next passage and decide which option is **NOT** correct.

> On a hot summer day or a wet winter night, when there are high winds or snow storms, it is always the relationship between air, water, and heat that is responsible for those weather conditions. Ever-changing quantities of these three elements produce a wide variety of weather systems experienced around the world. Our weather occurs in the lowest part of the atmosphere, which extends about 12 km above Earth.
>
> The pattern of weather in a particular area over many years is referred to as 'climate'. At the Equator, the weather is always warm and often wet. Near the poles, conditions are cold and often dry. In between, weather conditions vary.

According to this passage, which of these statements is **NOT** true about weather?

A   It varies considerably depending on area. ✓

B   It depends on the relationship between air, water and temperature. ✓

C   It occurs in the lowest part of the atmosphere.

D   It remains the same in a particular area over several years.

You should have chosen option **D**. All of the other options are true according to the text.

[continued from previous page]

Here is a longer passage. Quickly **skim** the passage to get the main idea.

1. Buses spew clouds of black exhaust fumes in Mexico City while, in India, wood burnt in rudimentary stoves fills houses with sooty smoke. Methane leaks from gas pipelines in Russia and rice paddies in China, eventually breaking down in sunlight and contributing to the production of smog and ozone. In each of these cases, simple steps to curb air pollution would promote public health; scaled up, they may offer the only realistic way to tame global warming over the next few decades.

2. Rapid measures to reduce emissions of black carbon, which soaks up solar energy, and methane, a greenhouse gas that is 25 times more potent than carbon dioxide, could cut the rate of global warming in half between now and 2050, according to an analysis published last week. Such numbers have spurred political interest, and next month a small coalition of countries is aiming to launch an initiative that would target these 'short-lived climate forcers'. If successful, the effort could have an immediate impact on global temperatures while countries grapple with efforts to regulate emissions of carbon dioxide, the most important greenhouse gas.

3. 'We're in a gridlock over carbon dioxide, and we're losing time,' says Veerabhadran Ramanathan, an atmospheric scientist at the Scripps Institution of Oceanography in La Jolla, California, and a co-author of the *Science* analysis. 'This is one way to buy back some of that time, and the co-benefits are huge.' By 2030, these reduction measures could prevent anywhere from 700,000 to 4.7 million premature deaths from air pollution annually, the study found. And because ozone is toxic to plants, such measures could boost global crop production by 1–4%.

4. The United Nations Environment Programme explored the potential gains in a detailed assessment last June. Chaired by Drew Shindell of the NASA Goddard Institute for Space Studies in New York, the assessment ranked hundreds of options for reducing black carbon and ozone pollution according to their potential to reduce warming. A follow-up report, released in November and funded by the Swedish government, further analyzed opportunities and impacts at national and regional levels. This work served as the basis for the *Science* study.

5. For methane, the study identified 14 control measures that would target leakage from coal mining and oil and gas operations, emissions from landfills, wastewater systems, livestock manure and rice paddies. Black-carbon reduction would focus on cleaning up diesel vehicle emissions, biomass stoves, brick kilns and coke ovens. Other measures would reduce the burning of agricultural waste and provide alternatives to wood, dung and charcoal for cooking and heating in poor countries.

6. It could take decades to slow global warming through reductions in carbon dioxide emissions, whereas cutting soot and methane would have immediate climate payoffs because they are quickly purged from the atmosphere.

Jeff Tolleson

Now try to match each of the following questions with the paragraph on which it is based. You may write that question on the blank line below that paragraph.

1. Which gas affects the growth of plants? (paragraph ...)

2. What human activities contribute to global warming? (paragraph ...)

3. In what ways can the amount of methane being released into the atmosphere be reduced? (paragraph ...)

4. What three substances lead to global warming? (paragraph ...)

Try to think of your own answers to the questions. Then look at the multiple-choice questions below and choose one correct option for each.

5. According to the text, what can help slow down global warming?
    A promoting public health
    B not using stoves
    C reducing air pollution
    D not using buses

6. Which of these is not mentioned as a contributing factor to global warming?
    A carbon dioxide
    B oxygen
    C black carbon
    D methane

[continued from previous page]

7. According to the text, which of these affects the growth of plants?

    A ozone

    B oxygen

    C carbon

    D carbon dioxide

8. Which of these is said to produce and release methane into the atmosphere?

    A vehicles running on diesel

    B faulty wastewater systems

    C burning wood fires

    D heating in poor countries

Activity 3.2: Exam-style practice

In this activity, you will just be given the passage and the questions, as you would in the exam. When you've finished, check your answers in the Answer Key in Appendix 1.

    Suggested time: 10 minutes

Black Gold for Green Cars

The next generation of electric-car batteries may thrive on a liquid that looks like crude oil.

Ferris Jabr

The tiny glass bottle in my hand is filled with what looks like crude oil, but it's actually oil's nemesis. If it works, this black sludge will transform the rechargeable battery, doubling the range of electric cars and making petroleum obsolete.

    Today's electric cars are handicapped by batteries that are heavy, expensive and a waste of space. Two-thirds of the volume of the battery in Nissan's Leaf electric car, for example, consists of materials that provide structural support but generate no power. And those materials cost more than the electrically active components.

    One way to vastly improve rechargeable batteries is to put more of that deadweight to work. That's the purpose of the secret sauce in the bottle, nicknamed 'Cambridge Crude' by Yet-Ming Chiang and his colleagues at the Massachusetts Institute of Technology, who developed it.

    In a standard battery, ions from one solid electrode travel to the other through a liquid or powder electrolyte. This in turn forces electrons to flow in an external wire linking the electrodes, causing a current. In Chiang's battery, the electrodes take the form of tiny particles of a lithium compound mixed with a liquid electrolyte to make slurry. The battery uses two streams of slurry, one positively charged and one negatively charged. Both are pumped across aluminium and copper current collectors with a permeable membrane in between. As they flow the streams exchange lithium ions across the membrane, causing a current to flow externally. To recharge the battery, you apply a voltage to push the ions back across the membrane.

The MIT creation is a type of flow battery, which normally has a liquid electrolyte that moves past stationary electrodes. Chiang reckons that the power per unit delivered by his lithium 'semi-solid' flow battery will be ten times that of conventional designs.

'This is probably the most exciting development in electrical energy storage in the last couple of years,' says Yuri Gogotsi of Drexel Nanotechnology Institute in Philadelphia, Pennsylvania. 'Chiang offers a unique hybrid between a flow battery and a lithium-ion battery.'

Drivers could have three ways of recharging the semi-solid flow battery. They could pump out spent slurry and pump in fresh; head to a recharge station where tanks of spent slurry would be replaced with fresh ones; or recharge the slurries with an electrical current. In the first two cases, regaining full power should only take a matter of minutes.

Rechargeable batteries are the heaviest and most expensive components of electric cars by a large margin. Chiang estimates that the cost of manufacturing his team's battery will be $250 per kilowatt-hour of generating capacity. So if one were built to replace the 24-kilowatt battery in the Nissan Leaf, it would cost $6000. This is about one-third the cost of existing batteries, and just low enough to compete with gasoline. Chiang also calculates that Cambridge Crude would let a car travel at least 300 kilometres on a single charge, double what is possible with today's batteries.

'This is an especially beautiful technology,' says Dan Steingart, of the City University of New York Energy Institute, because you can recharge the spent slurry. But he adds that even if the team manages to create a prototype car battery within five years, building the recharge stations to support it would take much longer.

Last year Chiang, his colleague Craig Carter and entrepreneur Throop Wilder founded a company called 24M Technologies to develop the battery. They have raised $16 million in funding so far, and plan to have a compact prototype ready in 2013.

---

*Choose the appropriate letters **A**, **B**, **C** or **D** to answer questions 1–6.*

1. This passage is about Yet-Ming Chiang's work on

    A developing a new car.

    B developing a new car that works on a battery.

    C developing a new car battery that is rechargeable.

    D developing a new rechargeable car battery that uses a new fuel.

[continued from previous page]

2. What is not true about the batteries in today's electric cars?

   A They are difficult to recharge.

   B They are too expensive.

   C They take up a great deal of space.

   D They are much heavier than a standard battery.

3. Chiang's battery

   A combines elements of lithium battery and flow battery.

   B moves ions through a powder electrolyte.

   C will allow cars to travel ten times as far on a single charge.

   D can be produced for $250.

4. 'Cambridge Crude'

   A could never replace petroleum.

   B has taken five years to develop.

   C is similar to crude oil in appearance.

   D will be cheaper than gasoline.

5. Drivers who want to recharge their batteries

   A will usually be able to do so within minutes.

   B will need an electric current.

   C must replace the slurry.

   D can go to their local gas station.

6. A prototype of the battery

   A requires a great deal more funding.

   B had been built at the time of writing.

   C could be available to buy by 2013.

   D will be developed before recharge stations are built.

When you have finished, check your answers in the Answer Key in Appendix 1.

UNIT 4

True/False/Not Given Questions

12:15

What do they test?

In this kind of question you are asked to identify factual information in the text. You are given a list of statements, and you must decide whether they match the information in the text (**TRUE**), contradict the information in the text (**FALSE**), or there is no information in the text (**NOT GIVEN**).

What do you need to do?

- Read each statement carefully, paying special attention to any qualifying words.
- Identify key words from the sentence and **scan** the text to find those words or synonyms.
- If you can find information in the text, decide whether it matches or contradicts the statement.
- If you cannot find the information in the text, choose the option of **NOT GIVEN**.

> **TIPS** Qualifying words include adverbs such as 'always', 'usually' and 'never', and quantifiers such as 'all', 'most' and 'none of'. They can change the meaning of a statement significantly.
>
> You can only use information **from the text** to choose your answer, not your own outside knowledge.

Activity 4.1: Guided practice

Here are some statements that relate to the text below. Before deciding whether each statement is true, false or not given, read and answer the 'clue' questions. These will help you to choose the correct answer. You can check your answers in the Answer Key in Appendix 1.

1. Turtles have existed since the prehistoric era.
   According to the text, when did turtles appear? Does this have the same meaning as 'the prehistoric era'?

[continued from previous page]

2.   Australia's land tortoises are unique.
     Which kind of turtles 'appear nowhere else'? What does the text say about land
     tortoises?

3.   The western swamp turtle is on the brink of extinction.
     What is the status of the western swamp turtle? Does this mean it is very close to
     extinction?

4.   Eastern long-necked turtles are often hit by cars when they are searching for food.
     Is there a synonym for 'cars' in the text? Are eastern long-necked turtles hit by
     cars? What are they looking for when they are hit?

5.   Because they spend their time under water, it is impossible to monitor freshwater
     turtles.
     Where do freshwater turtles 'spend most of their time'? Is it difficult to monitor
     freshwater turtles? Is it impossible?

6.   Turtles in Australia are producing fewer hatchlings.
     How many eggs do turtles lay? Has this number changed?

7.   Predators who eat turtle eggs pose the greatest threat to turtle populations.
     Do predators eat a lot of turtle eggs? Is this a big problem for turtles?

8.   The population of eastern long-necked turtles is now smaller than that of Murray
     turtles.
     Do we know the number of eastern long-necked turtles? Do we know the number of
     Murray turtles? Can we compare them?

Turtles in Trouble

Bruce Chessman

Imagine a world without turtles and tortoises. Unfortunately, many of the world's turtle and
tortoise species are at risk of extinction within a few decades, as more of their habitats are
lost or degraded and they are killed for their meat or shells, or their eggs are dug up and
eaten. Australia's turtles, though better protected than those in many countries, are not free
from hazards – in fact, the signs are that introduced predators, drought and the new threat of
climate change add up to an uncertain future for our unique turtle species.

Turtles and tortoises are great survivors. They first appear in the fossil record some
220 million years ago, about the same time as the first dinosaurs. But today, turtles rank among
the most endangered of animals, with nearly half of the world's species now regarded as
threatened, largely by excessive harvesting and habitat loss or degradation.

Australia lacks the land tortoises found on most other continents, but has a rich variety of marine and freshwater turtles. Most of Australia's freshwater turtles occur nowhere else in the world, and those few that extend beyond our borders range only as far as Papua New Guinea and eastern Indonesia. Our 24 or so freshwater species include the critically endangered western swamp turtle, which is restricted to a few wetlands near Perth. We also have much more widespread and abundant species like the eastern long-necked turtle, a frequent victim of motor vehicles when it crosses roads after rain in pursuit of new habitat.

We have little idea of their conservation status or population trends of many of our turtle species. Spending most of their time on the bottom of rivers and lakes, freshwater turtles are usually out of the public eye, and they are rarely included in long-term monitoring programs. There are, however, good reasons for concern about the future of our freshwater turtles. Research has shown that most turtle eggs, which nesting females bury in shallow sand or soil, are dug out and eaten by predators – mainly introduced species, such as foxes and feral pigs. Still, adult turtles can live for decades and lay hundreds of eggs in a lifetime, so even if only a few eggs survive, the resulting hatchlings may be enough to sustain turtle populations.

But if hatchlings, juvenile turtles and adults also suffer a heavy mortality, turtle populations may slowly wither away. And turtles are assailed by many hazards in today's Australia. In addition to road kills, turtles are drowned in fishing nets and struck by boats. They are eaten by dogs, cats, foxes, pigs and some native animals. During the recent 'millennium drought' in south-eastern Australia, some dry lake beds were littered with the remains of dead turtles. And in the lakes at the mouth of the Murray River in South Australia, where salinity rose during the drought, many turtles perished after becoming weighed down by massive growths of estuarine tubeworms on their shells.

In the last few years I have been revisiting turtle populations on the Murray River near Yarrawonga that I first studied as a PhD student in the 1970s. Changes in catch rates suggest that one of the three species inhabiting this area, the eastern long-necked turtle, has declined in abundance by about 90 per cent over the past 30 years. The Murray turtle appears to have declined by about 70 per cent. The broad-shelled turtle does not seem to have become less abundant, but was scarce in the 1970s and remains so today.

The population structures of the first two species – the eastern long-necked and the Murray turtles – have also changed. They are now dominated by older turtles, with a small proportion of juveniles. Such population structures are also seen elsewhere, suggesting that population ageing may be widespread. Turtles are an integral part of our natural heritage and widely recognised in Indigenous culture. Only through a sound understanding of their population trends and the threats that they face, gained through adequate monitoring and research, can we plan effective conservation actions to ensure their future.

Activity 4.2: Exam-style practice

This time you will be given only the statements and the text, the way you would be in the exam. Try to ask yourself the same kinds of questions as in Activity 4.1.

Suggested time: 12 minutes

Do the following statements agree with the information given in the reading passage?
Write:

TRUE *if the statement agrees with the information*
FALSE *if the statement contradicts the information*
NOT GIVEN *if there is no information on this.*

1. Cape Breton Island is in Quebec.

2. All of the Magdalen Islands are connected by Route 199.

3. Sea ice helps to protect the islands from storms.

4. Researchers began to notice the sea ice decreasing in the 1990s.

5. Before 1990, the ferry to the Magdalen Islands operated only for half the year.

6. As water freezes, it causes sandstone to break apart.

7. Each island loses 10–110 centimetres of coast per year.

8. A number of homes were swept away by storms the previous year.

Islands in the Storm

Nick Walker

Québec's Îles-de-la-Madeleine (Magdalen Islands) lie in the heart of the Gulf of St Lawrence, about 90 kilometres north-west of Cape Breton Island. Twelve islands make up the small, sandy archipelago, the six largest connected by many kilometres of thin sand dunes, across which runs Route 199. Open sea and salty lagoons stretch out on both sides of the scenic thoroughfare. In recent years, the islands' 13,000 residents have watched intensifying natural forces threaten the boundaries of their home. Warmer winters and fiercer storms, rising seawaters and the slow sinking of the islands are responsible for an alarming loss of coastline, and the erosion appears to be accelerating.

For locals, called Madelinots, high winds and ocean storms have always been a part of life on the islands. Dominant north-west winds blow through the Gulf of St Lawrence throughout the winter; typically, ice cover in the north is driven south and accumulates along the north side of the island chain. A high concentration of sea ice (30 per cent of the water surface or more) obstructs the storm waves that would otherwise batter cliffs and reshape road-bearing stretches of dune. Coastal ice shields the archipelago's shores from the destructive effects of rainwater and sudden freezes. But according to ongoing studies by Montréal-based climate-research organization Ouranos, by somewhere between 2050 and 2090, there will be no ice formation in the gulf.

Researchers have noted a significant decrease in ice thickness and surface area in the gulf since the 1990s. This has benefited navigation and communication with the archipelago – the ferry from Souris, PEI, to Îles-de-la-Madeleine started to offer year-round service in 2009 – but is harmful to the fragile sandstone coasts.

Sandstone is susceptible to gelifraction or frost shattering. More frequent freezing and thawing cycles are characteristic of progressively mild gulf winters. Water either melts or is rained into cracked and porous sandstone and shale, where it expands and 'explodes' the rock as it freezes. Already, an annual average of 10 to 110 centimetres of coast are lost around the perimeter of the islands, though intense storms can destroy up to 10 metres along certain cliffs. With every storm comes the danger that the erosion of precious coastline will swallow sections of residents' properties or buildings (four summer homes were moved inland last year and a storm swept away another) or will compromise vulnerable stretches of the vital south and north islands connecting Route 199.

'Wherever we can, we will retreat,' says Mayor Joël Arseneau. 'Our priority must be the protection of the public infrastructure that we all need.' Yet it will not be easy for Madelinots to flee from the dangers of crumbling cliffs and rising waters. Many of them have centuries-old roots on the archipelago. Louis Vigneau, manager of the local Transports Québec office, says that he's been here since 1792. 'I have salt in my blood,' he laughs, 'and sand also!' Two hundred and twenty years ago, his ancestors crossed the blustery gulf from Saint Pierre et Miquelon, landing on Île du Havre Aubert, just 25 kilometres south of his present home in Cap-aux-Meules. He and the municipality are waiting for a Transports Québec study that will provide an action plan for the management of the islands' transportation infrastructure. While they wait, they reinforce threatened stretches of highway with sand dredged up from the major harbour on Île du Cap aux Meules.

Guglielmo Tita, scientific director of the Research Centre on Island and Maritime Studies at Université du Québec à Rimouski and a resident of the Îles-de-la-Madeleine for the past nine years, attests to the anxiety that pervades the archipelago, particularly during stormy weather. Yet Tita is originally from Sicily, Italy, where the island landscape is dominated by the active volcano Mount Etna. 'People live on and around the volcano just as people live here, where there are serious erosion problems,' he says. 'While we apprehend and fear the danger, it's our land. It's where we live, and we continue living.'

When you have finished, check your answers in the Answer Key in Appendix 1.

UNIT 5

Yes/No/Not Given Questions

What do they test?

This question type tests your ability to identify the writer's viewpoint, claim or bias. There are numbered statements in the question that are based on opinions or claims. You are expected to read the text and state whether each of the given statements agrees with the text writer's opinion or claims (choose **YES**) or not (choose **NO**). There may also be a situation when there is no information in the passage to suggest or contradict that it was the writer's opinion (choose **NOT GIVEN**).

What do you need to do?

* Read each statement in the question and underline key words.
* Scan the text and locate the section where the relevant information is given.
* Remember, synonyms of key words or paraphrased sentences will help you identify the appropriate section.
* Now read the section slowly and carefully to see if the statement in the question agrees or disagrees with the stated opinion or claim in the text. Accordingly, choose **YES** or **NO**. If the relevant information is not in the text, choose the option **NOT GIVEN**.

> **TIPS** An opinion is not necessarily based on fact or knowledge and it cannot be proved right or wrong. So, do not choose your answer on the basis of what you know as factually right or wrong.
> Be sure of the difference between 'NO' and 'NOT GIVEN'. If the views of the writer explicitly disagree with or are opposite to what the statement in the question says, the answer needs to be 'NO'.
> On the other hand, if the given statement can be neither confirmed nor contradicted on the basis of the reading passage, the answer should be 'NOT GIVEN'.

Activity 5.1: Guided practice

Let us now do a simple exercise in identifying sentences that agree, disagree or neither agree nor disagree with short samples of the reading passage 'Natural Disasters' given below.

Read the text samples 1–4. Then read each of the three statements that follow and write **YES** *if the statement agrees with the text;* **NO** *if it disagrees with the text; and* **NOT GIVEN** *if the information is neither supported nor contradicted.*

1

Natural disasters around the world last year caused a record US$380 billion in economic losses. That's more than ... according to a report from Munich Re, a reinsurance group in Germany. But other work emphasizes that it is too soon to blame the economic devastation on climate change.

a The world economic records for the previous year show losses of AU$380 billion.

b Some studies say that climate change cannot be blamed on natural disasters.

c Other studies insist that more research is needed to see the relationship between the economy and climate change.

2

Almost two-thirds of 2011's exceptionally high costs are attributable to two disasters unrelated to climate and weather: the magnitude-9.0 earthquake and tsunami that hit Japan in March, and February's comparatively small but unusually destructive magnitude-6.3 quake in New Zealand.

a In 2011, Japan's earthquake and tsunami and New Zealand's earthquake had a considerable financial impact.

b As it was quite small, the quake in New Zealand did little damage.

c The two disasters mentioned here could have been predicted to avoid losses.

3

And the long-term rise in the costs of global disasters is probably due mainly to socioeconomic changes, such as population growth and development in vulnerable regions.

a A growing population does not incur higher costs when dealing with world disasters.

b Population growth and development of disaster-prone areas are examples of socioeconomic changes.

c Several factors contribute to the rise in the costs of global disasters.

4

'It would not seem plausible that climate change doesn't play a role in the substantial rise in weather-related disasters,' says Ernst Rauch, head of Munich Re's Corporate Climate Centre.

a According to Ernst Rauch, climate change has contributed to the huge rise in weather-related disasters.

b Ernst Rauch says that it is reasonable to think that changing weather conditions causing disasters are going to rise substantially.

c Ernst Rauch does not think that climate change can cause natural disasters.

Check your answers in the Answer Key in Appendix 1.

Natural Disasters

Quirin Schiermeier

Natural disasters around the world last year caused a record US$380 billion in economic losses. That's more than twice the tally for 2010, and about $115 billion more than in the previous record year of 2005, according to a report from Munich Re, a reinsurance group in Germany. But other work emphasizes that it is too soon to blame the economic devastation on climate change.

Almost two-thirds of 2011's exceptionally high costs are attributable to two disasters unrelated to climate and weather: the magnitude-9.0 earthquake and tsunami that hit Japan in March, and February's comparatively small but unusually destructive magnitude-6.3 quake in New Zealand.

And the long-term rise in the costs of global disasters is probably due mainly to socioeconomic changes, such as population growth and development in vulnerable regions. That conclusion is backed up by a forthcoming study – supported by Munich Re – by economists Fabian Barthel and Eric Neumayer at the London School of Economics. Their analysis of events worldwide between 1990 and 2008 concludes that 'the accumulation of wealth in disaster-prone areas is and will always remain by far the most important driver of future economic disaster damage'. Any major weather event hitting densely populated areas now causes huge losses because the value of the infrastructure has increased tremendously, they note, adding that if the 1926 Great Miami hurricane happened today, for example, it would cause much more damage than it did at the time.

However, weather-related events are generally on the rise. Thanks to a relatively quiet Atlantic hurricane season, damage caused by extreme weather was actually lower in 2011 than in four of the previous five years. But weather accounted for about 90 per cent of the year's 820 recorded natural disasters, which caused at least 27,000 deaths. These disasters include flooding in Thailand, a series of tornadoes that hit the United States Midwest and southern states last spring, and storms and extreme rainfall over parts of the Mediterranean in November.

Since 1980, the report notes, the number of severe floods has almost tripled, and storms have nearly doubled, which insurance experts link, in part, to the impact of climate change. 'It would not seem plausible that climate change doesn't play a role in the substantial rise in weather-related disasters,' says Ernst Rauch, head of Munich Re's Corporate Climate Centre.

Activity 5.2: Exam-style practice

Given below are eight statements and a reading passage. Follow the steps in the beginning of this chapter and find out whether these statements agree with the writer's opinion or claims.

Suggested time: 12 minutes

Do the following statements agree with the information given in the reading passage?
Write:

YES *if the statement agrees with the writer's views or claims*
NO *if the statement contradicts the writer's views or claims*
NOT GIVEN *if there is no information to say what the writer thinks about it.*

1. People are normally afraid of change.

2. Groups opposing genetically modified foods were not being rational.

3. The practice of genetic modification does not indicate any scientific progress.

4. If we do not use genetically modified foods, we will face the problem of famine.

5. Genetic modification of foods will help to bring down the prices of pesticides.

6. Genetically modified plants should be able to grow in any environment.

7. Results of the research into the effects of GM foods are not reliable.

8. Changing the genes of plants could affect human beings' natural resistance to diseases.

Genetically Modified Foods

Thom Murphy

The furore over genetically modified food is just the latest in a long line of people reacting because they are frightened of change. Despite the strangely emotional lobby against GM food, the movement does raise some salient points.

The genetic modification of food is an important step on the ladder of scientific development, and can lead to plants becoming resistant to disease, yielding higher quality and quantity of fruits and even growing more quickly. These practices will enable the amount of food grown to be increased massively, which could potentially, if not solve, go a long way to alleviate the problem of famine or world hunger. It could lead to a fall in the use of pesticides, as they would not be needed for use on plants with natural genetic resistance to insects. GM crops will be able to grow in climates that would be totally inhospitable to unmodified plants, allowing new sources of food to be grown in countries without the environmental strain of flying in the foodstuffs from all over the world. The credibility of all research done regarding the ill effects of GM food is in doubt, and thus all evidence found here should be taken with a large pinch of salt.

There are several pieces of evidence that genetically modified food may be bad for people, and even if these results are not steeped in scientific credibility the findings should be researched, analyzed and developed to ensure the product is safe before they gain universal release. Farms specifically devoted to GM food, like most other dedicated agricultural establishments, will lead to a unilateral habitat being established that could not support other forms of life; due to a change of environment and other factors such as pesticides. These areas of cropland would destroy the places where countless insects and other small animals live, hunt and breed. By altering the genomes of these plants, this could easily give rise to new diseases in the future that human beings would have no genetic resistance to. This problem must be avoided at all costs. Similarly, like all branches of big business, genetically modified farming would lead to the people involved being solely focused on profit-making rather than ethical practices. This would lead to the soul of rural areas being ripped out, and many communities being destroyed.

In conclusion, it is integral that the process of created genetically modified foodstuffs must be closely monitored by independent, disinterested watchdog-style organizations. With these ombudsmen in place, the genetic modification of food can lead to massive developments in how we feed people and in the quality of foods.

When you have finished, check your answers in the Answer Key in Appendix 1.

UNIT 6

Short Answer Questions

What do they test?

These questions test your ability to identify and locate in the passage the precise information being asked for. Therefore, they are used with passages relating to factual information and specific details.

The questions are in the same order as the information is presented in the passage.

What do you need to do?

- You will need to skim-read the article to get a general idea and then scan the text for specific information that the question asks for.
- Note the instructions given with the short answer question, quickly.
- Skim-read the text to get a general idea of the text.
- Read the questions and underline key words.
- Scan the text for words, phrases or numbers that answer the given questions. (They may not be the same words as the key words you underlined in the question.)
- Write your answers: copy the words from the original text with correct spelling onto the Answer Sheet.

TIPS You must not write more than the number of words asked for.

Hyphenated words (e.g. 'medium-sized') are counted as single words.

You can write numbers using figures (77) or words (seventy-seven).

Activity 6.1: Guided practice

Read the passage below and do the task that follows.

1   Along with the physical changes that occur as we get older, changes to our sleep patterns are a part of the normal ageing process. As people age they tend to have a harder time falling asleep and more trouble staying asleep than when they were younger. It is a common misconception that sleep needs decline with age. In fact, research demonstrates that our sleep needs remain constant throughout adulthood. So, what's keeping seniors awake?

[continued from previous page]

2   Changes in the patterns of our sleep – what specialists call 'sleep architecture' – occur as we age and this may contribute to sleep problems. Sleep occurs in multiple stages including dreamless periods of light and deep sleep, and occasional periods of active dreaming (REM sleep). The sleep cycle is repeated several times during the night and although total sleep time tends to remain constant, older people spend more time in the lighter stages of sleep than in deep sleep.

3   Many older adults, though certainly not all, also report being less satisfied with sleep and more tired during the day. Studies on the sleep habits of older Americans show an increase in the time it takes to fall asleep (sleep latency), an overall decline in REM sleep, and an increase in sleep fragmentation (waking up during the night) with age.

4   The prevalence of sleep disorders also tends to increase with age. However, research suggests that much of the sleep disturbance among the elderly can be attributed to physical and psychiatric illnesses and the medications used to treat them.

5   The prevalence of insomnia is also higher among older adults. According to NSF's 2003 *Sleep in America* poll, 44 per cent of older persons experience one or more of the night time symptoms of insomnia at least a few nights per week or more. Insomnia may be chronic (lasting over one month) or acute (lasting a few days or weeks) and is oftentimes related to an underlying cause such as a medical or psychiatric condition. It is worthwhile to speak to your doctor about insomnia symptoms and about any effects these symptoms may have. Your doctor can help assess how serious a problem it is and what to do about it.

6   As we age, there is an increased incidence of medical problems, which are often chronic. In general, people with poor health or chronic medical conditions have more sleep problems.

Now, read the following three text outlines.
Indicate which of these three outlines matches the above passage most accurately.

Text outline (a)

General introductory statement + misconception + preview to the rest of the text
Normal sleep pattern – 'Sleep architecture'
Changes to normal sleep pattern
Sleep disorders
Sleeplessness
Concluding comment

Text outline (b)

General introductory statement + misconception + preview to the rest of the text
Normal sleep pattern + changes to it due to ageing
More description of such changes
Other sleep disorders brought on not directly by ageing but other related factors
Insomnia or sleeplessness: types, causes and treatment
Concluding comment

Text outline (c)

General introductory statement + misconception + preview to the rest of the text
Changes to normal sleep pattern due to ageing
Different sleep problems among older Americans
Sleep disturbance and sleep disorders
Insomnia and help for insomnia
Concluding comment

Now complete the table below. You will need to read one question at a time and underline the key words in the question.

Next, locate the relevant paragraph and the sentence in the reading passage with the answer.

From here you will choose and copy only the two or three most appropriate words as an answer to the given question.

Short answer question	Answer located in paragraph no.	Relevant text in the paragraph	Two- or three-word answer
1 What is incorrectly believed about the sleeping needs of an elderly person?	1	*It is a common misconception that sleep needs decline with age.*	**decline with age**
2 What happens to total sleep time when sleep pattern changes?			
3 What conditions increase sleep disorders among the elderly?			
4 People may suffer with one of the two types of conditions of sleeplessness. What are they?			
5 In general, what conditions cause people to suffer with more sleep problems?			

Activity 6.2: Exam-style practice

Read the passage below and then answer the questions that follow.

Suggested time: 8 minutes

1. The length of a day – as based on daylight or the period between sunrise and sunset – varies over the course of a year. While the days tend to be longer than nights in summer, they become shorter than nights in winter. The change in the length of day is gradual, starting from the longest day of the year to the shortest day. Similarly, starting from the shortest day of the year, the length of a day increases gradually until it is the longest day of the next calendar year.

2. The occurrence of the longest or shortest day of the year is attributed to the astronomical event known as 'solstice', which occurs twice in a calendar year – first when the apparent position of the Sun is at its northernmost limit (Tropic of Cancer/23.5° North), and again, when the apparent position of the Sun is at its southernmost limit (Tropic of Capricorn/23.5° South).

3. This event of astronomy is further categorized into two parts – **summer solstice**, which is the longest day of the year, and winter solstice, which is the shortest day of the year. When the Sun is at its northernmost limit at 23.5°N, it is referred to as summer solstice, and when it is at its southernmost limit at 23.5°S, it is referred to as winter solstice.

4. On the other hand, when the Sun's apparent position is just above the equator, it is referred to as equinox – which occurs twice a year. This, however, only applies to the northern hemisphere of the Earth.

5. In the southern hemisphere, summer solstice occurs when the Sun is at its southernmost limit at 23.5° South and winter solstice occurs when the Sun is at its northernmost limit at 23.5° North. Owing to the differences in apparent position of the Sun, each of the two hemispheres experiences summer solstice and winter solstice at different times of the year. When the Sun is positioned at the northernmost limit, the northern hemisphere experiences more daylight as compared to the southern hemisphere. Contrary to this, when the Sun is at its southernmost extreme the southern hemisphere experiences more daylight as compared to its northern counterpart. For a resident of the northern hemisphere, the longest day is when the Sun is at the Tropic of Cancer, and the shortest is when it is at the Tropic of Capricorn.

6. If you happen to be a resident of some country in the southern hemisphere, you will experience the longest day when the Sun is at the Tropic of Capricorn and the shortest day when it is at the Tropic of Cancer. Generally, the Sun is at the Tropic of Cancer on 20 or 21 June (sometimes on 19 or 22 June)

and at the Tropic of Capricorn on 21 or 22 December (sometimes on 20 or 23 December). Going by these dates, the longest day of the year has to be 20 or 21 June for the northern hemisphere, but 21 or 22 December for the southern hemisphere. Similarly, the shortest day of the year has to be 21 or 22 December for the northern hemisphere, but 20 or 21 June for the southern hemisphere.

7.   Interestingly, when the Sun is positioned at the 23.5° North latitude, the region around the North Pole experiences 24 hours of daylight (day) while the region around the South Pole experiences 24 hours of darkness (night) at a stretch. Similarly, when the Sun is positioned at the 23.5° South latitude the North Pole and surrounding areas experience 24 hours darkness while the South Pole and surrounding areas receive 24 hours of daylight.

American National Sleep Foundation

Do the following based on the text above.
*Write **NO MORE THAN THREE WORDS** to complete each sentence.*

1.   What two natural events mark the start and end of the daylight period of a day?

      _____

2.   In which season does the longest day of the year occur in the northern hemisphere?

      _____

3.   What other name is given to the shortest day of the year in the northern hemisphere?

      _____

4.   How often does equinox occur?

      _____

5.   Which region experiences darkness over a long period, when the Sun is positioned at 23.5° North latitude?

      _____

When you have finished, check your answers in the Answer Key in Appendix 1.

UNIT 7

Sentence Completion Questions

What do they test?

In this kind of question you are given a number of sentences with gaps (usually at the end of the sentence), which you must complete with words from the text. These questions are testing your ability to read for specific information.

What do you need to do?

- Read each sentence carefully and try to predict what could be missing.
- Identify key words from the sentence and **scan** the text to find those words or synonyms.
- Choose words FROM THE TEXT to complete the sentence.
- Reread your sentences to make sure they are grammatically correct.

> **TIPS** The questions in this exercise follow the order of the text.
>
> The missing section is usually, **but not always**, a noun phrase.
>
> Do not change the words from the text in any way: if they don't fit, it's the wrong answer.

Activity 7.1: Guided practice

Here are some incomplete sentences. Can you guess what kind of information might be missing from each one?

1. Stonehenge is being surveyed using _____.
   PARAGRAPH: ____

2. The ground-penetrating radar system scans to _____ under the ground.
   PARAGRAPH: ____

3. The surveyors must work around _____.
   PARAGRAPH: ____

4. Laser-scanning and magnetometer technology are to be utilised
    in addition to the _____.
    PARAGRAPH: ___

5. Below Stonehenge there may be undiscovered _____.
    PARAGRAPH: ___

6. Staff from VISTA will process the _____.
    PARAGRAPH: ___

7. The project is possible because data capture technology is now as advanced as
    _____.
    PARAGRAPH: ___

8. The University of Birmingham and the Ludwig Boltzmann Institute are providing
    project _____.
    PARAGRAPH: ___

   Now read the text below and identify in which paragraph the answer for each sentence
can be found.
Using the information that you have found, complete each sentence using **NO MORE THAN
THREE WORDS** *from the text.*

Virtual Excavation Aims to Unearth Stonehenge Secrets

James Hayes

1 What's claimed to be the world's most extensive 'virtual excavation' has begun at the Stonehenge prehistoric monument in Wiltshire. The Stonehenge Hidden Landscapes Project is using advanced geophysical imaging technology to survey the 14 sq km site over approximately nine weeks spread over a three-year period.

2 The project will be the first time that Stonehenge has been subjected to such a detailed archaeological survey, with every inch of the targeted terrain scanned to a depth of three metres using high-frequency ground-penetrating radar (GPR) systems from Swedish firm MALÅ Geoscience. The survey is scheduled around the needs of farmers and small-holders whose lands abut the Stonehenge site.

3 Led by the University of Birmingham's Institute of Archaeology and Antiquity, the project brings together a 12-member multi-disciplinary team that includes archaeologists, geophysicists, historians, and computing specialists. As well as the GPR they will use laser-scanning and magnetometer technology to enhance their understanding of the site.

4 'The Stonehenge landscape is one of the most intensively examined in the world, but despite this much of it remains *terra incognita*,' says project leader Professor Vince Gaffney. 'We don't even know if we are aware of all the monuments that may exist under the Stonehenge site itself. Even people connected with Stonehenge are surprised that it has not been surveyed in this level of detail before. We can discover the "hidden landscape" in a way that you can't really do through invasive work.'

5 The excavation data will be processed by the University of Birmingham's IBM Visual and Spatial Technology Centre (VISTA), which supports academic research and development for spatial analysis, visualisation, and imaging applications. Using the University's BlueBEAR high-performance computing resource running on Scientific Linux 5.2, the project will eventually produce two- and three-dimensional images of the mapped areas.

6 'Technology has taken a massive step forward in recent years,' adds Professor Gaffney. 'The data capture side is now on a par, capability-wise, with the data-processing systems. We now have mobile ground-penetrating radar working through close-spaced cluster-form sensors that enable us to digitally chart this famous landscape.'

7 Funding for the project has come from the Ludwig Boltzmann Institute for Archaeological Prospection and Virtual Archaeology in Vienna and the University of Birmingham, with additional support from English Heritage and the National Trust.

TIP   Words that are hyphenated (e.g. long-sleeved) are counted in English as **one** word.

Activity 7.2: Exam-style practice

Here is another, similar exercise. This time you will only be given the text and the questions as you would in the exam. Follow the same steps as you did in Activity 7.1 to find the answers, and then when you have finished check the Answer Key in Appendix 1.
    Suggested time: 12 minutes

Transformer – Dark Past of the Moon

David Shiga

Family squabbles rarely result in cannibalism, but that may be just what happened in the moon's youth. It may have gobbled up a smaller sibling, making itself permanently lopsided. The moon is thought to have formed when a Mars-sized body slammed into the infant Earth. This threw a cloud of vaporised and molten rock into orbit, which coalesced into the moon.

Simulations have previously shown that additional moons could have formed from the debris cloud, sharing an orbit with the one large moon that survives today. Eventually, gravitational tugs from the sun would destabilise the moonlets, making them crash into the bigger one.

New simulations now suggest such moon-on-moon violence could explain the long-standing puzzle about the moon's two-faced nature. The moon's crust is thicker on its far side and differs in composition from rocks on the side facing Earth.

Previous explanations for the difference have created their own puzzles. For example, a giant, high-speed impact could have blasted away much of the crust from the near side. But this would probably have led to a global magma ocean that would have cooled and erased the initial thickness difference.

Now Martin Jutzi and Erik Asphaug at the University of California, Santa Cruz, have simulated the effect of an impact between the moon and a smaller sibling 1300 kilometres across, about one-third as wide.

Crucially, such an impact would have happened at about 2 kilometres per second, which, although fast in everyday terms, is very low compared with the typical speeds of asteroids and comets that blast out craters on the moon. Like racing cars that swerve and hit each other on a circular track, the moons' speed relative to each other is low because they travel in nearly the same orbit.

Such a low-speed impact does not melt or vaporise rock like a high-speed crash. Nor does it form a crater – it actually adds material to the moon. 'In a way you do make a crater, but you fill it all in with the impactor material,' says Asphaug. The smaller moon breaks up and spreads out from the collision points like a landslide, thickening the larger moon's crust on one side. 'It basically looks like you are smearing the impactor across the face of the moon,' says John Chambers of the Carnegie Institution for Science in Washington DC, who was not involved in the study.

Like squashing one end of a tube of toothpaste, the impact also pushes subsurface magma to the opposite side of the moon from the crash point. This could explain why rocks on the moon's near side are richer in potassium, phosphorus and other elements that suggest they were among the last rocks to solidify out of the moon's primordial magma ocean.

One way to test the idea is to get rock samples from the far side, says Maria Zuber of the Massachusetts Institute of Technology. The simulation suggests rocks on the far side come mostly from the smaller moon, which should have previously cooled and solidified faster than the main moon, making its rocks older.

Low-speed collisions have also been proposed to explain some comets' layered structures. If a smaller comet hit a larger one, its icy remains might be plastered on the surviving sibling.

Complete questions 1–8 below using **NO MORE THAN THREE WORDS** *from the text.*

1. The moon may have been created by the collision of Earth and _____.

2. There could have initially been a number of moons inhabiting the same _____.

3. If the moons crashed, it would explain why one side of the moon is _____.

4. A loss of crust from one part of the moon would likely have resulted in a _____.

5. Moon craters can be created by _____.

6. A low-speed crash would spread _____ around the moon.

7. Rocks on one side of the moon contain more of elements such as _____.

8. The collision hypothesis could be tested by examining _____.

When you have finished, check your answers in the Answer Key in Appendix 1.

Diagram/Flow Chart Completion Questions

What do they test?

In this kind of question, you are given a diagram or flow chart that you must label using words from the reading. You are being tested for your intensive reading skills and your ability to understand visual information.

What do you need to do?

- Find the section of the text that describes the diagram or flow chart.
- Read that section as many times as necessary to understand it well.
- Look at the information in the diagram or flow chart that you have already been given.
- Label the diagram or flow chart using words FROM THE TEXT.

> **TIPS** The description of the diagram or flow chart will almost always be concentrated in one section of the text, sometimes even in just a few lines.
>
> You cannot change the form of the words from the text.

Activity 8.1: Guided practice

Skim the following article to find a description of a STANDARD SOLAR CELL. Is the description all in one paragraph, or does it span more than one paragraph?

Performance Degradation in Solar Plants

Lars Podlowski and Daniel Hundmaier

A

A solution to prevent potential induced degradation, a recently discovered new trend in high-voltage solar systems throughout the world, has been researched by SOLON SE's Dr Lars Podlowski and Daniel Hundmaier.

B

In photovoltaic (PV) modules, an initial drop in efficiency is a well-known phenomenon. Known as light induced degradation, it has long been included in the performance guarantees offered by producers in the industry or the calculations of project developers and plant operators. Light induced degradation can cause an approximate 2 per cent decrease in system performance in the first few hours of operation of any new PV installation.

C

In 2006, a new form of performance degradation began to be noticed. The effect was first discovered in solar plants whose modules used a certain type of high-performance cells. Initial suspicions turned to the specific technology of these cells, which differed substantially from industry-standard cells. In these cases, a concentration of charge carriers at the cell surface was suggested to be the cause of the potential difference between the cells and the ground potential.

D

It has now been established that this new type of degradation – known as potential induced degradation (PID) or high-voltage stress – is indeed promoted by the special technology used in these cells. However, the phenomenon has also been observed in standard and thin-film cells. As these panels are serially interconnected modules of all cell types, the more modules you connect, the higher the voltage gets. It is the high voltage that causes PID.

E

In order to understand PID, it is important to understand how a solar cell works and how it interacts with other materials in the module. In simple terms, a standard cell consists of a thin film of negatively doped (polarised) silicon on top of a thicker layer of positively doped silicon. When exposed to sunlight, so-called electron-hole pairs are produced in the space between the two layers – the depletion zone or space-charge region. Positively charged holes move in the direction of the positively doped superconductor, whereas negatively charged electrons move to its negatively doped counterpart. The charge carriers are then conducted to the next cell.

F

The serial array of the cells means that the voltage increases from cell to cell in the module. The same applies to the individual modules in the system, also connected in series. The maximum voltage in such a system can easily reach up to 1000 volts – this is basically a positive effect, because the higher the voltage is, the lower the electrical resistance. In this way, high voltage helps to increase the capacity of the system.

G

At the same time, these high system voltages can lead to unwanted leakage currents between the solar cells, the bedding materials, glass, and the grounded module frame. This allows a positive charge to build up on the anti-glare coating at the surface of the cells. The result is a temporary short circuit in the affected cells, which means a decrease in cell voltage and a drop in efficiency – an effect that is reinforced by high temperatures or humidity around the modules.

Look below at the diagram of a standard solar cell and try to complete it with between one and three words from the text in each gap. The questions would not ordinarily be in the text, but are designed to help you find the answers.

Standard solar cell

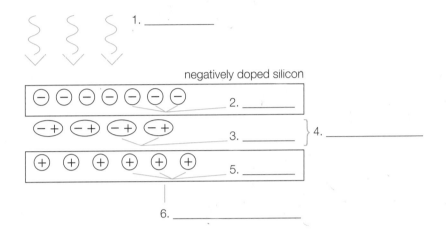

1. Gap 1 shows something from outside the cell feeding into the cell. What powers the solar cell?

2. Gap 2 has the symbol −. What does this symbol usually mean?

3. Gap 5 has the symbol +. What does this symbol usually mean?

4. Gap 3 has both symbols, − and +. Can you find a word in the text that refers to two things together?

5. The top layer of the cell is labelled *negatively doped silicon*. What, then, do you expect the lower layer (Gap 6) to be labelled?

6. Gap 4 shows the space between the layers. How is this referred to in the text?

Activity 8.2: Exam-style practice

Here is a similar exercise, where you must label a flow chart. This time you will only be given the text and the questions. Try to follow the same steps as in Activity 8.1.

Suggested time: 14 minutes

The Tyre: Where does it Come From and Where does it Go?

WME Magazine

A standard car tyre consists of three components: the carcass, belts and tread. The carcass – in essence the main body of the tyre – is made of a synthetic rubber sheet with radial polyester or rayon cords running through it for strength.

The belts are rubber sheets embedded with brass-coated steel wire used to give additional strength and support under the tread, which is the layer of grooved rubber that makes contact with the road. The synthetic rubber and polyester are produced from fossil fuels, the steel is mined from iron ore and the rayon is a form of cellulose produced from wood pulp. These components are assembled and 'vulcanised' – pressed at around 198°C to make the sandwich of rubber tough and resilient to heat.

Creation of a standard family car tyre uses 27 kg of raw material and 584 L of water. In the process, it produces 4.4 kg of waste and 13.5 kg of materials extracted but not used. Australia disposes of 20 million car tyres annually. Once the tread has worn away – after an average life of 50,000 km – tyres in Australia go to one of four destinations: landfill, incineration, retreading or recycling.

Around 57 per cent of Australian tyres go to landfill each year but this is by far the worst option environmentally. Without sunlight a tyre takes up to 30,000 years to degrade, taking up valuable space, providing havens for vermin and mosquitoes, and posing a fire hazard. A further 13 per cent are dumped.

Since tyres are essentially just processed hydrocarbons, they burn readily. The calorific value of a tyre is 34 MJ/kg, better than Australian black coal at 28 MJ/kg. In Victoria tyres are used to power a cement factory. The drawback is that only a small proportion of the energy taken to create the tyre is recovered. Incomplete combustion can also occur if the tyres are not incinerated at sufficiently high temperatures, creating gases such as carbon monoxide.

Retreading extends the life of a tyre, so it seems like the best end-of-life use. However, the jury is still out on this one. While retreads do postpone the need for a new tyre, they have a higher rolling resistance than a new tyre and as most of a tyre's impacts come about as a function of this resistance, some studies have shown the environmental benefits of avoided resource use are outweighed by running an inefficient tyre. Others say the scale tips about even.

Belgian tyre researcher BLIC says the best use for a used tyre is to pulverize it into crumbs and reuse it in another guise. In both the Eco-Indicator 99 and Environmental Policy Strategies (EPS) method of lifecycle analysis, recycling is good for the environment. Crumbed tyres make good road bases and playground and sporting surfaces, and can be used in construction as a replacement for gravel or, in some cases, processed into building materials.

Complete the following flowchart using **NO MORE THAN THREE WORDS AND/OR A NUMBER FROM THE TEXT**.

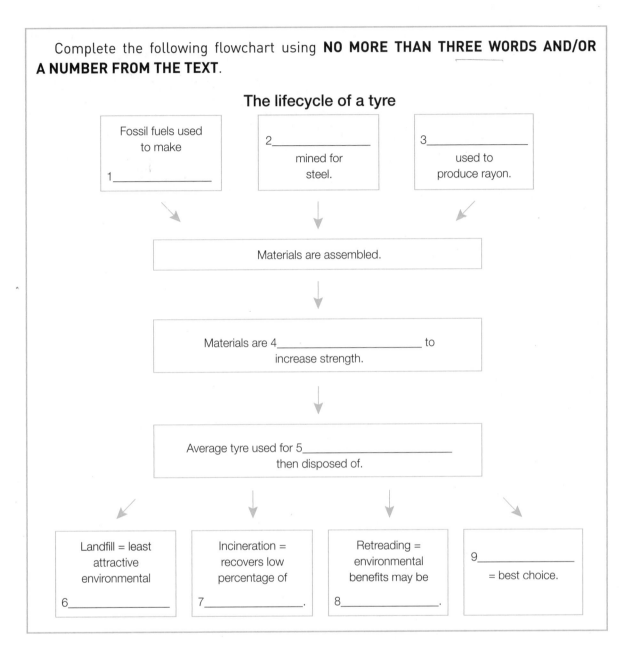

The lifecycle of a tyre

Fossil fuels used to make

1_____

2_____ mined for steel.

3_____ used to produce rayon.

Materials are assembled.

Materials are 4_____ to increase strength.

Average tyre used for 5_____ then disposed of.

Landfill = least attractive environmental

6_____

Incineration = recovers low percentage of

7_____.

Retreading = environmental benefits may be

8_____.

9_____ = best choice.

When you have finished, check your answers in the Answer Key in Appendix 1.

9:30

Table/Note Completion Questions

What do they test?

In this type of question you are given a table or a series of notes which you need to complete with information from the text. These questions are testing your ability to identify specific factual information and categorise it.

What do you need to do?

- Identify the type of information needed to complete the table or set of notes.
- Scan for keywords or synonyms in the text.
- Complete the table or notes with the required number of words FROM THE TEXT.

> **TIP** Look carefully at the numbers to make sure you put your answers in the correct place on the answer sheet.
>
> Because the answers to these questions are in note form, articles are usually unnecessary.

Activity 9.1: Guided practice

Look at the following table and answer the questions below.

SHIP	Titanic	Wilhelm Gustloff	Dona Paz	Russian ship
YEAR	1912	1_____	1987	2011
DEATH TOLL	1514	More than 9000	2_____	–
CAUSE	Hit iceberg	Sunk by 3_____ _____	Hit 4_____	5_____ _____

CONTRIBUTING FACTOR/S	(i) Not enough 6_____ (ii) Poor 7_____ procedures	–	Too many 8_____	Dangerous and 9_____ waters
TYPE OF SHIP	Passenger liner	10_____	Passenger ferry	Fishing vessel

1. How many questions are there?

2. What information do you need for question 1?

3. What does 'death toll' mean? Do you need to know the death toll for the Russian ship?

4. What information do you need for questions 3 and 4? How is question 5 different?

5. What part of speech do you need for questions 6, 7 and 8?

6. What part of speech do you need for question 9?

7. What information do you need for question 10?

8. What information should you **scan** for in the text to find the answers?

Now, complete the table using **NO MORE THAN THREE WORDS** *from the text.*

Could the *Titanic* Disaster Happen Today?

Stephanie Pappas

A century ago on Sunday, the RMS *Titanic* hit an iceberg and sank to a watery grave, killing 1514 passengers. The disaster conjures images of luxury and hubris, cowardice and heroism, as well as one haunting question: could it happen again?

In many ways, it already has, according to maritime experts. The Northern Maritime Research shipwreck database, for example, lists more than 470,000 shipwrecks in North America in the 20th century alone. Extremely deadly shipwrecks are much more rare, of course, but even the infamous *Titanic* disaster was only the sixth-deadliest shipwreck in history. The deadliest, the sinking of the German hospital ship the MV *Wilhelm Gustloff* by Soviet torpedoes, killed more than 9000 people. That disaster occurred in 1945 – long after the *Titanic*'s wreck in 1912.

Certain facets of the *Titanic*'s sinking are likely not to be repeated. But other risks still remain, said Mahlon 'Chuck' Kennicutt II, an oceanographer at Texas A&M University. 'You never can completely eliminate risk,' Kennicutt told LiveScience. 'It's just a matter of trying to minimize it.'

In fact, the *Titanic* disaster taught shipbuilders and crew plenty about minimizing risks. Famously, the ship had too few lifeboats for its passengers, and the evacuation procedure was disastrous.

'There are documented cases of people refusing to get into boats,' said Charles Weeks, an emeritus professor of marine transportation at the Maine Maritime Academy, and a member of the Titanic International Society. It wasn't immediately obvious how much danger the *Titanic* was in, Weeks told LiveScience, so people hesitated to jump into lifeboats being lowered into the frigid North Atlantic. 'The lights were on, the heat was on, so it was warm and comfortable, particularly if they stayed inside,' Weeks said.

Lives could have been saved if *Titanic* officers were more forceful in loading passengers onto boats, said George Behe, a member of the Titanic Historical Society and author of several books on the disaster. Behe credits one man, Fifth Officer Harold Lowe, with saving many lives due to his insistence that passengers board lifeboats. Lowe also rowed back to the wreck site after the ship sank, looking for survivors.

'Having said that, though, Fifth Officer Lowe was also responsible for the deaths of a certain number of well-to-do first-class passengers, since he later boasted to survivor Margaret Brown that he personally saw to it that none of the *Titanic*'s "rich nabobs" would find a seat in the lifeboats and that those "nabobs" must take their chances on the ship with "good men",' Behe told LiveScience.

Better officer training and sufficient lifeboats would eliminate many of these issues today, Kennicutt said. So, too, would better navigation aids that would have been more likely to prevent the iceberg strike in the first place. Modern communication would have made rescue more likely. 'If another ship mid-ocean had an accident, I would expect a much higher survival rate,' Weeks said. 'More crew trained to handle lifeboats, sufficient lifeboats, better radio communications.'

Shipbuilding technology is certainly better today, Kennicutt said. For instance, though *Titanic* was built to high standards in her day, 1912 steel contained more impurities than modern steel and was more brittle in the cold.

But as Kennicutt stresses, there are always risks to taking to the sea. At any given time, he said, there are an estimated 4 million commercial fishing vessels on the ocean, with tens of thousands more cruise liners, oil tankers, military ships and private vessels beside. 'Because there are so many more ships, there are that many more opportunities for mishaps to occur,' Kennicutt said.

Ships are increasingly venturing into Arctic and Antarctic waters that may be poorly mapped and treacherous, Kennicutt added. In December 2011, for example, a Russian fishing vessel hit an iceberg in the Ross Sea of Antarctica and took on water. The vessel was stranded for almost two weeks and risked spilling its fuel into an important emperor penguin feeding ground. Eventually, crew members were able to make enough repairs to get the damaged ship to New Zealand.

Human error plus laxity around safety regulations are often to blame for maritime disasters, Kennicutt said. In one deadly accident in 1987, the passenger ferry *Doña Paz* collided with an oil tanker. After the collision, a fire spread to the *Doña Paz*, which was loaded down with perhaps twice as many passengers as it could safely handle. Only 24 people survived the wreck, and the death toll is estimated at more than 4,000. 'If you're operating outside the capabilities of the system, then you've really increased the risk of a bad accident,' Kennicutt said.

Activity 9.2: Exam-style practice

Now look at the following note completion task. In this task you will only be given the questions and reading, as in the exam.

Suggested time: 14 minutes

*Complete the notes below. Choose **NO MORE THAN TWO WORDS OR A NUMBER** from the passage for each answer.*

Hypothyroidism:

- caused by malfunction of the **1** _____, which controls the **2** _____
- insufficient **3** _____ released into bloodstream
- affects approximately **4** _____ of people
- can be extremely difficult to **5** _____
- cannot be cured, but is **6** _____ with daily **7** _____ of Thyroxin
- more common in **8** _____ than **9** _____
- becomes significantly more common after **10** _____.

A Demon Hides Under a Cloak of Tiredness

Workplace stress and the heavy demands of life generally can mask the onset of a serious medical condition.

Report: Jeanne-Vida Douglas

'The thing about stress is that it plays havoc with your health precisely at the time you need to stay well,' the owner and founder of corporate training company Cheeky Food Group, Leona Watson, says. 'Last year I was seriously wondering how we were going to survive. The financial crisis had really started to hit in November 2008, so we had a quiet Christmas then started January without the normal cash reserves. I wasn't sleeping well, my hair seemed to be coming out in handfuls and it was a couple of months before I actually went and had something done about it.'

Watson's symptoms may have seemed like the classic stresses of running a business but they had a much more specific origin. Like more than 500,000 other Australians, she suffers from a condition called hypothyroidism. The thyroid is a small gland that sits around the windpipe delivering hormones into the blood stream. Hormones produced by the thyroid regulate the entire metabolic process by which food is converted into energy and delivered into every cell in the body. Blood sugar levels, circulation, appetite, cardiac rate, muscle tone, vitamin uptake, all depend on the thyroid producing the correct amounts of hormones at the right time.

Hypothyroidism, where the thyroid does not produce enough hormones, affects about 7 per cent of the population, although its symptoms are varied and can often be mistaken for other mental and physical conditions. Its twin, hyperthyroidism, where the thyroid is overactive and releasing too many hormones, hits only 1 per cent of the population but can be equally hard to identify. With a family history of hypothyroidism, Watson knew what to look out for and had been diagnosed in her early twenties. Sufferers need to take a small dose of Thyroxin every day to replace the hormone that is no longer produced by the thyroid.

Although the condition is treatable, it is also permanent and can be exacerbated by stress. 'I was a really young person when I was first diagnosed, so when the doctor gave me the prescription it initially didn't compute that I'd need to be on this medication for the rest of my life,' Watson says. 'But even last year when I had all the symptoms again, it was two months before I made the connection and went to my doctor to get my blood tested again.'

Thyroid conditions are about four times as prevalent in women as they are in men and the incidence increases significantly in women over the age of 50. The conditions are of particular concern to business owners and managers such as Watson because the symptoms are easy to dismiss as the result of a heavy workload.

Watson says: 'It was late February by the time I was doing something about it, and it wasn't until we got near the end of the financial year that companies began to realise that they had a little extra to spend and business really started to pick up again. By that time I was on the right level of Thyroxin and so I had the energy and the clarity I needed to find solutions for the business.'

When you have finished, check your answers in the Answer Key in Appendix 1.

What do they test?

In this kind of question, you are required to complete a summary of the text or a part of the text. You either will be given a list of words to choose from or will need to choose words from the text. The examiners are testing your ability to understand main ideas.

What do you need to do?

*   Read the gapped summary to get an overall understanding.
*   Decide whether it is a summary of the whole text or just part of the text.
*   Identify the part of speech needed for each gap.
*   Look for key words before and after the gap.
*   Choose either words from the list or exact words from the text to complete the summary.
*   Once you have finished, reread the summary to check that it makes sense.

Activity 10.1: Guided practice

Here is an example of a gapped summary. Can you identify the part of speech that is missing in each case?

Since cinema was **1** _____ at the **2** _____ of the nineteenth century, it has been used in Australia to explore the relationship of white and **3** _____ Australians to the outback, a dry and lightly populated area covering the **4** _____ of the country. Indigenous Australians were some of the first people to be on **5** _____. At first, Aborigines were not given the chance to express their own **6** _____ or control how they were represented. However, after the 1960s, films such as *The Land My Mother* and *On Sacred Ground* **7** _____ Aborigines to speak for themselves. These films looked at how the **8** _____ Aboriginal connection to the land was affected by European development and practices such as **9** _____. Later, Aborigines started to make their own films in which they examined their **10** _____, their stories and their feelings about the land.

> **TIP**   As well as thinking about grammar, you should also be thinking about collocation: which words tend to go together. For example, what nouns usually go with the verb *express*?

Now look at the list of words to choose from and put them into categories according to part of speech.

majority	forced	mining	appeared	new
end	European	enabled	most	viewpoints
traditional	introduced	Aboriginal	past	camera
Aborigines	bush	cinema	gave	beginning

NOUN	VERB	ADJECTIVE

Read the text, and choose the best words to complete the summary above, making sure they are the correct part of speech.

Outback on Screen

Shirley Graham

Many of Australia's creative interpretations of the outback over the last two centuries have reflected a mostly immigrant people's interpretation of a landscape very different to the lands which they or their forebears came from. But like artists, poets and novelists, Australian film makers from the beginning have used the outback to define a sense of belonging.

Covering 70 per cent of Australia, the outback is remote, arid and lightly populated. Most of the remaining continent has been defined as 'the bush', comprising the well-watered domesticated or semi-domesticated coastal fringes east and south of the Great Dividing Range flanking eastern Australia, moving west via Melbourne to Adelaide as well as incorporating the island of Tasmania. Today, when most of Australia's almost 23 million people live in urban areas, the character of the outback survives as a major ingredient in the nation's novels, poetry, paintings, feature and short films, TV drama and advertising.

In 1896 cinema made its first global appearance at a time of intense nationalism for Australian identity, especially as interpreted through literature and painting. Australian novelists, short story writers and ballad writers of the 1880s and 1890s used the bush and outback to define what it was to be Australian. The painters Tom Roberts, Frederick McCubbin and Arthur Streeton created their own myths about frontier and farm life. From the 1890s onward Australian cinema would perpetuate these myths, eventually questioning and extending them.

Prior to white settlement, Aboriginal people had occupied Australia for at least 50,000 years – not a single Aboriginal nation but a gathering of several hundred communities or tribes, each with its own language, set of beliefs and territory on which many lived a nomadic and spiritual existence that recognised a community's unique relationship with the land. Whites occupied much of that land after European settlement in 1788, dispossessing most tribes except those living a very remote existence.

Aboriginal people were first officially recognised as Australian citizens in 1967, one year after the Northern Territory Gurindji tribe launched the first Indigenous bid to obtain title to traditional land. They were among the earliest Australians filmed in the 1890s. In 1898 Cambridge University anthropologist Alfred Cort Haddon filmed Torres Strait Islanders and mainland Aborigines, making this the world's first film of an anthropological field trip. In 1901 and 1912 Professor Walter Baldwin Spencer filmed the lifestyles and spiritual activities of the tribes of Central and Northern Australia.

Aborigines on screen in early filmmaking were often exploited subjects rather than people who had any say in how they were filmed and who would see the results. With rare exceptions, it was not until the 1960s and '70s that documentary filmmakers sought to include the perspective of Aboriginal people. David Roberts in 1976 made the documentary *Walya Ngamardiki: The Land My Mother*, featuring Arnhem Land Aboriginal people talking about traditional attachment to their land and their attitudes to the uranium mining that could change it irretrievably. Oliver Howes's documentary *On Sacred Ground* (1981) looks at the dispossession and loss of identity that provides a background to the late 1970s Noonkanbah land rights confrontation between traditional Aboriginal owners and miners in the Kimberley region of Western Australia.

Over time, Aboriginal people gained opportunities to speak for themselves about their relationship to and ownership of land, a number of whose landforms had sacred associations. More recently a new generation of Aboriginal filmmakers, producing for a variety of screen media including television, have been telling stories of Aboriginal history, myths, legends and connections with the land.

Courtesy of the National Film and Sound Archive of Australia. The full essay appears at aso.gov.au

Activity 10.2: Exam-style practice

Here is another, similar exercise. In this case you will only be given the text and the questions, and you will need to choose the words from the text.

Suggested time: 14 minutes

Complete the following summary using **ONE** *word from the text.*

The company Harley-Davidson has profited considerably from the desire of people to **1** _____. Harley-Davidson motorcycles are often associated in the minds of the public with members of criminal **2** _____, but the Australian managing director says that sales to outlaw bikers make up only a very small **3** _____ of their **4** _____. The increase in the number of people **5** _____ motorcycles in Australia shows that many kinds of people ride them, whether to **6** _____ to work or just for fun. The global president of the company feels that everyone has a Harley **7** _____ waiting to be activated. Once it has, many owners become addicted to the **8** _____ feeling of riding and the special **9** _____ they form with other riders.

Wild and Free and Off to Work

They may hint at a life lived on the edge but motorbikes are also practical, economic and fun.

Report: Dan Hall

One of the world's biggest brands has made a lot of money out of youthful rebellion – or, in many cases, nostalgia for it. 'Who doesn't have a little something to rebel against in their life?' Harley-Davidson's global chief marketing officer, Mark Hans-Richer, says about the raw attraction of the big, high-powered motorcycles. Blame Peter Fonda and the late Dennis Hopper in the 1969 classic film *Easy Rider* for producing instant, iconic images of freedom, rebellion and the desire to push back.

The appeal of rugged individualism is occasionally tarnished by association with outlaw biker crime, as was the case in Sydney last year when a violent brawl between rival outlaw motorcycle gangs at Sydney airport resulted in a death.

But Australians are signing up to the ranks of motorcycle owners in droves, whether it is for the pure exhilaration of riding or the convenience and low cost of commuting on a motorcycle. Motorcycle registrations have risen by almost 10 per cent a year since 2004, with more than 620,000 now registered across the country. This is 57.4 per cent more motorcycles on the road than in 2004.

It isn't just leather-clad members of bikie gangs who are buying motorcycles. For people who have to commute to work, choosing two wheels can lessen the travel time in a fun and economical way. Motorcycles come in all shapes and sizes, from wasp-sounding scooters to giant, gurgling monsters adorned with polished chrome and accessories, and not one stereotype defines the average motorcycle rider.

In fact, everyone, whether they have flirted with the idea of riding or not, has it in them to be a motorcycle rider, Harley-Davidson global president and chief operating officer Matt Levatich says. He calls this 'the Harley gene' and says everyone has it. It's just that for some, the Harley gene is dormant and waiting to be roused by the roar of a turbo-charged engine. 'Ten years ago, Harley-Davidson did some research and the research agency came up with the idea of the Harley gene,' Levatich says.

'A big part of the company's strategy is to encourage people with a dormant interest in motorcycles to bring their Harley gene to life, because typically, when you get someone on a Harley-Davidson, they don't get off.'

Activating this interest is a big part of Harley-Davidson's marketing strategy: turning dreams and latent interest into a full-blown motorcycle addiction. 'Really subtle things push someone that is generally curious about motorcycles to act on that curiosity,' Levatich says. 'First-time riders are usually engaged through an experience with a dealership; they feel welcome, it gets demystified for them and they do a test ride.' The feeling, so riders say, is liberating.

'[A Harley-Davidson motorcycle] is not a like a soft drink. This is not a commodity product. This is an experiential product,' Hans-Richer says. 'I have ridden all over the world and the people you meet all have the same joy of life. They come from all walks of life and yet they will form an immediate bond; it's a cool leveller.'

But not all motorcycle owners are on the straight and narrow – and Harley as a brand has to deal with association with the wilder fringes of the motorcycling world. The image of outlaw motorcycle gangs is the same all over the world, Hans-Richer says.

The fact that the image of bike riders is quite rugged and includes elements of risk is part of what attracts people to motorcycles and this naturally attracts a fair number of risk-takers.

'Harley-Davidson is a little more rebellious than your average everyday brand,' Hans-Richer says. 'You can push that way to the edge and become an outlaw, but the motorcycle doesn't make you do that; that's just who [outlaw bikers] are and it just happens a motorcycle might be part of that.'

Sales to outlaw motorcycle gang members make up about 1 or 2 per cent of the company's business, Harley-Davidson's Australian managing director Peter Nochar says.

'While outlaw gangs are in the headlines quite a bit, they are actually a small proportion of the business,' Nochar says. 'These are the folks that define the outer edge of the biker identity.'

When you have finished, check your answers in the Answer Key in Appendix 1.

9:35

What do they test?

In this kind of question you are asked to match a number of paragraphs or sections in the text to the most appropriate heading. This kind of question tests your understanding of main ideas, and your ability to distinguish between main ideas and details.

What do you need to do?

- If there is an example given, look at it carefully (and cross out that heading from the given list of headings).
- Read one paragraph and think about what the main idea is.
- Choose a heading from the list that most closely matches your idea.
- Cross out headings as you use them, but remember you may have to go back and change one.

Activity 11.1: Guided practice

Read the following text. After each paragraph you will be given a choice of two headings, one of which is the main idea and one of which is a detail. Choose the main idea.

A

> As WA tries to keep pace with a growing population and a resources boom, the strain on road infrastructure is clear. But a new independent report commissioned by the RAC to assess how much road-related tax is collected in WA, and how much is reinvested, has found a gaping hole in the budget. Only a fraction of the money collected in taxes related to road use and sent to the Federal Government is returned in the form of better roads and bridges, despite millions heading into Commonwealth coffers.

Heading 1: A report reveals an inequity
Heading 2: WA's growing population

B

Economics group ACIL Tasman looked at the amount sent east in the excise duty charged on petrol and diesel, the cost of luxury car tax on vehicles worth more than $57,100, and customs duties paid on motor vehicles for the State. It also calculated the amount of GST paid on petrol, and GST for new cars and fleet vehicles. In total the revenue heading from those sources to the Federal Government works out at approximately $2 billion a year. But when the amount transferred back to WA for road funding is considered, the gap is substantial.

ACIL Tasman estimated that only 33 cents in every dollar raised in federal road-related taxes from WA is returned to the state for road projects, mostly in grants to local governments or in specific funding, like that for Black Spot projects. This leaves the state and local governments picking up the rest of the tab to build, maintain and repair the 175,000 km of roads in WA.

Heading 1: *Only a third of revenue returned*
Heading 2: *A breakdown of the numbers*

C

RAC Head of Member Advocacy Matt Brown said the report found that an additional billion dollars that was collected from road users by the State Government was reinvested in the network. But this only looked at direct charges, such as registration fees, and didn't reflect the real economic gain to the government from an effective road system.

'There is enormous additional economic benefit from the road network,' he said. 'Governments in general aren't investing enough in the road network, and that is particularly emphasised with Canberra getting the better part of $2 billion directly from WA motorists and only returning 33 cents in the dollar. When you look at the challenges of our road network compared to other states, and you look at the size of our state, it is simply unsustainable for Canberra to refuse to increase the proportion of motoring taxes they actually return to WA in road funding.'

Heading 1: *Why the government should invest more*
Heading 2: *How much Canberra receives in taxes and fees*

D

The funding collected from Western Australia out of road-related taxes will hit an estimated $3 billion this year, the ACIL Tasman report says, and by 2014–15, it will be close to $3.5 billion. Over that time expenditure on roads in WA is projected to fall, not rise.

The picture worsens when you consider that a major source of federal funding for the 126,000 km of local roads could vanish within two years. About 80 per cent of Australia's roads are owned and maintained by local governments, paid for in part by property taxes raised by councils, but also through federal grants.

WA Local Government Association President Mayor Troy Pickard estimated about 27 per cent of the funding for local government roads comes from the Federal Government, through the Roads to Recovery program and other grants. But the Roads to Recovery money is due to run out when the program ends in 2014, leaving many routes that are already under-funded in a worse state.

'There are situations across Western Australia where local roads need to be upgraded and incur higher maintenance costs in order to support the development of industries, including a range of mining and agricultural activities,' Mr Pickard said.

'Local governments believe that there is an additional role for the Federal Government to financially support the upgrade of regionally important local roads to enable this economic development to occur.'

Heading 1: *Projected changes in funding and expenditure*
Heading 2: *The end of a key program*

E

Mr Pickard said this funding should be continued and indexed, so the funds reflect the real cost of building and maintaining the road network. 'Local governments recognise that in many areas there is a gap between expenditure on local roads and the lifecycle cost of maintaining those roads,' he said. 'Unless this gap is addressed, the quality of local government roads will decline.'

While the Federal Government promises it will put more money into WA infrastructure in the next few years, this will not come from the $2 billion of road-related taxes identified in the ACIL report.

Instead, the Commonwealth contribution to projects such as Gateway WA – the upgrade to the area around the airports, including Tonkin Highway – will be paid for out of a separate pool of money, called the Regional Infrastructure Fund, which the Federal Government plans to build with revenue from the proposed Minerals Resource Rent Tax.

The mining tax, which has not yet been voted on in Federal Parliament, is due to start 1 July next year. But even this promised pool of cash has been clouded by tense political relations.

The Federal Government has said that while the money for Gateway WA will be there regardless of recent moves by WA to increase its royalty taxes, other infrastructure funding may be in doubt as the state jostles for a better slice of revenue.

Heading 1: *Funding affected by political relations*
Heading 2: *Sources of funding*

F

Mr Brown said that Canberra's failure to invest more in WA roads would ultimately hurt both the state and national economy. 'Canberra always says that in WA you have roughly 10 per cent of the population, therefore you get roughly 10 per cent of the land transport funding,' Mr Brown said. 'That simply ignores the fact that WA is the growth state for population and economic development and that we are driving the country's economy.

'If they don't invest in the network, they are cutting their own throats because it is our state that has helped push Australia through the global financial crisis, and it is our state that will keep the country growing in the future.'

Heading 1: *The proportion of funding WA receives*
Heading 2: *An engine of economic growth now and in the future*

Source: Ruth Callaghan, RAC Horizons Magazine

Activity 11.2: Exam-style practice

This time you will only be given the list of headings and the text, as you would in the exam. *Choose the correct heading for sections **A–G** from the list of headings below.*

List of headings

i.   How Different Kinds of People Use Language

ii.   How Content Words Reveal Thoughts

iii. Potential Uses of this Knowledge

iv. Three Distinct Styles of Speech

v.   Differences Between Men and Women

vi. Language and Health

vii. Neurological Differences

viii. Ways of Writing

ix. Words of Meaning and Style

x.   A Few Words Used Often

xi. A Program to Analyse Language

The Secret Life of Pronouns

James W. Pennebaker

A

In the early 1980s, I stumbled on a finding that fascinated me. People who reported having a traumatic experience and kept the experience a secret had far more health problems than people who talked openly. If you asked people to write about their secrets, would their health improve? The answer, I discovered, was yes.

As part of this work, we developed a computer program to analyse the language people used when they wrote about traumas. We made numerous discoveries using this tool. However, our most striking discovery was not about the content of people's writing but the style. In particular, we found that the use of pronouns mattered enormously. The more people changed from using first-person singular pronouns (I, me) to using other pronouns (we, you), the better their health became. Their word use reflected their psychological state.

B

What do I mean by style? In any given sentence, there are two basic types of word. The first is content words, which provide meaning. These include nouns (table, uncle), verbs (to love, to walk), adjectives (blue, mouthwatering) and adverbs (sadly, hungrily).The other type are 'function' words. These serve quieter, supporting roles – connecting, shaping and organising the content words. They are what determines style.

Function words include pronouns (I, she), articles (a, an), prepositions (up, with), auxiliary verbs (is, don't), negations (no, never), conjunctions (but, and), quantifiers (few, most) and common adverbs (very, really). By themselves, they don't have much meaning. Whereas a content word such as 'table' can trigger an image in everyone's mind, try to imagine 'that' or 'really'.

C

Function words are psychologically very revealing. They are used at high rates, while also being short and hard to detect. They are processed in the brain differently from content words. And, critically, they require social skills to use properly. A very small number of function words account for most of the words we hear, read and say. English has about 450 common function words in total, which account for 55 per cent of the words we use.

To put this into perspective, the average English speaker has a vocabulary of perhaps 100,000 words. More than 99.9 per cent of this is made up of content words but these account for less than half of the words we use.

D

Function words are both short and hard to perceive. One reason we have trouble spotting their high rate of usage is that our brains naturally slide over them. We automatically focus on content words as they provide the basic who, what and where of a conversation.

This distinction can also be seen in people with brain damage. Occasionally, a person will have a brain injury that affects their ability to use content words but not function words. Injuries in other areas can produce the opposite results.

The two brain regions of interest are Broca's and Wernicke's areas. If a person with damage to their Broca's area were asked to describe a picture of, say, a girl and an old woman, he or she might say, 'Girl … ummm … woman … ahh … picture, uhhh … old.' Someone with a damaged Wernicke's area might say, 'Well, right here is one of them and I think she's next to that one. So if I see over there you'll see her too.' To say that Broca's area controls style words and Wernicke's controls content words is a gross oversimplification. Nevertheless, it points to the fact that the distinction between content and style words is occurring at a fairly basic level in the brain.

E

The ability to use function words is a marker of basic social skills – and analysing how people use them reveals a great deal about their social worlds. That is not to say a single sentence is particularly revealing. If you mention 'a chair' versus 'that chair', it says very little about you. But what if we monitored your words over the course of a week? What if we found that you use 'a' and 'the' at high rates, or hardly at all?

In fact, there are people who use articles at very high rates and others who rarely use them. Men tend to use them at higher rates than women. Gender aside, high article users tend to be more organised, emotionally stable, conscientious, politically conservative and older.

F

In one experiment, we analysed hundreds of essays written by my students and we identified three very different writing styles: formal, analytic and narrative.

Formal writing often appears stiff, sometimes humourless, with a touch of arrogance. It includes high rates of articles and prepositions but very few I-words, and infrequent discrepancy words, such as 'would', and adverbs. Those who score highest in formal thinking tend to be more concerned with status and power and are less self-reflective. They drink and smoke less and are more mentally healthy, but also tend to be less honest.

Analytical writing, meanwhile, is all about making distinctions. These people attain higher grades, tend to be more honest, and are more open to new experiences. Narrative writers are natural storytellers. The function words that generally reveal storytelling involve people, past-tense verbs and inclusive words such as 'with' and 'together'. People who score high for narrative writing tend to have better social skills, more friends and rate themselves as more outgoing.

G

This work on personality only scratches the surface. We have also found that function words can detect emotional states, spot when people are lying, predict where they rank in social hierarchies and the quality of their relationships. They reveal much about the dynamics within groups. They can be used to identify the authors of disputed texts, and much more.

[continued from previous page]

A. _____

B. _____

C. _____

D. _____

E. _____

F. *Example* F <u>viii</u>

G. _____

When you have finished, check your answers in the Answer Key in Appendix 1.

UNIT 12

Matching Features Questions

What do they test?

In this kind of question you are given a list of people, organisations or places. You have to match them to information about them in the text.

What do you need to do?

- Scan the text to find all the places where the names of people, organisations or places are mentioned.
- Read the parts of the text surrounding the names and try to match the text to the information in the questions.
- These types of questions are NOT in order, so be prepared to read various parts of the text.

> **TIP** Read the instructions carefully: you can often use letters more than once.

Activity 12.1: Guided practice

Underline or circle all the places in the following reading where these names are mentioned. The first one (Francis Collins) has been done for you as an example. Note that there is no answer for this part of the Activity in the Answer Key. However, there is discussion below the reading.

A Francis Collins

B Andrew von Eschenbach

C Eric Lander

D Steve Elledge and Greg Hannon

E Harold Varmus and Bruce Stillman

F Elian Zerhouni

Cancer Genome Atlas Pilot Launched

Kevin Davies

Researchers from the US National Cancer Institute (NCI) and the National Human Genome Research Institute (NHGRI) have launched a three-year, US$100 million pilot program for the Human Cancer Genome Project. Highlighted by the landmark completion of the human genome project two and a half years ago, researchers have completed the genome catalogues of more than 300 organisms, including, this year, first drafts of the dog and chimpanzee genomes. But the complete inventory of human genes does not by itself provide a huge advance in scientists' understanding of the molecular biology of cancer. Many senior US researchers have publicly posited launching a more ambitious cancer genome project.

Earlier this year, Broad Institute director Eric Lander floated the idea of a nine-year, US$1.3 billion cancer genome project, backed by former NIH director Harold Varmus and others. Lander suggested surveying 250 genome samples from each of 250 tumour types, producing a comprehensive catalogue of cancer-causing mutations. In a press conference in Washington DC to mark the launch of the project, NHGRI director Francis Collins noted that the first call for the human genome project, in 1986, was made by a cancer biologist, Renato Dulbecco. But while 'more than 300 genes contribute to the diabolical transformation of normal cells into cancer cells', a complete inventory of the genetic aberrations in cancer was urgently needed.

Collins said the unique collaboration between the NCI and the NHGRI would 'go beyond and behind the frontlines to create the first list of genomic insurgents that lead to cancer'. The project will be called The Cancer Genome Atlas – TCGA for short. The abbreviation, made up of the four letters of the genetic code, was no accident, said Collins. Collins said the TCGA pilot project would unite the 'powerful resources and experience of the [NCI], with the genome attitude of the [NHGRI]. Together, we've committed to investing $100 million over the next three years to construct a powerful network of researchers, technology and resources to tackle the cancer problem like never before.' 'This is an audacious project,' said Collins. 'We could not have undertaken this project until now. The biomedical research projects are aligned, the time is right.' Andrew von Eschenbach, director of the NCI, said the TCGA pilot project would help make cancer a chronic manageable condition. 'Mapping the cancer genome will be an important step in the understanding of the genetic component of the cancer process and the genetic susceptibility of people who are threatened by cancer.'

Not all cancer researchers support the idea of the HCGP. Two distinguished cancer biologists, Steve Elledge and Greg Hannon, recently criticised the project on the grounds that it would fail to meet its goals, and siphon money away from more fruitful investigator-driven research. Similar objections to the human genome project were raised two decades ago. Those complaints were rebutted by Nobel laureate Harold Varmus and Cold Spring Harbor Laboratory director Bruce Stillman. 'The cancer research community now needs a much better description of the genetic damage that drives human cancers,' Varmus and Stillman wrote in a letter to *Science*. 'This will form the basis for all future studies of cancer in the laboratory and the clinic and will provide immediate benefit for molecular diagnosis of human cancers.'

Collins acknowledged that there has been some anxiety about the total cost of the TCGA. 'We have no idea' of the ultimate cost, he admitted, adding that lessons learned in the coming three years will determine the cost of expanding the project from two or three tumours to 50 or more. 'Having a pilot project is a strong inspiration for the development of new technologies and the optimisation of existing ones,' said Collins. NIH Director Elian Zerhouni added that major initiatives such as TCGA are 'not designed to consume money but to provide new opportunities, new hypotheses that researchers will use. Even in tight budget times, we intend to make sure that balance [with investigator-driven funding] is preserved.'

Now, look at the information in the passage before and after the names to find the opinions of each person.

TIP When you're trying to find someone's opinion, keep an eye out for speech verbs such as 'said', 'claimed', 'suggested' and so on.

You should have found the following opinions:

Eric Lander

- *suggested surveying 250 genome samples from each of 250 tumour types, producing a comprehensive catalogue of cancer-causing mutations.*

Francis Collins

- *a complete inventory of the genetic aberrations in cancer was urgently needed.*
- *would 'go beyond and behind the frontlines to create the first list of genomic insurgents that lead to cancer'.*
- *We could not have undertaken this project until now.*
- *'We have no idea' of the ultimate cost.*

Andrew von Eschenbach

- *would help make cancer a chronic manageable condition.*

Steve Elledge and Greg Hannon

- *would fail to meet its goals, and siphon money away from more fruitful investigator-driven research.*

Harold Varmus and Bruce Stillman

- *'The cancer research community now needs a much better description of the genetic damage that drives human cancers.'*

- *'This will form the basis for all future studies of cancer in the laboratory and the clinic and will provide immediate benefit for molecular diagnosis of human cancers.'*

Elian Zerhouni

- *Even in tight budget times, we intend to make sure that balance [with investigator-driven funding] is preserved.*

Here is the list of names again, along with a series of statements. Match each opinion to the person who expressed it. All of the answers can be found in the extracts above.
  NB: Any letter can be used more than once.

A   Francis Collins

B   Andrew von Eschenbach

C   Eric Lander

D   Steve Elledge and Greg Hannon

E   Harold Varmus and Bruce Stillman

F   Elian Zerhouni

1.   The project will have benefits now and in the future.

2.   The project would not have been feasible in the past.

3.   Scientists should create a database of genetic material from different kinds of tumours.

4.   It may be possible for people to live with cancer.

5.   The project may cost more than expected.

6.   The project will divert funds from other research.

7.   The economic climate should not dictate funding.

Activity 12.2: Exam-style practice

This time you will only be given the reading and the questions as you would in the exam.

Suggested time: 12 minutes

Match each company with the information given about them.

NB: *Any letter may be used more than once.*

A   Google

B   Apple

C   Twitter

D   Facebook

1.   ... is planning to make it easier for users to keep information private.

2.   ... said that it had been collecting information by accident.

3.   ... is being forced to pay a considerable financial penalty.

4.   ... is required to be regularly monitored by an outside organisation.

5.   ... argued that security breaches had no serious effects.

6.   ... must let its users know what information it is collecting.

7.   ... has been accused of facilitating online crime.

8.   ... must keep the data it has collected until otherwise notified.

Who Owns Your Personal Data?

Kris Sangani

Attracting users to social networking sites and cloud computing sites is all about building trust. However, if recent news is anything to go by, consumers would be right to consider that the trust they have put into the internet companies that run these services has been betrayed. In recent months, it seems that not a day has gone by without another revelation that the private and personal data, the currency of these websites, has been compromised, misused or surreptitiously collected without the owner of the data's permission.

Between 2006 and the beginning of 2010, search engine giant Google started a project to map and digitally photograph every road in every major city in more than 30 countries for its product Google Streetview. This soon became a hate symbol among privacy and civil rights advocates, who claimed that Google were pushing the envelope on what type of information you could collect and publish on the Internet. But images, it appears, is not all that the Streetview cars collected. It now turns out that Google collected over 600 gigabytes of data from users of public and unprotected Wi-Fi access routers – which included Web pages visited and emails.

All this only came to light when German data privacy regulators investigated Google's Streetview project – and Google had to admit to collecting the data – although the company claimed they were not aware of their own data collection activities until the request was received and that none of this data was used in Google's search engine or other services. Google has said it will not destroy the data until permitted by regulators.

Even consumer tech companies such as Apple cannot escape criticism from the eagle-eyed German regulators. Apple must immediately 'make clear' what data it collects from users of its products and for what purposes, Germany's justice minister was quoted as saying by *Der Spiegel* magazine. 'Users of iPhones and other GPS devices must be aware of what kind of information is being collected,' Sabine Leutheusser-Schnarrenberger told the German weekly. The minister's criticism was aimed at changes Apple has made in its privacy policy whereby the company can collect data on the geographic location of its users – albeit anonymously. Leutheusser-Schnarrenberger said she expected Apple to 'open its databases to German data protection authorities' and clarify what data it was collecting and how long it was saving the data. The justice minister said it would be 'unthinkable' for Apple to create personality- or user-based profiles. 'Apple has the obligation to properly implement the transparency so often promised by [CEO] Steve Jobs,' she said.

Microblogging service Twitter recently agreed to a settlement with the US Federal Trade Commission over charges it put its customers' privacy at risk by failing to safeguard their personal information. This agreement stems from a series of attacks last year on Twitter, the service that lets people send short messages to groups of followers. Lapses in Twitter's security allowed hackers to send out fake tweets pretending to be from US President Barack Obama and Fox News. Hackers also managed to take administrative control of Twitter and gain access to private tweets, or messages. Between January and May 2009, hackers were 'able to view non-public user information, gain access to direct messages and protected tweets, and reset any user's password' and send tweets from any user account, according to the original FTC complaint. Twitter acknowledged 45 accounts were accessed by hackers in January last year and 10 in April 2009 'for short periods of time'. Twitter claims the January attack resulted in 'unauthorised joke tweets' from nine accounts. But the company also admitted that the hackers may also have accessed data such as email addresses and phone numbers. In April, when another incident occurred, Twitter claims to have cut off the hacker's administrative access within 18 minutes of the attack and quickly informed affected users. Under the terms of the settlement, Twitter will be barred for 20 years from 'misleading consumers about the extent to which it maintains and protects the security, privacy, and confidentiality of non-public consumer information'. Twitter must also establish a comprehensive security program that 'will be assessed by a third party every year for ten years', according to the FTC.

But most criticism surrounding data privacy is currently reserved for Facebook, which has faced the wrath of a consumer backlash when millions of users suddenly found their private details exposed and searchable on Google, Bing and Yahoo. Facebook, whose privacy policies have come under attack both at home and abroad, now faces a stiff fine from Germany's Hamburg Commissioner for Data Protection and Freedom of Information for storing non-users' personal data without their permission. The issue came to the fore in recent months amid criticisms that Facebook's confusing privacy settings were making it possible for Internet stalkers, cyber criminals and even nosy neighbours to gain a wealth of information about its users without their knowledge or permission. Facebook has now started to roll out changes that would give users more powerful tools to prevent personal information being accessed by others. For instance, Facebook will allow users to block all third parties from accessing their information without their explicit permission. It will also make less information available in its user directory and reduce the number of settings required to make all information private from nearly 50 to less than 15.

The back tracking by internet companies on how they use our private data has demonstrated that they cannot take our trust for granted. If social networking becomes increasingly important to companies such as Google, Apple and Microsoft, they will have to be careful not to violate their users' trust in the future.

When you have finished, check your answers in the Answer Key in Appendix 1.

UNIT 13

Matching Sentence Endings Questions

What do they test?

In this kind of question you are given a number of sentence 'stems', or beginnings, and you must choose the correct ending in order to make a complete sentence that expresses one of the main ideas of the text.

What do you need to do?

- Identify the key words in the sentence stem and scan the text to find those words or synonyms.
- Read that section of the text carefully and look for the sentence ending that most closely fits the information in the text.
- Think about the grammar: sometimes in a matching exercise some options are not grammatically possible.
- Use logic: some options will not make sense, even if they are grammatically possible.
- Once you have chosen your answers, look at them all again to check that they all fit.

> **TIPS** The questions in this exercise follow the order of the text.
> There will be more sentence endings than sentence stems, so you won't use them all.

Activity 13.1: Guided practice

Read the passage on pp. 71-2. Here are some sentence stems from the passage. Can you identify the key words in each one?

1. According to Amnesty International,

2. Although a court ordered Taser International to pay damages of ten million,

3. When a police officer fired a taser at Douglas Turner,

4. In Taser demonstrations,

5. If subjects are tased multiple times,

6. According to the Taser manual,

7. Taser International argued that

Now, **scan** the following text to find those words (or synonyms), and read the section surrounding the words.

Taser Stunned

Paul Marks

A US court has found Taser guilty of lax training practices, but doesn't query the stun gun's use.

Taser International, the maker of the electric-shock stun gun, has seen off 127 lawsuits from families who have claimed that its 50,000-volt weapon, in the hands of police, killed a relative. In all but one case the firm's lawyers have successfully argued that mitigating circumstances – mainly the victim's alleged drug use or pre-existing cardiac condition – meant they would have died from the trauma of being physically subdued by police officers in any case. In the one case the company lost, it paid out $150,000 in damages. But on 19 July the Arizona-based firm lost a major decision when a jury in a US District Court ruled that Darryl Turner, a 17-year-old shop assistant in Charlotte, North Carolina, had been killed by a police taser after receiving an extended 37-second shock. The ruling orders the firm to pay Turner's family $10 million in damages.

Amnesty International estimates that 450 people in the US have died after being tased since 2001. It welcomed the verdict. 'This important verdict confirms our long-held position that tasers are potentially lethal and therefore should only be used in a limited set of instances where there is a very serious and real threat to loss of life,' says Oliver Sprague, Amnesty's UK arms program director. The court's ruling does not question the safety of the weapon itself. Instead, it finds the firm negligent for improperly instructing and training the officers of the Charlotte-Mecklenburg Police Department (CMPD).

The Turner case concerned an incident in a Charlotte supermarket on 20 March 2008. Police were called when Turner, an employee, had an argument with a manager. When Turner lunged at a CMPD officer, the latter fired the taser probes into Turner's chest. He then kept the current applied for 37 seconds. After that, Turner was not moving. The Mecklenburg County medical examiner found he had died from a cardiac arrest.

This is not how a taser is supposed to be used. When you see a taser demonstration, the volunteer usually gets a half-second burst – enough to fell most people with excruciating muscle spasms. In practice, officers use a 5-second burst. This can be repeated – and often is – but officers should be well aware that research shows multiple bursts are a health risk. In 2009, despite winning legal challenges, Taser International revised its training manuals to warn users that they should avoid firing at people's chests owing to the proximity of the heart to the electric pulses.

Toxicology tests revealed no drugs in Turner's bloodstream and that his heart was in good shape. Death was caused by 'agitated state, stress and use of a conducted energy device', according to the medical examiner. Taser International disputed this, arguing Turner had a pre-existing risk of cardiac arrhythmias of a type exacerbated by drugs – and that he was carrying marijuana. What was clear to the jury, however, was that the CMPD officer should have been trained to avoid the chest and they found Taser International had been negligent in not doing this. John Burton, legal counsel for Turner's parents, proclaimed the case would mark the beginning of the end for the energy weapon. 'I think the taser is on the way out,' he told *New Scientist*.

When contacted by *New Scientist*, Taser International said it plans to appeal the verdict. But whatever the outcome, the use of tasers remains controversial. Just hours after the Turner verdict was delivered, another CMPD officer tased a 21-year-old man. He died an hour later.

You should have identified these sections of the text:

1. 'This important verdict confirms our long-held position that tasers are potentially lethal and therefore should only be used in a limited set of instances where there is a very serious and real threat to loss of life,' says Oliver Sprague, Amnesty's UK arms program director.

2. The ruling orders the firm to pay Turner's family $10 million in damages … The court's ruling does not question the safety of the weapon itself.

3. When Turner lunged at a CMPD officer, the latter fired the taser probes into Turner's chest. He then kept the current applied for 37 seconds.

4. When you see a taser demonstration, the volunteer usually gets a half-second burst.

5. … officers should be well aware that research shows multiple bursts are a health risk.

6. Taser International revised its training manuals to warn users that they should avoid firing at people's chests owing to the proximity of the heart to the electric pulses.

7. Taser International disputed this, arguing Turner had a pre-existing risk of cardiac arrhythmias of a type exacerbated by drugs.

Now, look at the sentence endings and choose the one that matches the information in each section of the text.

A. it was applied for far longer than advisable.

B. Turner's bloodstream was found to be free of drugs.

C. they may suffer health problems.

D. tasers should only be used in life-threatening situations.

E. Douglas Turner had a heart condition that contributed to his death.

F. it did not find tasers to be inherently unsafe.

G. the current is applied for less than a second.

H. subjects should not be tased in the chest.

I. police officers use the taser in 5-second bursts.

Activity 13.2: Exam-style practice

Here is another, similar exercise. This time you will only be given the text and the questions as you would in the exam. Follow the same steps as you did in Activity 13.1 to find the answers, and then when you have finished check the Answer Key in Appendix 1.

Suggested time: 12 minutes

Paint

WME Magazine

With Australia's craze for home renovation, we are going through paint by the truckload. In 2003, almost 124 million litres of paint was manufactured in Australia. What are the environmental implications of changing colours?

The ingredients in paint are a well-kept secret. Most paint manufacturers will only divulge the four broad categories of ingredients: pigments, solvents, resin or binder, and other additives.

Colour comes from the pigment, which is usually a mineral (such as Fe_2O_3 for red, TiO_2 for white) or a complex organic molecule (such as dioxazine violet for purple). The solvent and resin/binder provide the base for the pigment. In enamel paints the solvent is a hydrocarbon, while in water-based paints it is mostly water.

The remaining additives, usually some kind of hydrocarbon, are used for purposes such as controlling drying, as in preservatives or thickeners, preventing mildew formation in damp houses or to aid in the formation of the resin film.

All these components – as many as 40 separate materials in some paints – are extracted from the earth's crust. Most of the pigment materials are mined, while the others are usually refined from crude oil. Some paint manufacturers have begun replacing the resins in enamel paint with alkyds sourced from vegetable oils and there are also 'natural paint' manufacturers who use ingredients such as beeswax and milk proteins.

While determining what goes in paint is highly complex, making it is relatively simple. The ingredients are added to a mixer in the right order, stirred in and then packaged into steel cans. The paint shop is then supplied with cans of base paint and of tinter, a concentrate of the pigment that is added to the base according to a customer's colour preference.

Paint is environmentally advantageous in that it protects wood or metal surfaces from decay, reducing resource use and the generation of building waste. It also has negative impacts. The greatest of these occurs during application, with enamel paints in particular releasing volatile organic compounds as the solvents evaporate and the paint dries. This can give rise to 'Painter's Syndrome', which has been known to affect the central nervous system of professional decorators. In Europe it is estimated three per cent of total VOC emissions come from paint. One leading paint manufacturer estimates the lifecycle impact of painting 100 m² with enamel paint every seven years for 40 years would include release of up to 12 kg of VOCs, 171 kg of CO_2 and generate a similar amount of waste. It would need just 2,360 MJ but would also contribute 2.3 kg of acid-forming SO_4.

The impacts don't end with a coloured wall. DIY home decorators, despite the best educative efforts of councils, EPAs and paint companies, often wash their brushes in the sink or over a drain, sending diluted paint into waterways. Similarly, half-empty cans are sent to landfill, causing toxins to leach into the soil and groundwater. Recent programs such as Victoria's 'Paintback' trial aim to collect leftover paint. This not only pulls steel cans out of the waste stream, but also sees the paint reused, commonly on public property where specific colour is less vital.

---

*Choose one phrase from the list of phrases (**A–J**) to complete each sentence (**1–8**) below. There are more phrases than sentences, so you will not use them all.*

A.   environmental benefits.

B.   paint-related waste.

C.   animal products.

D.   the components of paint.

E.   a serious health problem.

F.   landfill.

G.   deciding its ingredients.

H.   paint companies.

I.   enamel.

J.   the earth.

1.   Paint companies are reluctant to reveal

2.   Paint additives generally come from

3. Producing paint is considerably easier than

4. While it releases dangerous chemicals, paint also has

5. A career as a painter can lead to

6. Water-based paint presents fewer dangers than

7. Home painters often ignore the advice of

8. The scheme in Victoria is trying to reduce

When you have finished, check your answers in the Answer Key in Appendix 1.

UNIT 14

Academic Reading Practice Tests

In the following pages you will find four full practice tests of academic reading, designed to give you an idea of how you might do in the real IELTS exam. It is strongly advised that:

- you work through all the units in this book BEFORE attempting the practice tests. This way you will have a solid grounding in the various question types and how to approach them.
- you get the most authentic result by putting yourself under exam conditions: give yourself only **60 minutes** and do not use a dictionary, any electronic devices or any notes during the test.
- you write your answers directly on the answer sheet as you would in the real test. Remember that you do not get any extra time to do so.
- you aim to get at least 65–70 per cent (i.e. around 26–28 correct answers). If you consistently receive lower scores, it's a good idea to wait a while, do a second round of these practice tests and score better results before you book an IELTS test.
Good luck!

IELTS
ACADEMIC READING PRACTICE
TEST 1

TIME ALLOWED: 1 hour
NUMBER OF QUESTIONS: 40

Instructions

All answers must be written on the answer sheet.

The test is divided as follows:

Reading Passage 1 Questions 1–13
Reading Passage 2 Questions 14–26
Reading Passage 3 Questions 27–40

Start at the beginning of the test and work through it. You should answer all the questions. If you cannot do a particular question, leave it and go on to the next. You can return to it later.

READING PASSAGE 1

You should spend about 20 minutes on Questions 1–13, which are based on Reading Passage 1.

Fact Sheet on Meteorites

Western Australian Museum

A

Meteorites are travellers through time and space that plunge to Earth, sometimes trailing a brilliant light and with a noise like thunder, at the end of a journey that began in the farthest reaches of the solar system as long ago as 45,000 million years.

They are solid bodies of crystalline matter thought to have originated deep inside planet-like bodies that were later fragmented. Unlike Earth rocks, the oldest of which date back about 3,800 million years, they have been isolated in deep space since the birth of the solar system.

While in space, they are known as meteors. Though their origins cannot be known for sure, there are indications that they are associated with comets, and that they originate from the asteroid belt between Mars and Jupiter. There they remain orbiting the Sun, but any that stray too close to Earth find themselves caught in its gravitational pull and begin to plummet towards its surface. Tearing through the atmosphere they are heated and their surfaces melted by friction. Between 100 and 150 kilometres above Earth they become incandescent and the larger ones are visible as bright lights trailing luminous tails. Some explode with a brilliant flash and a roar like thunder.

Most meteors burn up completely on entering the atmosphere, but some survive the journey and land on Earth's surface. They then become known as meteorites.

Meteorites vary in size. Some are the size of small pebbles, others weigh many tonnes. Scientifically, they are extremely valuable. Studying their chemical and mineralogical composition helps us to interpret the origins and nature of the solar system, as well as of Earth itself.

B

The study of meteorites is a comparatively young science, but meteorites have been known to man since the earliest days of prehistory.

Meteorite falls were described by writers of the Han Dynasty in China and by the philosophers of ancient Greece. In Mecca, Moslems pay homage to the sacred stone of Kaaba, which is apparently a meteorite. American Indians are also known to have paid homage to meteorites and members of two tribes made yearly pilgrimages to a hill in southern Alberta where the Iron Creek meteorite lay.

During the Iron Age, many meteorites were destroyed to make implements and weapons – among some peoples, these weapons were believed to confer supernatural powers on the bearer.

In the Middle Ages meteorites were regarded with awe as signs of God's wrath, so they were rarely preserved. It was not until the early 19th century that scientists became convinced that they were perfectly natural bodies; the scientific study of them is only about 150 years old.

C

There are three main types of meteorite – irons, stones and stony-irons.

Irons are mainly composed of nickel–iron alloy and have a characteristically dense and metallic appearance. They originate from the 'core' of their parent body and because of their metallic nature are more resistant to atmospheric friction than other meteorites. The largest meteorites are usually irons. The first meteorites found in Western Australia were irons discovered by a policeman named Alfred Eaton towards the end of the 19th century.

Stones consist largely of magnesium-rich silicate minerals, with varying amounts of nickel–iron. There are two main classes of stony meteorites – those that contain substances called chondrules, and those that do not. The chemical composition of the first group – known as chondrites – is very similar to that of the Sun.

Stony-irons contain about equal amounts of metallic nickel-iron alloy and silicate material. They are less common than the other two types of meteorite. The stony portion generally occurs as fragments welded by metal. They are probably the result of a high-speed collision in space between a body of iron and one of stone – the metal would have melted at the time of impact.

D

A meteorite 'fall' is a meteorite recovered after a witnessed fireball. A meteorite 'find' is a meteorite found by chance long after it fell to Earth.

Seeing a meteorite fall can be quite spectacular. For example, residents and visitors in Wiluna, Western Australia, for the Annual Race Meeting festivities on 2 September 1967 saw the night sky lit by a flash 'like a welding arc – white and blue'. One man reported seeing 'an object about 20 feet [six metres] long throwing out balls of fire'. Others reported 'a terrific rumbling noise' and 'six or seven bangs'. These explosive noises were caused by atmospheric shock waves as the meteorite fragmented on its journey to Earth.

E

The surface of a meteorite is quite different from that of most ordinary rocks. This is a result of entering the atmosphere at high speed and the outer portions of the meteorite being melted or burned off.

Stony meteorites have a glassy, dull black to deep brown fusion crust. This coating is only a few millimetres thick and if part of the surface is broken, the interior looks quite different.

Iron and stony-iron meteorites also have fusion crusts, but they are not quite so obvious.

Most meteorites contain some metallic iron. This can be recognised as silvery areas or grains on broken surfaces. It means that meteorites are usually heavier than ordinary rocks of the same size. Also, they will attract a magnet.

Making a positive identification and classifying a meteorite requires expert knowledge and sophisticated equipment.

QUESTIONS 1–5

Reading Passage 1 has five sections, A–E.
Choose the most suitable heading for each section from the list below.
Write the correct letter A–E in boxes 1–5 on your answer sheet.

1. Meteorites: *Falls* or *Finds*

2. Types of meteorites

3. Origins and journeys

4. Early beliefs

5. Appearance and other features

QUESTIONS 6–10

Complete the sentences below using words from the passage.
Choose NO MORE THAN TWO WORDS from the passage for each answer.
Write your answers in boxes 6–10 on your answer sheet.

6. Meteorites consist of solid bodies of …

7. Some American Indian tribes went on … to a meteorite in southern Alberta.

8. The chondrites are very similar to the Sun in their …

9. The surface of a meteorite gets melted as a result of travelling at …

10. To identify and classify a meteorite requires specialist knowledge and …

QUESTIONS 11–13

Do the following statements agree with the information given in Reading Passage 1?
In boxes 11–13 on your answer sheet, write
TRUE *if the statement agrees with the information*
FALSE *if the statement contradicts the information*
NOT GIVEN *if there is no information on this*

11. On Earth we can find meteorites, but never meteors.

12. A meteorite 'find' may also have been a meteorite 'fall'.

13. Meteorites are like any ordinary Earth rock.

READING PASSAGE 2

You should spend about 20 minutes on Questions 14–26, which are based on Reading Passage 2.

Internet Censorship

Cory Bernardi

To some, censorship is a powerful example of the loss of personal freedom and a step towards totalitarianism. Others see it as a necessary part of protecting the values that have provided the moral foundation to our society for generations.

Censorship is a double-edged sword with the potential to provide great benefits to society or to become itself the rot that destroys the democratic ideal.

At some level, censorship is practised by individuals, families, communities and nations. Our personal moral code, laws and regulations restrict and prohibit all manner of content or behaviour based on personal standards or societal expectations. Of course, no level of censorship can ever be 100 per cent effective. Prohibited material will always be available to those who are prepared to break the rules in order to obtain it.

While there are a few civil libertarians who advocate for personal choice to reign supreme and will oppose any form of censorship, mainstream Australia accepts that the appropriate classification and filtering of content is a reasonable thing to do.

The questions then remain, what is appropriate content and who should be the arbiter of it?

The government already appraises most modern forms of media and regulates when and where certain content can appear. This has proved to be a reasonably effective process.

However, there is now a suggestion that all internet content should be filtered at the ISP (Internet Service Provider) level and only 'acceptable' content be available to home and business users. Apart from the technical aspects of the scheme (which have come under fire from many areas and which I am not appropriately qualified to address), there are a number of more fundamental principles for people like myself.

I identify myself as a social and fiscal conservative and most people who know me would agree with that assessment. As such, one could reasonably expect me to support ISP filtering as a means of ensuring inappropriate content remains unavailable via the internet.

Yet I have grave reservations about the Labor Party proposal on mandatory ISP filtering which is described as 'a clean feed' – words that just sugar-coat compulsory censorship of whatever the government deems you are not allowed to see.

While I strongly believe that anything we can do to prevent access to illegal material is a lawful and moral obligation, there is a world of difference between illegal and inappropriate. The latter is a personal assessment in which I also recognise that my own standards and beliefs are not shared by all in our community.

Further, the nature of the internet means that we can't really classify content for availability only at a certain time or for certain ages like we can with television, movies or some printed content. This is a concern where young people may be exposed to inappropriate content inadvertently.

There are also broader philosophical reservations about allowing government to be the ultimate judge of what people should or should not have access to. I believe in small government – not Big Brother where personal responsibility is subservient to the State.

There are already many PC-based filters available that will prevent access to 'blacklisted' sites and allow PC end users to tailor the filters to meet the particular requirements of their households. Critics of these filters claim that they are easily disabled, but as I wrote earlier, prohibited material will always be available to those willing to break the rules.

In recent times we have seen evidence of this where paedophiles have been caught using peer to peer networks, bypassing mainstream networks to exchange files. I am advised that such peer to peer networks would not be captured by current ISP filtering technology.

Where there is evidence of illegal conduct or content online then filtering is certainly no substitute for sophisticated and well-resourced law enforcement. Wouldn't it make more sense to increase resources for our law enforcement agencies to strike at the heart of illegal content production and distribution rather than penalise millions of law-abiding citizens?

Where material is legal (many forms of pornography for instance), whilst many will object to its abundant availability, a blanket ban on accessibility via the internet is simply wrong.

Among the many advocates for ISP filtering that I have spoken with, no one has been able to explain to me exactly how it will work and what content will (or should) be filtered. It has been suggested that there should be a rating system for internet content similar to how Australian Communications and Media Authority (ACMA) rates media content. When I have asked how this could work, no one that I have spoken to has any clear idea, yet they all maintain that 'it needs to be done'. That may be so, but at what cost?

There is no stronger supporter of families than myself. My political life is a commitment to strengthening families and changing our nation through the development of our children. However, I also believe that in most circumstances, families know better than government what is best for their children. Parental responsibility cannot and should not be abrogated to government – if it is, our society will only become weaker.

Yes, illegal content should be banned from the web. It is illegal after all, but it is wrong to give the government a blank cheque to determine what is appropriate for us to view on the internet. That is a job for families, working with government.

QUESTIONS 14–18

Choose the correct letter **A**, **B**, **C** *or* **D**.
Write the correct letter in boxes **14–18** *on your answer sheet.*

14. In the passage, which of these is not stated as a result of censorship?

    A restricts an individual's liberty

    B conflicts with democratic principles

    C safeguards a society's moral values

    D reflects a community's living standards

15. Which of the following may not be used to impose restriction or prohibition?

    A rules and regulations

    B policies and laws

    C freedom of choice

    D codes of conduct

16. Why is the 'filtering' of all internet content at ISP level being recommended?

    A to ensure inappropriate content remains available

    B to allow acceptable content to be available

    C to prevent access to legal material

    D to avoid inadvertent exposure to appropriate content

17. Legally banned material will always be available to those who are

    A eager to learn the rules

    B ready to follow the rules

    C happy to bend the rules

    D willing to break the rules.

18. 'A blanket ban on accessibility via the internet' implies

    A keeping the whole internet blank

    B banning the entire illegal material on the internet

    C prohibiting access to the entire illegal material on the internet

    D an extended ban on accessing legal material through the internet.

QUESTIONS 19–21

*Look at the following list of items 19–21 and the list of items **A–D**.*
*Match each meaning 19–21 with the correct words **A**, **B**, **C** or **D** from the passage.*
*Write the correct letter: **A**, **B**, **C** or **D**, in boxes **19–21** on your answer sheet.*

19. Those who make judgements about the good and bad qualities of something

20. Those who live in a particular country or state and have rights and responsibilities there

21. Those who believe that people should be free to do and think what they want to

    A Totalitarians   **B** Libertarians

    C Critics   **D** Citizens

[continued from previous page]

QUESTIONS 22–26

Complete the summary below.
*Choose **NO MORE THAN THREE WORDS** from the passage for each answer.*
*Write your answers in boxes **22–26** on your answer sheet.*

The writer calls censorship a .... **[22]** and thinks the phrase
.... **[23]** is merely to make compulsory censorship appear less
threatening. According to him, there is a vast difference between .... **[24]**.
He recommends increasing resources for the country's .... **[25]** so
that they control the production of illegal content rather than giving the government
.... **[26]** to decide for us what is appropriate on the internet for viewing.

READING PASSAGE 3

You should spend about 20 minutes on Questions 27–40, which are based on Reading Passage 3.

Cross-cultural Communication

Melvin Schnapper

A

A Peace Corps staff member is hurriedly called to a town in Ethiopia to deal with reports that one of the volunteers is treating Ethiopians like dogs. What could the volunteer be doing to communicate that?

Another foreign volunteer in Nigeria has great trouble getting any discipline in his class, and it is known that the students have no respect for him because he has shown no self-respect. How has he shown that?

Neither of these volunteers offended his hosts with words. But both of them were unaware of what they had communicated through their non-verbal behaviour.

In the first case, the volunteer working at a health centre would go into the waiting room and call for the next patient. She did this as she would in America – by pointing with her finger to the next patient and beckoning him to come. Acceptable in the States, but in Ethiopia her pointing gesture is for children and her beckoning signal is for dogs. In Ethiopia one points to a person by extending the arm and hand and beckons by holding the hand out, palm down, and closing it repeatedly.

In the second case, the volunteer insisted that students look him in the eye to show attentiveness, in a country where prolonged eye contact is considered disrespectful.

B

While the most innocent American-English gesture may have insulting, embarrassing, or at least confusing connotations in another culture, the converse is also true. If foreign visitors were to bang on the table and hiss at the waiter for service in a New York restaurant, they would be fortunate if they were only thrown out. Americans might find foreign students overly polite if they bow.

C

It seems easier to accept the arbitrariness of language – that dog is *chien* in French or *aja* in Yoruba – than the differences in the emotionally laden behaviour of non-verbal communication, which in many ways is just as arbitrary as language.

Secondly, we assume that our way of talking and gesturing is 'natural' and that those who do things differently are somehow playing with nature. This assumption leads to a blindness about intercultural behaviour. And individuals are likely to remain blind and unaware of what they are communicating non-verbally, because the hosts will seldom tell them that they have committed a social blunder. It is rude to tell people they are rude; thus the hosts grant visitors a 'foreigner's licence', allowing them to make mistakes of social etiquette, and they never know until too late which ones prove disastrous.

An additional handicap is that the visitors have not entered the new setting as free agents, able to detect and adopt new ways of communicating without words. They are prisoners of their own culture and interact within their own framework. Yet the fact remains that for maximum understanding the visitor using the words of another language also must learn to use the tools of non-verbal communication of that culture.

D

Non-verbal communication – teaching it and measuring effect – is more difficult than formal language instruction. But now that language has achieved its proper recognition as being essential for success, the area of non-verbal behaviour should be taught to people who will live in another country in a systematic way, giving them actual experiences, awareness, sensitivity. Indeed, it is the rise in linguistic fluency that now makes non-verbal fluency even more critical. A linguistically fluent visitor may tend to offend even more than those who don't speak as well if that visitor shows ignorance about interface etiquette; the national may perceive this disparity between linguistic and non-linguistic performance as a disregard for the more subtle aspects of intercultural communication. Because non-verbal cues reflect emotional states, both visitor and host national might not be able to articulate what's going on.

E

While it would be difficult to map out all the non-verbal details for every language that the Peace Corps teaches, one can hope to make visitors aware of the existence and emotional importance of non-verbal channels. I have identified five such channels: *kinesic, proxemic, chronemic, oculesic*, and *haptic* …

These five channels of non-verbal communication exist in every culture. The patterns and forms are completely arbitrary, and it is arguable as to what is universal and what is culturally defined.

Of course, there is no guarantee that heightened awareness will change behaviour. Indeed, there may be situations where visitors should not alter their behaviour, depending on the status, personalities, and values in the social context. But the approach seeks to make people aware of an area of interpersonal activity that for too long has been left to chance or the assumption that visitors to other countries will be sensitive to it because they are surrounded by it.

QUESTIONS 27–31

Reading Passage 3 has five sections, **A**–**E**.
Choose the correct section for each main idea from the list of main ideas given below.
*Write the correct number, **i–vii**, in boxes **27–31** on your answer sheet.*

List of Headings

i.	How Americans would interpret the non-verbal behaviour of foreigners
ii.	How Africans would interpret the non-verbal behaviour of American volunteers
iii.	Non-verbal behaviour of foreigners in Africa
iv.	Five channels of non-verbal communication as identified by the writer
v.	A word of warning from the writer
vi.	Non-verbal fluency as necessary as linguistic fluency
vii.	Why one needs to learn about intercultural behaviour

27. Section **A** _____

28. Section **B** _____

29. Section **C** _____

30. Section **D** _____

31. Section **E** _____

QUESTIONS 32–36

*Choose the correct letter **A**, **B**, **C** or **D**.*
*Write the correct letter in boxes **32–36** on your answer sheet.*

32. In Ethiopia, to call someone, one can

    A point at them with one finger

    B call out their name aloud

    C beckon them with head movement

    D beckon with whole arm and hand.

33. The assumption that leads to an ignorance about intercultural behaviour is

    A our own cultural practices are normal and natural

    B we need not know what we are communicating non-verbally

    C we are allowed to make mistakes in social etiquette

    D we can notice and learn new non-verbal behaviour in a new environment.

34. Which one of these is not listed as part of the suggested training in non-verbal behaviour?

A real experience

B critical attitude

C enhanced awareness

D heightened sensitivity

35. A linguistically fluent visitor to a new country is likely to offend the locals if

A they are ignorant about the local social etiquette

B they show off their linguistic skills to locals

C they do not use their linguistic skills

D their non-verbal cues reflect their emotional states.

36. Which one is not true about the five channels of non-verbal communication?

A Visitors can be made aware of their existence.

B Visitors can be shown their emotional importance.

C They exist in every culture.

D Being aware of them will change interpersonal behaviour.

QUESTIONS 37–40

Do the following statements agree with the information given in Reading Passage 3?
*In boxes **37–40** on your answer sheet, write*
TRUE *if the statement agrees with the information*
FALSE *if the statement contradicts the information*
NOT GIVEN *if there is no information on this*

37. One of the Peace Corps volunteers was understood as treating the Ethiopians like dogs.

38. In a New York restaurant, banging on a table to call for service is usual.

39. A foreigner's licence allows visitors to make mistakes when travelling in a new country.

40. A linguistically fluent visitor will also have non-verbal fluency.

IELTS
ACADEMIC READING PRACTICE
TEST 2

TIME ALLOWED: 1 hour
NUMBER OF QUESTIONS: 40

Instructions

All answers must be written on the answer sheet.

The test is divided as follows:

Reading Passage 1 Questions 1–13
Reading Passage 2 Questions 14–23
Reading Passage 3 Questions 24–40

Start at the beginning of the test and work through it. You should answer all the questions. If you cannot do a particular question, leave it and go on to the next. You can return to it later.

READING PASSAGE 1

You should spend about 20 minutes on Questions 1–13, which are based on Reading Passage 1.

The Truth About Global Warming

Claudia Cornwall

A

Eleven of the hottest years since 1850 occurred between 1995 and 2006. Last year, the United Nations Intergovernmental Panel on Climate Change (IPCC) reported that the earth was about 0.75°C warmer than it was in 1850. While this doesn't sound like a lot, a small difference in average temperature can make a big difference in climate. During the last ice age, for example, the planet was only about 5°C colder than now.

B

The IPCC has concluded that human activity is very likely responsible, by increasing the concentrations of greenhouse gases and thus the greenhouse effect. More than 25 scientific societies, including the national science academies of the G8 nations, have endorsed the conclusion. Some scientists, however, still disagree, arguing that human contribution is minimal.

C

The effect, explains Robert Charlson, a professor at the University of Washington, 'has been on the scientific books for over a century. It has been tested very thoroughly.' Certain gases cause the atmosphere to trap heat energy at the earth's surface. Without the greenhouse effect, the earth's average global temperature would be −18°C, rather than the present comfortable 14.6°C. The concern is with the enhanced greenhouse effect that humans cause – specifically, that it will heat the planet too much.

D

The main greenhouse gases (GHGs) are carbon dioxide (CO_2), methane, nitrous oxide, chlorofluorocarbons (CFCs) and water vapour. Except for CFCs, which are for commercial purposes, these gases are found in nature. Burning fossil fuels, trees and agricultural waste adds to the CO_2, methane and nitrous oxide, as do landfills, oil refineries and coalmines. And we affect water vapour indirectly, too. As the earth warms because other GHG levels increase, evaporation ramps up, creating more water vapour.

E

'CO_2 has increased 35 per cent since the beginning of the industrial era,' says Gavin Schmidt, a climatologist with NASA's Goddard Institute for Space Studies in New York. 'Methane has more than doubled. Nitrous oxide has gone up 17 per cent.'

F

Scientists are particularly concerned about CO_2 because it is the most abundant of the gases that we affect directly. While we have stabilised our CFC and methane emissions, we have not done the same with CO_2 so far. The carbon dioxide in the atmosphere continues to rise by about 0.4 per cent a year – because the fossil fuels that produce it fill 85 per cent of our energy requirements.

G

According to NASA's Schmidt, 'CO_2 stays around for centuries.' Worldwide, we produce some 23.5 gigatonnes of CO_2 annually. (A gigatonne is a trillion kilograms.) Fortunately, only half of this amount stays in the atmosphere; natural systems absorb the rest. For instance, oceans, our largest repository of carbon dioxide, take in more than a quarter of our CO_2 emissions every year. They already hold about 50 times the amount in the atmosphere and ten times that in the land biosphere. But just how much more they can safely store is still not clear. In addition, forests and plants soak up less than a quarter of CO_2 emissions. Through photosynthesis, plants separate CO_2 into oxygen, which they emit, and carbon, which becomes part of their cells.

H

Climate change may also result from regular shifts in the orbit of the earth and the tilt of its axis changing how sunlight is distributed around the globe, and may explain why the ice ages came and went. These shifts take place slowly over hundreds of thousands of years.

I

Tiny particles pumped into the atmosphere by erupting volcanoes and industrial pollution reflect some solar energy back to space, with the effect of making things cooler. In 1991, Mount Pinatubo in the Philippines blew so much dust into the stratosphere that the temperature dropped by half a degree for two years.

J

Water in the form of vapour and clouds plays a role, but their impact is hard to predict. Water evaporating from warmer oceans creates clouds that can both trap heat and reflect it into space. 'Low clouds tend to cool the planet,' Professor Charlson says. 'High clouds warm it.'

K

Many researchers have concluded that natural forces alone do not explain the temperature increases over the past 30 or 40 years. Bruce Bauer, who studies ancient weather systems at the World Data Centre for Paleoclimatology in the US, says, 'When you try to do the maths, the only way you can calculate what's happening is to include the effects of artificial CO_2.'

L

The theory of heat-trapping gases projects that as CO_2 emissions go up, temperatures will rise in the lower atmosphere and at the surface of the earth. Thomas Karl, director of the National

Oceanic and Atmospheric Administration's National Climatic Data Centre in the US, says, 'The evidence continues to support human impact on global temperature.'

M

According to the IPCC, by 2100 the average temperature might rise by as much as 5.8°C. But its report also says we could hold temperature increases to a more bearable two degrees above pre-industrial levels. Getting that result means halving current CO_2 emissions by 2050, which is achievable if we lower them by slightly over 1 per cent of current levels every year until then.

QUESTIONS 1–5

*Reading Passage 1 has 13 paragraphs, **A–M**.*
Which paragraph contains the following information?
*Write the correct letter **A–M** in boxes **1–5** on your answer sheet.*

1. Of all GHGs, methane has had the highest increase in the age of industrialisation.

2. The greenhouse effect prevents the earth's atmosphere from becoming too cold.

3. Nearly 50 per cent of CO_2 produced is dissipated in our natural environment.

4. There are contradictory opinions about the role of human beings in enhancing global warming.

5. The atmosphere surrounding us has all but one of the greenhouse gases present in it.

QUESTIONS 6–9

*Answer the following questions using **NO MORE THAN THREE WORDS** from the text.*
*Write your answers in boxes **6–9** on your answer sheet.*

6. How did scientific societies and science academies respond to the result reached by the IPCC?

    _____

7. What are chlorofluorocarbons used for?

    _____

8. What environmental effect did the eruption of Mount Pinatubo have that lasted until about 1993?

    _____

9. What forms of water cause the earth's temperature to rise or to fall?

    _____

[continued from previous page]

QUESTIONS 10–13

*Complete each sentence with the correct ending **A–F** from the box below.*
*Write the correct letter **A–F** in boxes **10–13** on your answer sheet.*

10. According to Professor Robert Charlson

11. According to Bruce Bauer

12. According to Thomas Karl

13. According to the Intergovernmental Panel on Climate Change

---

A carbon dioxide remains for hundreds of years.

B one must take into account the effects of unnatural carbon dioxide.

C our planet is warmer than it was hundreds of years ago.

D the rise in the earth's temperature could be controlled.

E there is proof that global temperature has been affected by humans.

F science has known of the greenhouse effect for more than a hundred years.

READING PASSAGE 2

You should spend about 20 minutes on Questions 14–23, which are based on Reading Passage 2.

Unoriginal Sins

Victoria Laurie

Are we creating a generation of people unable to distinguish between an original idea and a borrowed one?

'Cyber-cheating' and 'cyber-shoplifting' are new words coined to describe the worldwide rise in plagiarism and abuse of copyright. Universities, in particular, are reeling from this new version of plain old academic dishonesty, with students copying entire slabs or essays with a click-and-drag motion, buying essays from cheat sites; or even paying people to write them. Jan Thomas, a pro-vice chancellor at Perth's Murdoch University, knows how easy it is to 'lift' information from the internet. On her desk is a 2000-word essay liberally highlighted with yellow markings. On a sheet beneath is the article the student cribbed from. His entire philosophy essay on friendship has been copied verbatim, with the exception of about 50 words. 'This student probably put "friendship" in the search engine and found a 1996 article about Aristotle's writing on achieving a good life,' says Thomas. 'But this is an extreme example.'

All Murdoch University first-year students are given mandatory instruction on referencing and critiquing other sources. 'It's three strikes and you're out,' says Thomas. 'But you can be excluded from the university on the first occasion if the breach is severe enough.'

If she has suspicions, Thomas uses a search engine such as Google or Yahoo! to enter key phrases and find out if slabs of text have been lifted. But it's time-consuming. 'In a division of 500 students last year I saw five definite cases. It probably means we are missing about 50.' One of Thomas's colleagues in another department says she deals with 20 cases of plagiarism a semester. She says some students change every third word to avoid detection on search engines. One student even plagiarised her bibliography – detected when eight of the sources she cited were not stocked in the university library.

Plagiarism and cheating are, of course, not new – what is new is the fact offenders are being caught, says Thomas. 'I think we're more rigorous now.'

Current reliable figures on the incidence of plagiarism are surprisingly scarce, perhaps because universities are loath to reveal them. This is one of the reasons CAVAL, a university-owned information resources group, conducted its own investigation last year on behalf of six Victorian universities. It checked nearly 2000 essays over 20 subjects using a new plagiarism-detection program called Turnitin.com, which can scan 2.6 billion journals for matching text. Plagiarised parts of an essay are highlighted in red and the original source displayed.

Research leader Steve O'Connor says one in eight students was found to have copied 25 per cent or more of an essay from the internet. But he believes this is just the tip of the iceberg and estimates as many as 500,000 essays a year could contain some plagiarism. Adding to the problem are a host of new websites such as 'School Sucks', 'Other People's Papers' and 'The Evil House of Cheat', which offer downloadable university papers and essays.

Dr Garry Allan, director of information technology at RMIT, says plagiarism 'needs to be addressed within the framework of academic integrity. [The problem is] social values and nature of learning are lagging behind technology.' Allan floats an intriguing idea: one day every computer user in the world may find themselves pressing an 'originality check' button on their keyboard. 'At the moment you have a spellchecker in your word processor. In the future you'll have an originality checking button and when you press it, it will underline in a particular colour all the text strings that are not identifiably original,' says Allan.

QUESTIONS 14–17

Do the following statements agree with the information given in Reading Passage 1?
*In boxes **14–17** on your answer sheet, write:*
TRUE *if the statement agrees with the information*
FALSE *if the statement contradicts the information*
NOT GIVEN *if there is no information on this*

14. Students fail to differentiate between an original idea and a borrowed idea.

15. There are two new terms to describe the ways copyright is breached.

16. Worldwide increase in the incidence of academic dishonesty is related to an increase in the use of computers.

17. Academic dishonesty includes cheat sites buying essays.

QUESTIONS 18–23

Using information in the reading passage, match each of the following actions with the purpose it was meant to achieve.
*Write the appropriate letters **A–G** in boxes **18–23**. There are more letters than you will need.*

ACTION	PURPOSE
18 ... giving mandatory instruction on referencing	**A** To access downloadable material as university assignment
19 ... using search engines to enter key phrases	**B** To prevent students from failing to give the source of their information
20 ... changing every third word	**C** To detect which parts of a student's essay have been copied
21 ... using the program Turnitin.com	**D** To detect if chunks of text have been copied from another source
22 ... using websites like 'School Sucks'	**E** To avoid detection of one's essay as a copied essay on search engines
23 ... paying others to write essays or buying essays from certain websites	**F** To avoid giving true figures on the incidences of plagiarism
	G To earn good scores without making the expected effort as a learner

READING PASSAGE 3

*You should spend about 20 minutes on Questions **24–40**, which are based on Reading Passage 3.*

The Eccentric Engineer

Justin Pollard

Genetic engineering gets a bad press with talk of 'playing God' and 'Frankenstein foods'. But in truth this had always been an area of engineering where precautionary principle has held sway that, in the absence of scientific consensus, the burden of proof lies in showing that an intended action is not harmful. This is largely thanks to one man.

In early 1971 Paul Berg and his team at Stanford University in California were working at the very edges of biological science. Following the pioneering work of Crick and Watson identifying the DNA helix, they were now looking at ways of splicing together sections of DNA from different organisms and then using a virus to inject the resulting genome into a living cell – a technique known today as Recombinant DNA (rDNA). This held out the prospect of identifying the effects of genes and perhaps later taking particular beneficial genes from one creature and inserting them into another. During the 1960s a lot of work had been done using the bacterium every handwash manufacturer loves to hate, E. Coli, and the virus 'lambda' which infects it. What had not been attempted was expanding this research into studying mammalian cells and the viruses that might be used to insert new genetic material into them. In the early 1970s, Berg wondered whether it might be possible to use the Simian Virus 40 (SV40) to carry novel DNA sequences into mammalian cells.

The problem with SV40 was that it was tiny – only 5000 base pairs long, encoding just five genes – so he realised he would have to tinker with it to enable it to pick up other genes and carry them into a living cell. To achieve this he decided to try to splice together SV40 DNA with a DNA fragment that could replicate independently a cell's genome (a plasmid) constructed from his old friend the lambda virus and three E. Coli genes. This recombinant DNA would then be inserted into living E. Coli cells.

Explaining this development to other pioneering genetic engineers at the Cold Spring Harbor Laboratory Tumor Virus Workshop, Long Island, in 1971, Berg's research assistant Janet Metz gained a reaction she was perhaps not expecting. Microbiologist Robert Pollack observed that the agent they were using, SV40, was a tumour-causing virus, which they had now given the ability to splice itself into the genome of E. Coli. E. Coli was, in turn, a very common bacterium resident in the human intestine. In an urgent call to Berg, Pollack asked: 'What if the E. Coli in your lab escaped into the environment and into people? It would be a real disaster if one of the agents now being handled in research should in fact be a real human cancer agent.' Could they have created a Frankenstein bacterium – a common human parasite now with the deadly ability to spread a cancer plague?

The deadly possibilities of recombinant DNA had suddenly become clear: so what was to be done? Concerned that Pollack was over-reacting, Berg canvassed more opinion. Many argued that the work was so vital that risks were worthwhile, others that it was a matter of ethics. One group claimed that the technique posed no particular threat and that 'over-regulating' research would be more dangerous.

It was a delicate situation. The first steps of Berg's work had been completed; the rDNA had been painstakingly created. All that remained was to insert it into a living cell. But what would result? A miracle or a monster or just something interesting in between? With the certainty that executing the last step in the experiment would be Nobel-worthy stuff, many would have carried on regardless, leaving the theoretical problems for others, but Berg chose not to. On 26 July 1974 he published an open letter in *Science* calling for a voluntary moratorium on some areas of rDNA research (including his own) until the risks were better understood.

This was followed up the next year at the Conference on Biohazards in Biological Research. Here genetic engineers openly discussed the possible outcomes of their research, bringing the subject to public and government attention and leading to the laying down of strict guidelines on the creation and use of rDNA. In the meantime another team had successfully spliced a gene from a toad into an E. Coli bacterium, effectively stealing Berg's thunder.

But Berg's insistence on being an ethical engineer did bear fruit, ushering in a new era of openness in science. Far from restricting research, it also brought the ideas and terminology of genetic engineering into the public domain where they belong.

QUESTION 24

*Choose the correct letter: **A**, **B**, **C** or **D**. Write the correct letter in box **24** on your answer sheet.*

24. The reading passage highlights which particular aspect of Paul Berg as a scientist?

    A that he was a genetic engineer

    B that he created a new recombinant DNA

    C that he acted in an ethical manner instead of in his own interest

    D that he sought the opinion of other scientists on the possible outcomes of his research.

QUESTIONS 25–28

Complete the following table outlining various research-related works or programs mentioned in the reading passage, using words and phrases from the box on the next page.
*Write the appropriate letters **A–H** of your answers in boxes **25–28** on your answer sheet.*

Year/date	Scientist/researcher	Research on/work on
25 …		E. Coli and the virus 'lambda'
	Watson and Crick	DNA helix identified
Early 1970s	Paul Berg and team	**26** …
27 …	**28** …	Voluntary moratorium on rDNA research

A	1960s	B	1970s
C	1974	D	Janet Metz
E	Paul Berg	F	Watson and Crick
G	Robert Pollack	H	Simian Virus 40 (SV40)
I	A gene from a toad spliced into E. Coli		

QUESTIONS 29–32

Label the parts of the diagram illustrating a process described in the reading passage.
Choose your labels from the box below the diagram.
*Write your answers in boxes **29–32** on your answer sheet.*

The process of forming a recombinant DNA (rDNA)

29 _____ + 30 _____ = 31 _____ >>>> 32 _____

A The recipient living cell	**B** A section of DNA from organism A
C Injecting virus with genome	**D** A section of DNA from organism B
E Resulting genome within a virus	

QUESTIONS 33–35

*Choose the correct letter: **A**, **B**, **C** or **D**. Write the correct letter in boxes **33–35** on your*
answer sheet.

33. There were different responses when Paul Berg asked others how he should proceed
with his research using Simian Virus 40 (SV40). Which of the following reactions from
other scientists is not mentioned in the text?

A it was an ethical issue

B to continue his research even if it involved risks because it was an
important study

C to stop his research as it was dangerous for him to work with
cancer-causing agent

D to continue his research as there was no specific danger other than getting research
too controlled.

[continued from previous page]

34. What did Paul Berg eventually do after creating the new rDNA and after receiving different responses from other scientists?

A He continued his work using SV40 as he had planned.

B He stopped working as a scientist altogether.

C He started publishing articles on scientific topics.

D He temporarily stopped his work and asked others working in that area to do the same until the dangers involved in the work were clearer.

35. Which of these was NOT the outcome of what Paul Berg did in regard to his research with SV40?

A Genetic engineers openly discussed their research in a science conference.

B Genetic engineers wrote open letters in science journals.

C Strict rules were made about the making and using of rDNA.

D Berg lost a chance to win worldwide recognition for groundbreaking research.

QUESTIONS 36–40

*Using information in the reading passage, match each of the items in **List A** with the related information in **List B**.*

*Write appropriate letters in boxes **36–40**.*

List A	List B
36 ... E. Coli	**A** a DNA fragment able to replicate independently
37 ... SV40	**B** a bacterium infecting the human body
38 ... Lambda	**C** combining two strands of DNA
39 ... splicing	**D** a virus infecting a bacterium
40 ... a plasmid	**E** a tumour-causing virus

IELTS
ACADEMIC READING PRACTICE
TEST 3

TIME ALLOWED: 1 hour
NUMBER OF QUESTIONS: 40

Instructions

All answers must be written on the answer sheet.

The test is divided as follows:

Reading Passage 1 Questions 1–13
Reading Passage 2 Questions 14–26
Reading Passage 3 Questions 27–40

Start at the beginning of the test and work through it. You should answer all the questions. If you cannot do a particular question, leave it and go on to the next. You can return to it later.

READING PASSAGE 1

You should spend about 20 minutes on Questions 1–13, which are based on Reading Passage 1.

Science and Human Life

Bertrand Russell

1

Science and the techniques to which it has given rise have changed human life during the last hundred and fifty years more than it had been changed since men [sic] took to agriculture, and the changes that are being wrought by science continue at an increasing speed. There is no sign of any new stability to be attended on some scientific plateau. On the contrary, there is every reason to think that the revolutionary possibilities of science extend immeasurably beyond what has so far been realized. Can the human race adjust itself quickly enough to these vertiginous transformations, or will it, as innumerable former species have done, perish from lack of adaptability? The dinosaurs were, in their day, the lords of creation, and if there had been philosophers among them, not one would have foreseen that the whole race might perish.

2

But they became extinct because they could not adapt themselves to a world without swamps. In the case of man and science there is a wholly new factor, namely, that man himself is creating the changes of environment to which he will have to adjust himself with unprecedented rapidity. But, although man through his scientific skill is the cause of the changes of environment, most of these changes are not willed by human beings.

3

Although they come about through human agencies, they have, or at any rate have had so far, something of the inexorable inevitability of natural forces. Whether Nature dried up the swamps or men deliberately drained them makes little difference as regards the ultimate result. Whether men will be able to survive the changes of environment that their own skill has brought about is an open question. If the answer is in the affirmative, men will have to apply scientific ways of thinking to themselves and their institutions.

4

One of the most obvious problems raised by a scientific technique is that of the exhaustion of the soil and of raw materials. This subject has been much discussed and some governments have actually taken some steps to prevent the denudation of the soil. But I doubt whether, as yet, the good done by these measures is outweighing the harm done in less careful regions. Food, however, is such an obvious necessity that the problem is bound to receive increasing attention as population pressure makes it more urgent. Whether this increased attention will do good or harm in the long run is, I fear, questionable. By a spendthrift use of fertilisers, food production in the present can be increased at the cost of food production in the future.

5

The question of raw materials is more difficult and complex than the question of food. The raw materials required at one stage of technique are different from those required at another. It may be that by the time the world's supply of oil is exhausted, atomic power will have taken its place. But to this sort of process there is a limit, though not an easily assignable one. At present there is a race for uranium, and it would seem likely that before very long there will be no easily accessible source of uranium. If, when that happens, the world has come to depend upon nuclear energy as its main source of power, the result may be devastating. All such speculations are of course very questionable, since new techniques may always make it possible to dispense with formerly necessary raw materials. But we cannot get away from the broad fact that we are living upon the world's capital of stored energy and are transforming the energy at a continually increasing rate into forms in which it cannot be utilised. Such a manner of life can hardly be stable, but must sooner or later bring the penalty that lies in wait for those who live on capital.

6

The problem which most preoccupies the public mind at the present moment is that of scientific warfare. It has become evident that, if scientific skill is allowed free scope, the human race will be exterminated, if not in the next war, then in the next but one or the next but two – at any rate at no very distant date. To this problem there are two possible reactions: there are those who say, 'Let us create social institutions which will make large-scale war impossible'; there are others who say, 'Let us not allow war to become too scientific. We cannot perhaps go back to bows and arrows, but let us at any rate agree with our enemies that, if we fight them, both sides will fight inefficiently.' For my part, I favour the former answer, since I cannot see that either side could be expected to observe an agreement not to use modern weapons once war had broken out. It is on this ground that I do not think that there will long continue to be human beings unless methods are found of permanently preventing large-scale wars. I shall return to it presently.

…

7

Apart from the more general duties of scientists towards society, they have a quite special and exceptional duty in the present critical condition of the world. All men of science who have studied thermonuclear warfare are aware of two superlatively important facts: first, that whatever agreements may have been reached to the contrary, thermonuclear weapons will certainly be employed by both sides in a world war. Second, that if such weapons are employed there can be no hope of victory for either side, but only of universal destruction involving, quite possibly, the end of all human and animal life and almost certainly, failing that, a complete reversion to barbarism.

QUESTIONS 1–5

*Choose the correct letter: **A**, **B**, **C** or **D**.*
*Write the correct letter in boxes **1–5** on your answer sheet.*

1. In the passage, the changes that are being referred to are

    A the changes that took place in the last fifty years

    B the changes caused by science and scientific techniques

    C the changes that caused dinosaurs to disappear

    D the changes that are unforeseen and unpredictable

2. Depletion of nutrients from agricultural soil is caused by

    A adopting unscientific techniques

    B implementing government measures

    C the overuse of fertilisers

    D the increase in population size

3. Which of the following is not true about the 'world's capital of stored energy' (paragraph 5)?

    A There is only a limited supply of it.

    B It may be replaced by another form in the future.

    C We are using and transforming it continually.

    D It provides long-term stability to our lives.

4. 'At present there is a race for uranium …' (paragraph 5) means that

    A these days people are running to catch uranium

    B the race for uranium is a present

    C a human race in favour of using uranium

    D currently, there is a competition for uranium

5. What does the passage say about thermonuclear weapons?

    A They will destroy the enemy.

    B It was part of the scientists' duty to produce them.

    C Scientifically advanced countries will use them to win wars.

    D They will cause large-scale destruction.

QUESTIONS 6–8

Do the following statements agree with the information given in Reading Passage 1?

In boxes 6–8 on your answer sheet, write:

YES *if the statement agrees with the writer's views*
NO *if the statement contradicts the writer's views*
NOT GIVEN *if there is no information on this.*

6. Science is bringing about changes to our environment at an ever-increasing pace.

7. Most of the environmental changes are a result of our own intentions.

8. No matter what, we will be able to survive the effects of environmental changes.

QUESTIONS 9–13

Complete the sentences below using words from the passage.
*Choose **NO MORE THAN TWO WORDS** from the passage for each answer.*

Write your answers in boxes 9–13 on your answer sheet.

9. We will have to use _____ of thinking to ensure our survival despite the environmental changes.

10. _____ will make the need for food a problem requiring urgent attention.

11. Some people think that setting up _____ will help to prevent future world wars.

12. Others are of the view that setting up agreements banning the use of

    _____ will help to reduce devastation.

13. In the present critical climate, world scientists have a special duty

    _____

READING PASSAGE 2

You should spend about 20 minutes on Questions 14–26, which are based on Reading Passage 2.

Capitalism

Mayday

Capitalism is the system under which we all live, which is failing so miserably to meet the needs of the vast majority of the world's population. Under capitalism, a small minority of people are in control of the money and resources of the planet.

They accumulate wealth and power and move their money and factories around at will to keep their profits high and wages low. Profit comes before people and the environment.

We are forced to compete with each other to work for low wages in order to buy necessities, and as a result the bosses and shareholders of the companies we work for and buy from make profits for themselves.

We work long hours with little say over our pay and conditions, no security, no control over what we are producing and why, or what happens to the profits. We have to try and accumulate money, because there is no security in our communities for when we are ill or old or out of work.

Most work is useless and tedious, making unnecessary new products and services which waste resources and generate pollution. They are usually products which are unaffordable to most of the world's population, which means we have to work harder to afford them.

Bosses, owners and share holders have control over industry, factories, machinery and profits. Last year the directors of Britain's top 1000 companies earned on average over 20 times the average salary of their employees, and the gap is increasing every year. Meanwhile, according to UN figures, one in five children in Britain live in families below the official poverty line.

The established unions have played a role in protecting and promoting workers' rights in some circumstances, but they do not challenge the true injustice, the idea that it is OK for the few to make the decisions, own the factory, and keep the profits.

By acting as intermediaries between the workforce and the bosses, the big established unions simply make the whole system run more smoothly.

If we try and survive outside this system, we end up poor, homeless, in prison. Under capitalism, money, background, education, and class determine how much freedom and control people have in their lives.

If you are poor, working class, black, female, foreign you are likely to have worse education and job opportunities, worse housing conditions, poorer health care provision, you are more likely to go to prison, and for longer terms, and you will die earlier, than those who come from wealthier, more privileged backgrounds.

All over the world people are being forced from their lands so oil, timber and mining companies can move in. Robbed of their land, cultures and communities, they have no choice but to labour for the profit of the global corporations just to survive, and to buy necessities which they would once have been able to grow or make for themselves.

The wealth of many industrialised countries has often come from exploiting the resources, labour and people of the 'third world', from historical slavery to the Nike sweat shops of today.

What resources many of these countries possess they must use to pay interest on their debts to the World Bank and Western countries, while their health and education systems collapse.

Is this a just way to run society, where a small number of people live in luxury while most of us have little control over our lives and more and more live in poverty and hunger?

Some people say that capitalism is based on human nature, and is therefore the best way to run things. But this isn't true. Human nature varies from human to human, and we are all capable of love and hate, compassion and coldness, generosity and selfishness, co-operation and competitiveness.

For most of human history societies have been based on people co-operating to survive and flourish. Capitalism suppresses most of our best qualities by forcing us to compete for necessities.

The thing about human beings is that we have choices. We can choose how to run things. Capitalism creates a minority who are free to suppress the freedom of choice of everyone else. This is not human nature. This is a system imposed upon us.

QUESTIONS 14–18

*Look at the following list of items **14–18**. Match each of them with the items **A–G**.*

*Write the correct letter: **A**, **B**, **C**, **D**, **E**, **F** or **G** in boxes **14–18** on your answer sheet.*

14. a small number of people

15. vast majority of workers

16. workers' unions

17. oil, timber and mining companies

18. industrialised countries

> **A** work against each other for employment and income
> **B** unfairly use people and resources in third-world countries
> **C** pay interest on debts to the World Bank
> **D** own and control wealth, power and resources
> **E** care for people and the environment
> **F** displace landowners
> **G** protect and promote the rights of employees.

QUESTIONS 19–24

Complete the summary below.

*Choose **NO MORE THAN THREE WORDS** from the passage for each answer.*

*Write your answers in boxes **19–26** on your answer sheet.*

The reading passage describes capitalism as a system under which **19** _____;

though it empowers only a **20** _____ people to live a life of luxury and

privileges. These people have the freedom to keep their **21** _____ and

workers' **22** _____.

[continued from previous page]

Instead of challenging the unfairness of the system, workers' unions help the system to **23** _____. Outside the system, one is worse off than those from a **24** _____.

Historically, societies have been based on people co-operating to **25** _____; but capitalism forces people to **26** _____.

READING PASSAGE 3

*You should spend about 20 minutes on Questions **27–40**, which are based on Reading Passage 3.*

Controlling the Car of the Future

Chris Wild

A

The car is not what it used to be. Styling, safety and performance have undergone radical changes and improvements in the last 40 years. Drivers from the 1960s, perhaps a Ford Anglia owner, would recognise that a BMW Series 5 was a car, but that is about as far as their understanding would go.

What would such a person make of air-bags, navigation, cruise control and rear-seat entertainment? The evolution which has led to these features is unlikely to slow down any time soon. In fact, in certain areas it may be about to accelerate.

B

One of the areas which is going to exhibit rapid and radical evolution is the car interior, in particular the interfaces between the car systems and the occupants. The interior systems are evolving as the **Original Equipment Manufacturers** (OEMs) react to a number of factors acting on the basic idea of the car itself.

C

These factors arise out of a number of external and internal influences, the latter being brought in by the automotive industry itself:

- economics – cars need to be cheaper to produce and rich in features to sell well
- energy issues – energy efficiency in the design and operation of cars is now a key selling point for the industry
- consumer connectivity (from within cars) – these are being set by the mobile device market, not the automotive industry
- safety concerns – governments and insurers are making increasing demands to reduce accident and mortality rates associated with road use

- congestion in the cities – city authorities require that road traffic is managed, potentially actively and intrusively, to allow cities to carry on functioning
- market types – non-Western markets and associated cultures such as those in China and India are becoming the major target for growth in car sales.

D

For car occupants, the first and the most visible impact of the influences described above will be the way information is presented and how the **Human-Machine Interaction** (HMI) occurs. As a result of changing market and consumer demands, a number of new features, and systems to deliver them, will appear in the car interior in the next decade.

Some of the features we will begin to see will include increasing connectivity to infrastructure to support security, traffic management and infotainment. As a result, commercial services for insurance, car maintenance and even advertising will appear in our cars. In-car media systems will offer multiple web and/or media streams to different parts of the car. Media will be available for playback in the car from mobile devices, in-car media support or from connectivity.

We should also expect to see systems in place to impose or coach eco-driving as standard. In the case of electric cars, this will range from systems for locating, scheduling and booking access, through to charging infrastructure. Such systems may include intelligent and connected agents which propose alternative modes of transport as a better way to travel under difficult traffic conditions.

E

But with such evolutions comes a major challenge. As more information is brought into the car, with more diversity of style, priority and urgency, interfacing to these features within the constraints of the vehicle will require new and innovative methods of interaction, and a new set of paradigms for the design of in-car HMI.

The challenge here has multiple facets. Firstly, much of the information being presented is relevant to the driver who is occupied with a critical task, that of safely operating the car. Secondly, the safety constraints of vehicle design preclude certain styles of technology; it is not acceptable that a mouse or a keyboard can move freely in space as the result of a rapid deceleration, during an accident for example. Thirdly, any design approach has to support cultural localisation in a manner which is economically viable; the basic design paradigm should be cheaply customisable for Delhi and London alike.

F

All of these evolutions are just the beginning of another round of change to the car as we know it. We may even see changes to the driving controls themselves; joysticks and fly-by-wire could soon make their appearance. Like the 1960s Ford Anglia owner, the BMW Series 5 owner of today will look at cars of 2020 and wonder where the ignition key is.

QUESTIONS 27–32

Reading Passage 3 has six sections, **A–F**.

Choose the correct section for each main idea from the list of headings given below.

*Write the correct number, **i–vii**, in boxes **27–32** on your answer sheet.*

List of Headings

i.	Fast and extreme modification of car's interior
ii.	Differences between BMW Series 5 and Ford Anglia
iii.	The facility of increased communication inside the car
iv.	Types of changes in a car's body and its performance
v.	The new changes presenting new problems
vi.	The latest features in a car and their future
vii.	Cars of the future to be very different from cars of today
viii.	Types of influences causing the changes

27. Section **A**   **28.** Section **B**

29. Section **C**   **30.** Section **D**

31. Section **E**   **32.** Section **F**

QUESTIONS 33–40

Complete the labels in the flow chart listing different reasons for the changes in the designing of cars.

Use **NO MORE THAN TWO WORDS** *from the reading passage for each label.*

*Write your answers in boxes **33–40** on your answer sheet.*

Types of reasons for making changes in the designing of cars

33 _____
_____

38 _____
_____

A
34 _____
_____

A
39 _____
_____

B
Insurers and governments having

35 _____
_____

B
40 _____
_____

so that cars are cheaper to run.

C
Management of

36 _____
_____

in the cities.

D
37 _____
_____

as in China and India.

IELTS ACADEMIC READING PRACTICE TEST 4

TIME ALLOWED: 1 hour
NUMBER OF QUESTIONS: 40

Instructions

All answers must be written on the answer sheet.

The test is divided as follows:

Reading Passage 1 Questions 1–13
Reading Passage 2 Questions 14–26
Reading Passage 3 Questions 27–40

Start at the beginning of the test and work through it. You should answer all the questions. If you cannot do a particular question, leave it and go on to the next. You can return to it later.

READING PASSAGE 1

You should spend about 20 minutes on Questions 1–13, which are based on Reading Passage 1.

Visual Art Education: A Frill or a Necessity?

Willemina Foeken

The following essay was originally written for a postgraduate unit, Art in Education 6, Curtin University, 1990. It was later published in the Artists' Chronicle, *issue 18, 1992, and has been adapted slightly to suit the present day.*

Art education fluctuates in popularity and presently seems to have sunk into an all-time low, with large numbers of art teachers retraining in other directions or joining Centrelink queues. Many parents believe that art education is a waste of time, and with the problems of unemployment faced by those with Visual Arts degrees, this view is reinforced. In times of economic stability, schools are typically expected to develop individuals and prepare them for life, as intelligent, well adjusted and thinking people. However, at times of economic stress, education is suddenly expected to change to job preparation. As there's little money to be gained by studying art, many people reason, there is no point in doing it. What is more, those students who wish to continue to university will find themselves severely handicapped if they choose to do TEE Art, as their examination results will automatically be scaled down, resulting in lower aggregates than those of students studying mathematics and sciences. Where university entry levels are important, this becomes a major factor in steering students away from art.

Elliot Eisner called the arts a 'fundamental part of the human language system' and went on to say that 'a school system that deprives children of the forms of literacy that art education makes possible, will graduate from its schools less than semi-literate children' (Lowenfeld and Brittain, 1987, p11).

Lowenfeld considered the arts to be 'more basic to the thinking process than the traditional school subjects'. He emphasized that all drawings, whether made by a small child or an adolescent, demanded 'a great deal of intellectual involvements' (Lowenfeld and Brittain, 1987, p53).

The two above educators have probably influenced art education, in America and elsewhere, more than anyone else during the twentieth century. Were they totally one-eyed and misguided, or are we in fact seriously depriving our children?

Goulding considered that part of our problem was that art was generally grouped with practical subjects such as Home Economics and the Manual Arts. This is due to a very old misconception that artists have been trying to put right for a long time. Even Leonardo da Vinci had a lifelong battle trying to convince people that art was not made with the hands but with the mind! Bramly (1992, pp261–2) stated that da Vinci considered painting, long thought of as a craft, as the greatest of all the arts and that it should be elevated to the level of the seven liberal arts. He considered it a *qualitative* science and the highest intellectual activity in which people could engage. Goulding quoted Ross as saying that not enough attention had been given to symbolism and meaning in the arts (Goulding, 1982, p326).

Powerful support for the arts in education can be found in numerous experiments carried out with underprivileged children in NY in the 1960s and 1970s. As a result of these programmes, it is now no longer a mere theory that a good art education can alter the attitudes and intellectual performances of underprivileged children. It is worthwhile to take a brief look at some of these programmes.

Joseph Deley and Stewart Kranz (1970, p65) reported on two such studies. The first one involved thirty normal teenagers who took part in a 'divergently oriented' art programme along with the usual subjects. Thirty others received no art education. They formed the control group. At the end of two and a half years it was found that the thirty children studying art were, in fact, now superior in every other area to those children who had received no art education! It was considered that the development of sensitivity and originality in the art programme was instrumental in producing greater achievements in other areas.

The second study concerned an early childhood compensatory programme in Harlem. This programme was skills-oriented and designed to help inner city children to 'catch up' with their more privileged peers. The goals were to develop language skills, perception, conceptual abilities, and a healthy self-image. The programme featured a range of games and art-related activities. All tests have shown that these children ultimately performed much better in all areas, especially in language, than the control group.

The case studies above should be sufficient reason for increasing art education at least in the lower and middle primary grades. However, there are more reasons for teaching art than provided by the above studies alone.

Goulding (1982) listed Bloom and Remer's reasons for including arts (including visual arts) in education. These have been summarized as follows:

A   The arts provide a medium for personal expression.

B   The arts focus attention on observation and self-awareness.

C   The arts are a universal means of communication.

D   The arts involve the elements of sound, movement, colour, mass, energy, space, line, shape and language.

E   The arts are part of our cultural heritage.

F   The arts reflect our perceptions of the world.

G   The arts offer a wide range of career choices.

H   The arts can contribute substantially to special education.

I   The arts provide us with pleasure and mental stimulation.

J   The arts are a useful tool for everyday living.

To deprive children and adolescents of a good art education is to deprive them of the chance to develop fully – mentally and emotionally. The world is full of emotional cripples. We can prevent much of that by doing all we can to teach the *whole* child. When we start teaching *people* rather than *subjects*, our emphasis also shifts from job training to education for a better quality of life. Ultimately, isn't that what we want for our children?

QUESTIONS 1–5

Match each person with the opinion attributed to them.
Write the correct letter A–E in boxes 1–5 on your answer sheet.

A Elliot Eisner   **B** Lowenfeld   **C** Goulding

D Ross   **E** Leonardo da Vinci

1.   Art is the most important pastime of the mind.

2.   It is impossible to achieve proper literacy levels without exposure to art.

3.   People should pay more attention to what art represents.

4.   Art is more fundamental than such subjects as maths or science.

5.   Art is often miscategorised.

QUESTIONS 6–8

Which three of these are listed as reasons to have art education in schools?
Write your answers in any order in boxes 6–8 on your answer sheet.

A Creating art can improve people's motor skills.

B Art is a way of getting across a message.

C Students may one day find employment in that field.

D Art may aid those with mental health problems.

E Students can utilise art in their daily lives.

QUESTIONS 9–11

Do the following statements agree with the information given in Reading Passage 1?
In boxes 9–11 on your answer sheet, write:
YES *if the statement agrees with the views given*
NO *if the statement contradicts the views given*
NOT GIVEN *if there is no information on this.*

9.   During a recession, education is expected to be more vocationally focused.

10. TEE Art should be valued equally with mathematics and science.

11. Educators need to take a holistic view of teaching children.

[continued from previous page]

QUESTIONS 12–13

Do the following statements match the information given in the text?

*In boxes **12–13** on your answer sheet, write:*

TRUE *if the statement matches the information given*

FALSE *if the statement contradicts the information given*

NOT GIVEN *if there is no information about this in the text.*

12. Two important studies on art in schools were carried out in New York by Deley and Kranz.

13. The study in Harlem involved thirty underprivileged children.

READING PASSAGE 2

*You should spend about 20 minutes on Questions **14–26**, which are based on Reading Passage 2.*

Beyond Copenhagen

The climate-change summit will not produce a plan. So it's time for a fresh approach.

Bjorn Lomberg

A

Should we be concerned that the Copenhagen Climate Change conference is not going to produce a concrete plan to produce greenhouse-gas emissions? Lots of people clearly are. Indeed, while activists prepare to unfurl protest banners, politicians are scrambling for a face-saving way to declare the summit a success. They should all save their energy. The failure of the summit may be a blessing in disguise, because when it comes to dealing with climate change, the last thing we need right now is yet another empty agreement and yet more moral posturing.

B

For years, we have been spinning our wheels on what I call the Rio–Kyoto–Copenhagen road to nowhere, slavishly following the notion – first endorsed at the 1992 Earth Summit in Rio de Janeiro and then extended in Kyoto 13 years later – that the only way to stop global warming is by means of draconian reductions in carbon dioxide emissions. All we have to show for this devotion is a continuing series of unmet targets, along with a startling increase in the number of people who no longer think climate change is worth worrying about.

C

Why has this approach led us to this dead end? Well, to begin with, it proposes a solution that costs more than the problem it's meant to solve. It is estimated that if we don't do anything about global warming, its damaging effects will cost the world close to $3 trillion by the end of this century. In an effort to avert this 'catastrophe', the industrialized nations have proposed a plan that would mandate cuts in carbon emissions in order to keep average global temperatures from rising any higher than 2°C above pre-industrial levels.

D

This is an enormously ambitious goal, but many experts agree it could make a real difference. The problem is that the cure may be worse than the disease. In a paper for the Copenhagen Consensus Center, climate economist Richard Tol, a lead author for the UN climate panel, determined that to cut carbon emissions enough to meet the 2°C goal, the leading industrial nations would have to slap a huge tax on carbon-emitting fuels – one that by the end of the century would reach something in the order of $4,000 per metric ton of carbon dioxide, or $35 per gallon of gas ($9 per liter). According to Tol, the impact of a tax hike of this magnitude could reduce world GDP 12.9 per cent in 2100 – the equivalent of $40 trillion a year. In other words, to save ourselves $3 trillion a year, we'd be giving up $40 trillion a year. No wonder we're not getting anywhere.

E

The problem isn't only a matter of economics. There's also technology to consider. On figures from the International Energy Agency, it is clear that to cut carbon emissions by three-quarters over the rest of this century while maintaining reasonable economic growth, we would have to develop alternative-energy sources capable of providing roughly 20 times the energy they do now. To be sure, there are plenty of promising alternative technologies on the horizon. But for all the optimistic talk of sustainable, non-carbon-emitting energy sources, none of them are remotely ready to shoulder such a load. The fact is, about half the world's electricity comes from coal. For emerging economies like those of China and India, the proportion is closer to 80%. Indeed, burning carbon-emitting fuels is the only way for such countries to rise out of poverty. No wonder so many of them have so much trouble with the largely Western plea that we all go on a carbon diet. It's simply not in their interest to do so.

F

It's time to stop trying to put the cart before the horse. Instead of trying to make fossil fuels more expensive, we should focus on making alternative energy cheaper. The cost of fully implementing the Kyoto Protocol (in terms of lost economic growth) has been estimated at roughly $180 billion a year. For just a little more than half that amount, we could fund a fiftyfold increase in spending on R&D for the kind of game-changing technological breakthroughs – like smart grids, ultra-efficient batteries or even cheap, manageable fusion – we will need to end our addiction to fossil fuels. Such a commitment would resolve many of today's political challenges. Developing nations would be much more likely to embrace a positive path of innovation than a punitive one that handicaps their abilities to grow their economies.

G

As things stand now, our political leaders continue to offer up little more than fanciful promises that either mean nothing or have little or no chance of being fulfilled. So let's not mourn the failure of the Copenhagen summit. If we are serious about tackling global warming, we need action that actually does good – as opposed to empty agreements and moral posturing that merely makes us feel good.

QUESTIONS 14–20

*This passage has seven sections, **A–G**.*
Choose the correct heading for each section from the list of headings below.
*Write your answers in boxes **14–20** of your answer sheet.*

List of Headings

i.	An enormous financial impact
ii.	Ill-prepared to meet the challenge
iii.	Fulfilling political promises
iv.	An alternative approach
v.	How developing nations will be affected
vi.	Why the current approach won't work
vii.	A long-held but mistaken idea
viii.	The beliefs of climate sceptics
ix.	Actions, not words
x.	Not worth worrying about

14. Section A _____

15. Section B _____

16. Section C _____

17. Section D _____

18. Section E _____

19. Section F _____

20. Section G _____

QUESTIONS 21–26

*Complete each sentence with the correct ending **A–J** from the box below.*
*Write your answers in boxes **21–26** of your answer sheet.*

21. The Copenhagen conference failed to bring about

22. The solutions proposed in Rio and Kyoto aim to restrict

23. It is hoped that temperatures can be kept close to

24. The benefits may be outweighed by the costs of

25. Developing nations get most of their energy from

26. It would be relatively cheap to fund

A new technology.	**B** a definite plan of action.
C industrial nations.	**D** political posturing.
E a carbon tax.	**F** coal.
G economic growth.	**H** carbon emissions.
I pre-industrial levels.	**J** two degrees.

READING PASSAGE 3

*You should spend about 20 minutes on Questions **27–40**, which are based on Reading Passage 3.*

Abuzz About Bee Genomics

Graeme O'Neill

Prof. Robert Page, founding director of the School of Life Sciences at Arizona State University, has spent 20 years investigating bee behaviour and its genetic underpinnings. He was intrigued that honeybee 'sisters', who share, live and work together, exhibit such contrasting but complementary behaviours late into their lives.

Page, a plenary speaker at the 2006 Lorne Genome Conference, says the division of labour is a hallmark of complex social systems, along with altruism – worker bees, which are all female, cede their reproductive privileges to their mother, the queen, and will lay down their lives to protect their sisters. He has been interested in how the division of labour during foraging evolved – and what light it can throw on the evolution of the honeybee social system.

Page says bees exhibit temporal polyethism – they change behaviours and specialisations as they age. The final transition involves a move from performing specialised tasks within the hive to foraging outside the hive. 'It's a very dramatic transition, involving lots of physiological changes, and requiring many genes to be upregulated or downregulated,' he says. Once they initiate foraging, they then tend to specialise either in collecting nectar or pollen. So first, they had to establish a division of labour between foraging and non-foraging bees, followed by a division of labour in the type of foraging.

'To a lesser extent, I'm interested in the evolution of the worker caste itself, because the females stay home to work for mother,' Page says. 'It's a black-box feature of complex insect societies – instead of going through a normal pattern of adult development, where they leave the nest, fly around and disperse, they stay home and engage in maternal behaviour.'

What has emerged from his research, says Page, is that bees that begin foraging slightly earlier in life specialise in pollen, while late starters tend to forage for nectar. Pollen foragers are more responsive to low sugar concentrations than nectar-foragers, and are also more responsive to light. 'If certain QTLS are common to different sets of traits, something very fundamental must be going on,' Page says. 'If the same genes are affecting whole sets of traits, why are they linked?'

Page says he remembered his first course in insect physiology, where he learned about the gonotrophic cycle in the female mosquito, involving major changes in foraging behaviour. 'She goes from foraging for nectar to foraging for blood meals high in protein. Her behaviour is related to the state of her ovaries. As the ovaries change, and begin to produce eggs, her behaviour changes too. When she has a blood meal, she tunes into a different set of stimuli – she seeks body heat, avoids light, avoids contact with the ground and seeks out low, dark places where she just sits while her eggs mature. Now her behaviour changes again – she seeks out water vapour, and lays her eggs on the water.'

Page says he wondered if bees had co-opted the ancient gonotrophic cycle into a system featuring specialised behaviours and division of labour. 'We looked at genes associated with the reproductive state, and knocked some out using RNA-induced silencing, and we were able to predict the resulting behavioural changes,' he says. 'For example, we found we could predict behavioural changes due to the gene knockouts, and we showed that the preference for pollen or nectar is related to the ancient gonotrophic cycle. So is the age of onset of foraging – bees performing different tasks get locked into them.'

By the time of the Lorne Genome Conference, Page and his colleagues will have published their latest findings in *Nature*.

'Going back to the solitary insect mode, we think what is happening is that the insect emerges from the cell without its ovaries activated, flies around and then disperses and mates,' he says.

'The ovaries are then activated by a hormonal signal involving ecdysone and juvenile hormone, and the ovaries become vitellogenic – they are ready to receive proteins produced from specialised fat-body cells and convert them into eggs.'

Page says this normally occurs after winter diapause, or a period of reproductive latency. The mosquito and bee have contrasting life histories – honeybees have pre-reproductive ovary activation, mosquitoes exhibit post-reproductive activation. 'In the honeybee, the hormonal signal to activate the ovaries occurs in the pupal stage, not in adulthood,' Page says. 'So when the honeybee emerges from its cell into the nest, it's not tuned for dispersing and mating. It has already undergone the equivalent of winter diapause or reproductive latency, and it's already in a maternal behaviour pattern.'

'In the maternal nest it's already responding to stimuli that would cause it to exhibit maternal behaviours – it has cells to clean, food to process, larvae to feed,' Page says. 'It's all fundamental reproductive behaviour, but with the timing of the activation signal changed. 'In honeybees, it denies the worker the opportunity to have all those pre-maternal behaviours we see in the mosquito and other insects that lead solitary lives.'

The genes that set the switches for these reproductive behaviours have not yet been cloned and studied in bees. Page says some likely candidate genes produce insulin-like signalling molecules similar to those found in humans. 'Now we have the complete genome sequenced from the honeybee, we can begin to identify candidate genes,' he says. He says natural selection has co-opted ancient patterns of behaviour in solitary insects and shaped them into unique patterns of social behaviour in bees.

QUESTIONS 27–30

Answer the following questions using **NO MORE THAN THREE WORDS** *from the text.*
Write your answers in boxes **27–30** *of your answer sheet.*

27. As well as the division of labour, what is a key characteristic of complex social systems? _____

28. Who do female worker bees sacrifice their reproductive privileges for?
_____

29. What term describes the way in which bees alter the way they behave as they get older? _____

30. What two substances do bees harvest? _____

QUESTIONS 31–35

Complete the following flow chart using **NO MORE THAN TWO WORDS** *from the text.*
Write your answers in boxes **31–35** *of your answer sheet.*

Gonotrophic Cycle of Female Mosquito

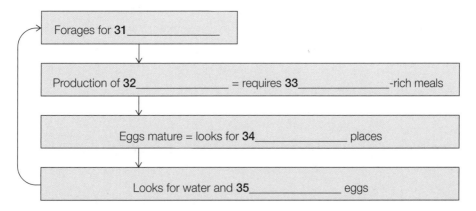

[continued from previous page]

QUESTIONS 36–40

Do the following statements match the information given in the text?
*In boxes **36–40** of your answer sheet, write:*
TRUE *if they match the information given in the text*
FALSE *if they contradict the information given in the text*
NOT GIVEN *if there is no information about this in the text.*

36. Page is primarily interested in why bees exhibit altruism.

37. Nectar-foraging bees respond more to lights than pollen-foragers.

38. At the time of writing, Page's research had not yet been published.

39. Honeybees and mosquitoes have similar reproductive timing.

40. The genes that control reproduction in mosquitoes have been cloned and studied.

Task 1 gives some data, for example, a graph or a diagram. You must find the patterns and important points, and write a report. For example:

> *The charts below show the number of visitors arriving in a particular country for a short trip, and the number of residents leaving that country for a short trip, from 2009 to 2011.*
>
> *Summarise the information by selecting and reporting the main features, and make comparisons where relevant.*
>
> *Write at least 150 words.*

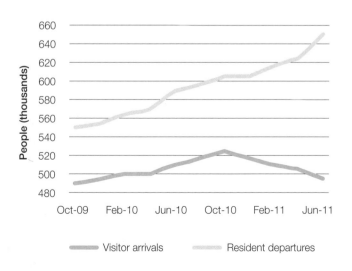

In Task 1, you must change images into words.

- You **must** only use the information that is given. For example, in the question above, we don't know *why* the people are travelling (business or holiday), and this doesn't matter.
- You must **not** add imaginary details. For example, don't try to imagine *why* the number of residents departing is higher than the visitors arriving. You are not asked to do this – Task 1 is not a guessing game!
- You must **not** add your own knowledge. Task 1 does not test your knowledge about a topic; it only tests your ability to write about data in English.
- You **must** use the information accurately. For example, in the question above, don't say '500 visitors arrived in the country in February 2010'. The scale is 'thousands', so 500,000 visitors arrived in the country.

How the task is marked

An examiner reads your answer and gives it points, from 1 to 9, for each of the following features:

- task achievement
- coherence and cohesion
- lexical resource
- grammatical range and accuracy.

The better your answer is, the more points it gets. Points are averaged to give your final 'Band'. If you write less than 150 words, the examiner subtracts points.

So what do they mean?

Task achievement means *How well did you answer the question?*

Did you describe the data clearly? Does it sound like a real report? For example, would a manager show it to a CEO? Did you include all the important points, such as overall trends or unexpected results? Did you do everything that the Task 1 question tells you to do?

> **TIP**   Task 1 imitates a research report. Imagine you are the researcher – what do you want to tell people about your research? Why did you collect the information? Why is it interesting?

Coherence and cohesion means *How clearly do ideas relate to each other?*

Is it easy to see how one sentence relates to the next one? Have you used a variety of linking words and pronouns? Have you used paragraphs, with one main idea per paragraph?

> **TIP**   When you check your writing at the end, look out for repetition. If lots of sentences start with the same word, you haven't used a variety of linking techniques.

Lexical resource means *Have you used a wide range of vocabulary? Have you spelled it correctly?* Have you used the same words over and over again, or have you used synonyms? Have you described things clearly, using exactly the right word? Have you spelled most words correctly?

> **TIP**   If you use a small range of words, with zero mistakes, you won't get a good score. If you use a wide range of vocabulary, you can get a good score even with a few mistakes. Don't play it safe – be adventurous!

Grammatical range and accuracy means *Have you used a wide range of verb forms and sentence structures? Are most of them correct? Have you used proper punctuation?*

> **TIP**   Grammar is only 25 per cent of your final mark, so don't focus on it too much.

Quiz 1
True or false?

1. Examiners subtract points for grammar mistakes.

2. It's important to use correct punctuation, like commas and full stops.

3. Because Task 1 is about graphs and data, you can write your answer as a list of points.

4. It's better to play safe and only use vocabulary that you're sure of. That way you won't make mistakes.

5. You must write more than 150 words.

You can check your answers for all activities in this Part in the Answer Key in Appendix 1.

The marking guide

IELTS examiners use a marking guide that describes the features of poor, good and excellent writing. A public version of this guide, called the 'IELTS Writing Band Descriptors', is freely available on the IELTS website at http://www.ieltsessentials.com/results/assessment_criteria.aspx

As you can see, examiners look at the *good* points of your answer, not the *bad* points. They are looking for what you *can* do.

> **TIP**   'Good' writing means that you use a **variety** or **range** of language, so when you are checking your answer at the end, don't just correct mistakes. You should also look for ways to add variety, for example, by replacing a word with a synonym or pronoun. This is described in Units 3 and 4.

Warning! Don't lose points

- You **must** write **more than** 150 words. If you write less, you will lose points. There is no maximum word limit – write as much as you like!
- You should spend around 20 minutes on Task 1 and 40 minutes on Task 2. This is because Task 1 is worth 33.3% of your mark, and Task 2 is worth 66.6% of your mark.
- You **must** use your own language. Do not use copied or memorised language – you will get zero points for it. For example, don't begin your answer by copying the Task 1 question: '*This graph shows the amount of money spent on household goods in three different countries between 2000 and 2010.*' This is a waste of time. The examiner will ignore it.
- You **must** write in connected sentences and use paragraphs. Do not write a list of bullet points.
- You **must** only write about the information that is given. The question does not ask for your own ideas or opinions about the data. For example, don't say that the graph shows a change that is good or bad for society.

Quiz 2

1. What happens if you write less than 150 words in Task 1?

2. What happens if you write more than 150 words in Task 1?

3. Can you copy the Task 1 title as your introduction?

4. Task 1 is an 'information transfer task'. What does this mean?

5. Should you give examples from your own knowledge and experience?

6. How long should you spend on Task 1?

7. Do you have to mention every piece of information in the diagram?

8. Can your answer be a list of important points?

Approaching the task

Analyse the data

You only have 20 minutes for Task 1. You need to use some of this time to look at the data and analyse it. Take notes about the important points, such as trends, differences and unexpected results. Decide what the most important pattern is, and think about how you can describe this. These skills are described in Unit 2 (Task Achievement).

Plan your report

Your answer will be around 150 words. This usually means three to four paragraphs. Before you start writing, decide on the main point for each paragraph. It is best to put your overview, or summary, in the first paragraph, so that the examiner can easily see it. These skills are described in Unit 3 (Coherence and Cohesion).

Write your report

Your overview should say what the main patterns are. Then the following paragraphs should prove that this is true by giving evidence and details. These skills are covered in Units 4 and 5 (Lexical Resource and Grammatical Range and Accuracy).

Check your report

At the end, spend a few minutes to check your answer and make changes to improve it. These skills are covered in Unit 6 (Practice Questions, Answers and Feedback). Always check these things.

Check for task achievement

Have you followed the instructions in the Task 1 question?
Have you described the main patterns in the data?
Have you quoted data accurately, to support your statements?

> **TIP**   Check that the data is accurate. For example, what is the unit of measurement? Is it 'litres' or 'thousands of litres'? Does the chart show 'number of dogs' or 'number of complaints about dogs'?

Check for coherence and cohesion

Is the information organised well?
Is it easy to see *why* you have ordered your answer like that?
Have you used a wide variety of linking words and techniques?

> **TIP**   Check whether you can change some nouns for pronouns. If you mention something twice, the second mention can be changed to a word like 'it', 'this' or 'them'. Doing this will improve your mark for coherence and cohesion.

Check for lexical resource

Have you used a wide variety of vocabulary?
Have you used collocations, phrasal verbs and academic English?
Are most words spelled correctly?

> **TIP**   Before the exam, memorise sets of synonyms such as [increase, grow, rise].
> Then, in the exam, you can look at your finished answer and substitute
> synonyms quickly.

Check for grammatical range and accuracy

Have you used a wide variety of grammar structures, including passives?

Are most of them correct?

Have you used correct punctuation?

> **TIP**   Write in pencil, so you can easily erase mistakes and write corrections.

UNIT 2

Task Achievement

TIP   To get a good mark, you need to make the report interesting.

Look at the data. Someone has collected this data for a reason, and it tells us something interesting. You need to explain *why* the data is important and interesting.

Example

The following tables describe bill-paying habits and attitudes to unpaid bills, by age group.

Table 1 Proportion of people who are worried about their unpaid bills, by age group.

	Worried
Under 30	74%
30–45	66%
45–60	33%
Over 60	20%

Table 2 Proportion of people who usually pay their bills on time, by age group.

	No
Under 30	65%
30–45	58%
45–60	30%
Over 60	15%

This data comes from a survey. A researcher asked the questions 'Are you worried about your unpaid bills?' and 'Do you pay your bills on time?' They asked thousands of people, and then put the results into these tables.

Activity 2.1

Imagine that *you* are the researcher who did this survey. Who paid you to do it? Why do they need the information? **Match the client (1–4) with the reason (a–d).**

Client	Need
1 A bank paid you …	a … to find out about their customers, who are people over 60.
2 You were paid by a government department that regulates the bank system …	b … to find out about their customers, who are people aged 30 to 45.
3 A private pension fund paid you …	c … to find out whether citizens are suffering financial stress.
4 A mortgage company paid you …	d … to find out about their customers for a new advertising campaign.

Your job now is to show the survey results to the bank, pension fund, government department, etc. They don't have time to look at every number in the tables – they just need the general idea. However, it is a technical report, so you need to prove that what you say is true by giving accurate details.

When people read data reports, they usually just skim-read the first sentences. Then they might read more, if it is interesting. That is why you should start with an 'overview' or 'executive summary' that summarises the most important information.

STEP 1. What is the main message you get from the data in the table?

Activity 2.2

Write TRUE, FALSE **or** NOT GIVEN.

1.   The majority of people under 30 are worried about their unpaid bills.

2.   More than half of people aged 30–45 are worried about their unpaid bills.

3.   The majority of people who are under 45 years old are worried about their unpaid bills.

4.   The majority of people aged over 45 aren't worried about their unpaid bills.

5.   The majority of people aged 30–45 and 45–60 pay their bills on time.

6.   The majority of people aged 45–60 and over 60 pay their bills on time.

7.   The older someone is, the more likely they are to pay their bills on time.

8.   There seems to be a change in behaviour and attitude around age 45.

9.   Most people aged 45–60 and over 60 don't have unpaid bills.

STEP 2. Write one or two sentences about the main message – this is your **overview**. It is best to give the overview at the beginning of your report. That way, the examiner is sure to notice it.

You should NOT copy the task prompt as your overview. For example: DO NOT write '*The tables describe bill-paying habits and attitudes to unpaid bills, by age group.*' This is a waste of time. It is not your own language, so the examiner will ignore it. It doesn't show how well you can use English, because you have copied it. It also doesn't show how well you have analysed the data because it doesn't say anything about the **results** of the study.

DO write: '*This survey of bill-paying habits and attitudes to unpaid bills shows that as people get older, particularly after age 45, they become better at paying their bills on time and become less worried about their unpaid bills.*'

> **TIP**   Do NOT use your own ideas to explain the data. For example, '*Older people have more money, so that's why they can pay their bills on time.*' This may be true, but the information is not in the graph, so don't write it.

STEP 3. Now you need to give details to prove that your main idea is correct. You need to quote some real survey results.

We made three main statements in the overview. We'll describe them one by one, with a paragraph for each one.

Activity 2.3

Match the overview statement (a, b, c) with the paragraph (D, E, F) that supports it.

a   '*The survey results show that as people get older, particularly after age 45, they become better at paying their bills on time.*'

b   '*The survey results show that as people get older, particularly after age 45, they ... become less worried about their unpaid bills.*'

c   '*There seems to be a relationship between these things.*'

Paragraph D

Overall, there seems to be a connection between not paying bills on time and being worried about unpaid bills. Where there is one, you also see the other.

Paragraph E

Most people aged under 45 (65 per cent of under 30s and 58 per cent of 30- to 45-year-olds) don't pay their bills on time. Meanwhile, most people over 45 do pay their bills on time, with 30 per cent of 45- to 60-year-olds and only 15 per cent of the over-60s not paying. It seems that bill-paying behaviour splits the population into two groups: under 45 and over 45.

Paragraph F

This is the same with worrying about unpaid bills. In the two younger age groups, most people are worried about them: 74 per cent of the under 30s and 66 per cent of the 30–45s. In contrast, only 33 per cent of 45- to 60-year-olds and 15 per cent of over-60-year-olds are concerned about unpaid bills.

Simple Present

Now, let's put the answer all together.

The survey results show that as people get older, particularly after age 45, they become better at paying their bills on time and become less worried about their unpaid bills. There seems to be a relationship between these things.

Most people aged under 45 (65 per cent of under 30s and 58 per cent of 30- to 45-year-olds) don't pay their bills on time. Meanwhile, most people over 45 do pay their bills on time, with 30 per cent of 45- to 60-year-olds and only 15 per cent of the over-60s not paying. It seems that bill paying behaviour splits the population into two groups: under 45 and over 45.

This is the same with worrying about unpaid bills. In the two younger age groups, most people are worried about them: 74 per cent of the under 30s and 66 per cent of the 30–45s. In contrast, only 33 per cent of 45- to 60-year-olds and 15 per cent of over-60-year-olds are concerned about unpaid bills.

Overall, there seems to be a connection between not paying bills on time and being worried about unpaid bills. Where there is one, you also see the other.

> **TIP**   In this example, there are probably other ways to explain the data, but you don't have that information. For example, people have more money as they get older, so they can pay their bills on time. This is why you should use Academic English expressions like 'there may be' / 'it seems' / 'there could be' / 'there appears to be'.

STEP 4. Check your work.

- Look back at the Task 1 instructions. Have you followed them? Yes, 'described the main trends and differences' and 'made comparisons'.
- Have you written an 'overview' (a short description of the main message)? Yes, the first sentence.
- Have you written about all the main points – the trends, differences or stages? Have you supported this with data? Yes. Every statement includes some numbers to explain it.
- Have you described the data accurately? Pay attention to any labels or headings. For example, does this table show number of people, or percentage of people? (Percentage of people.) Check that you have quoted numbers accurately. Yes.

> **TIP**   A good Task 1 should give a clear message. Imagine you are a bank director who requested this report. Does it give you a clear idea for action? Yes. You would probably start advertising to people aged around 45, because this seems to be a pivotal age.

Activity 2.4

The following graphs show exports from the UK, USA and China in one year.

1
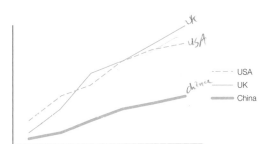

2
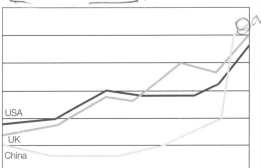

3
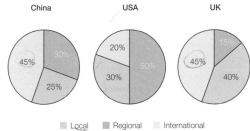

4
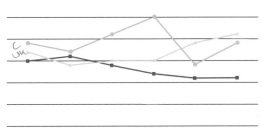

Which diagram (1–4) shows:

A. a big gap that shrinks over time?

B. a gradual increase that suddenly increases more quickly?

C. two things that show a similar growth for most of the period?

D. something that starts out highest, but becomes the lowest?

E. something that starts out highest, but becomes middle-ranked?

F. two things that show a similar growth for a part of the period?

G. two countries with the same share of something?

Activity 2.5

Match the graph (1–4) to the overview.

A. The USA had the highest proportion of regional exports, but the lowest proportion of international exports. China and the UK had similar proportions of international exports, but different proportions of the other categories.

B. Exports rose steadily in every country, but increased sharply in the USA and the UK, and gradually in China. The UK showed the greatest increase overall.

C. The USA showed a reasonably steady decline in exports over the period, while the UK's exports fluctuated, but showed an overall slight increase. China showed dramatic fluctuations in exports, but there was no overall increase or decrease over the period.

D. Exports showed an increasing trend, with some fluctuations, in every country over the period. However, in the future the most dramatic increase is predicted for China. It will go from the lowest of the three countries shown, to the highest.

Example activity

This activity is an example of how to do the following activities 2.6–2.8.

The following graph shows the population growth in developing countries and industrialised countries, with a prediction to 2050.

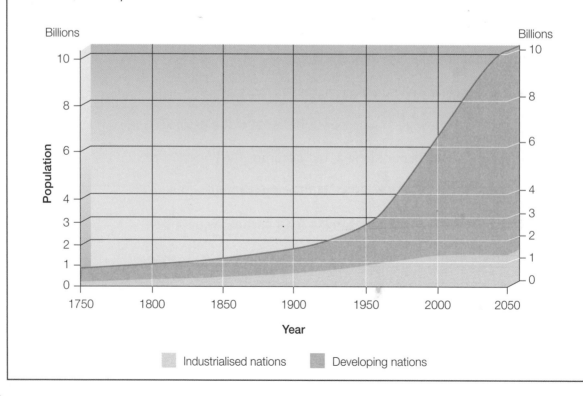

Industrialised nations   Developing nations

What are the main features?

Now write the overview.

Main features

1. Both populations increase slowly at first.
2. The increase in developing countries is much faster than in industrialised countries, especially after 1950.
3. After 2000, the population of industrialised countries stops growing.

Overview

The populations of developing countries and industrialised countries increased at about the same, steady rate until around 1950, when the population in developing countries skyrocketed. In 2000, while that rapid growth was still happening, the population in industrialised countries began to plateau. These contrasting trends are predicted to continue until 2050.

Activity 2.6

The following tables show the average age of students at a college, and how happy the students were with their courses.

What are the main features?

Now write the overview.

How happy students were with their courses

	Certificate	Diploma
very happy	73%	5%
happy	16%	12%
unhappy	10%	42%
very unhappy	1%	41%

[continued from previous page]

Average age of students

	Certificate	Diploma
15 to 25	79%	17%
25 to 35	18%	62%
35 to 45	1%	20%
45 and over	2%	1%

Activity 2.7

The following diagrams show changes to a museum.

What are the main features?

Now write the overview.

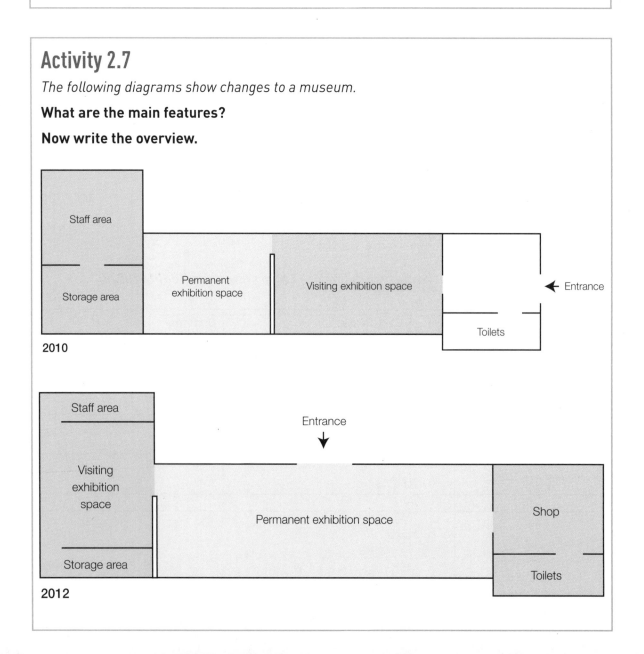

2010

2012

Activity 2.8

The following diagram shows the paper manufacturing cycle.

What are the main features?

Now write the overview.

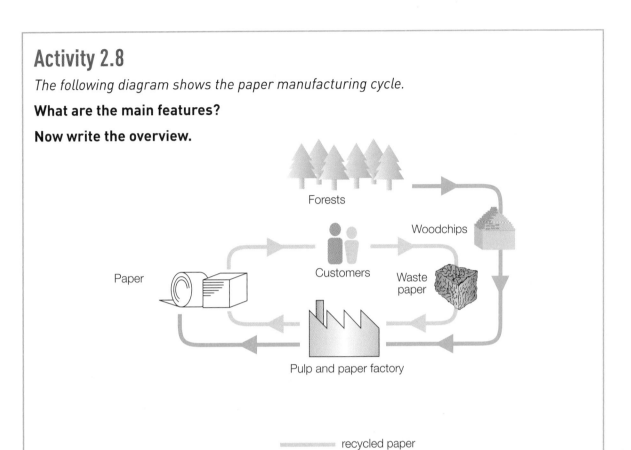

Activity 2.9: Spot the errors

These overviews have incorrect facts. Can you find them?

1.   *The following chart shows the population of a certain town from 1861 to 2002.*

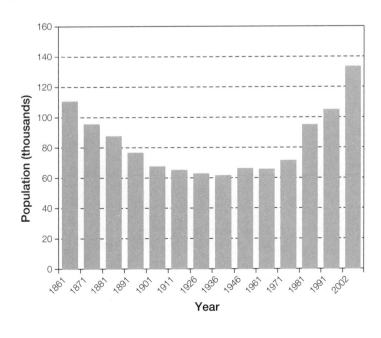

[continued from previous page]

The population fell and then increased over the period. At the start of the period, in 1861, the population was 110 people, and after decreasing to nearly half, the population only exceeded the 1861 level in 2002, when there were around 130 residents in the town.

2. *The following graph shows the number of widgets, by type (A–N), that were produced by a company in one year.*

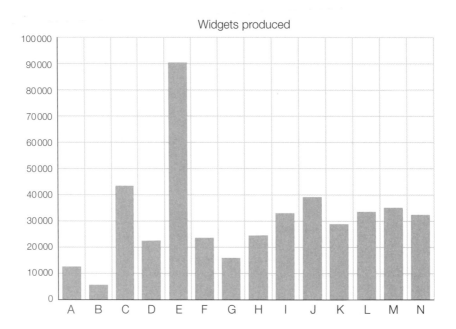

The graph clearly shows that, after some early fluctuation, the production of widgets levelled out towards the end of the year.

3. *The following graph shows the average monthly rainfall in two major cities.*

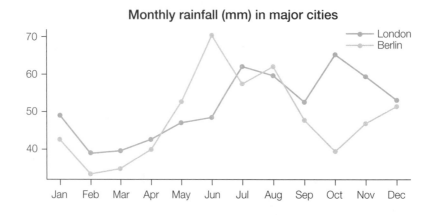

The monthly rainfall averages show similar patterns in the dry months (January to April), but different patterns in the rest of the year. Each city has two main peaks at different times and the highest monthly rainfall happens in London, in June.

4.   *The following graph shows the percentage of people who recycle their rubbish, in five countries, over 12 years.*

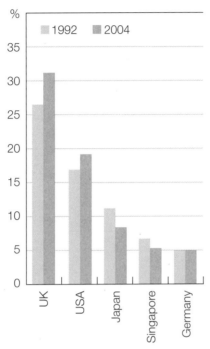

Between 1992 and 2004, there was a dramatic increase in the proportion of UK residents who recycle.

Presenting the data

After the overview, you need to write some more paragraphs to give the detail that proves your statements. For example, if your overview said 'men worked longer hours than women', you need to give data to support that statement. Do not list every single number. You need to organise the data and select the most important data.

Activity 2.10

Look at the answer and fill the gaps.

The following diagrams show international student enrolments at a university from 1975 to 2009.

Students' home region

	1975	2009
Asia	20%	65%
Europe	20%	20%
Africa	15%	10%
North America	15%	10%
South America	30%	0%

International student numbers

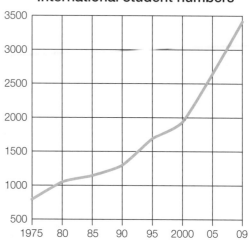

There were _____ stages of growth: a period of slow growth between

_____ and _____; a period of faster growth between _____

and _____; and a period of rapid increase between _____ and

_____.

It seems the increase came mainly from higher numbers of _____

students (up from _____ per cent in 1975 to _____ per cent in

2009). Proportions of students from other regions stayed roughly the same, or

fell slightly, except for students from _____. These students accounted

for _____ per cent of all international students in 1975, but by 2009 there

were no students from this region.

Activity 2.11

Look at this answer. What's wrong?

The following tables show the average age of students at a college, and how happy the students were with their courses.

How happy students were with their courses

	Certificate	Diploma
very happy	73%	5%
happy	16%	12%
unhappy	10%	42%
very unhappy	1%	41%

Average age of students

	Certificate	Diploma
15 to 25	79%	17%
25 to 35	18%	62%
35 to 45	1%	20%
45 and over	2%	1%

The tables show the average age of students at a college, and how happy the students were with their courses. There are certificate students and diploma students.

Certificate students were very happy with their course (73 per cent) or happy with their course (16 per cent) or unhappy with their course (10 per cent). Not many of them were very unhappy with their course (only 1 per cent). Diploma students were very unhappy with their course (41 per cent), unhappy with their course (42 per cent) or happy with their course (12 per cent) or very happy with their course (5 per cent).

Certificate students were 15 to 25 years old (79 per cent) or 25 to 35 years old (18 per cent). Not many of them were 35 to 45 years of age (1 per cent) or over 45 (2 per cent). On the other hand, 17 per cent of diploma students were 15 to 25 years old, and 62 per cent were aged 25 to 35, while 20 per cent were 35 to 45 years old and only 1 per cent were aged 45 and over.

Activity 2.12

Look at this answer. What's wrong?

The following tables describe bill-paying habits and attitudes to debt, by age group.

Worried about unpaid bills

Under 30	74%
30–45	66%
45–60	33%
Over 60	20%

Pay bills on time

Under 30	35%
30–45	42%
45–60	70%
Over 60	85%

The survey results show that as people get older, particularly after age 45, they become better at paying their bills on time and become less worried about their unpaid bills. There seems to be a relationship between these things.

Few people aged under 45 (only 35 per cent of under-30s and 42 per cent of 30- to 45-year-olds) don't pay their bills on time. Meanwhile, 70 per cent of 45- to 60-year-olds pay their bills on time. It seems that bill-paying behaviour splits the population into two groups: under 45 and over 45.

This is the same with worrying about unpaid bills. In the two younger age groups, most people are worried about them: 75 per cent of the under-30s and 66 per cent of the 30–45s. In contrast, only 33 per cent of 45- to 60-year-olds are concerned about unpaid bills.

Overall, there seems to be a connection between not paying bills on time and being worried about unpaid bills. Where there is one, you also see the other.

Checking

When you have finished writing your Task 1 answer, remember to check it. These are the important points to look for to get a good mark for task achievement:

Task Achievement	
Does it have an overview of main patterns?	✓
Does it have the most important details?	✓
Does it have any irrelevant information (for example, personal experience or opinions)?	✗ Do **not** include these.
Does it quote numbers and other data accurately?	✓

Activity 2.13

Check this example answer using the checklist.

The following tables compare the total value of exports and the amount of CO_2 produced per person for five countries.

Summarise the information by selecting and reporting the main features, and make comparisons where relevant.

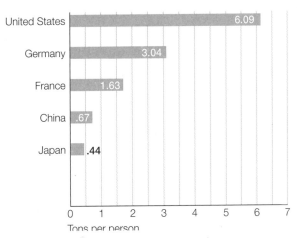

CO_2 produced per person (2010)

Country	Tons per person
United States	6.09
Germany	3.04
France	1.63
China	.67
Japan	.44

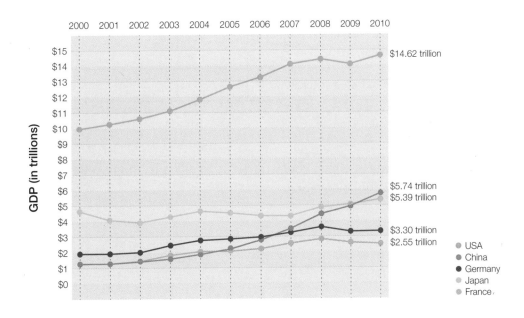

[continued from previous page]

Sample answer:

The data shows that the country with the largest GDP (the USA) also had the highest per-person CO_2 production. However, Japan and China, the countries with the second-largest GDPs, had the lowest per-person CO_2 production.

    Throughout the period (2000 to 2010), the USA had the highest GDP, rising steadily from $10 trillion to $14.62 trillion over the period, with only one small dip around 2009. This country also had the highest CO_2 production per person in 2010. In contrast, Japan's GDP fluctuated around $5 trillion, with no major growth over the period, and although Japan's GDP was around 30 to 50 per cent of the USA's, its CO_2 production was less than 10 per cent of the USA's.

    The GDPs of Germany and France remained fairly constant over the period, only increasing by about $1 trillion, to $3.30 trillion and $2.55 trillion, respectively. Although their GDPs were similar, Germany's CO_2 production was double that of France.

    China's GDP was the same as France's until 2005, when it began to increase rapidly. By 2010, China's GDP was $5.74 trillion, although it still only produced 0.67 tonnes of CO_2 per person.

Task achievement	Yes/no	Example
Does it give an overview of main patterns?		
Does it talk about the most important details?		
Does it have any irrelevant information (for example, personal experience or opinions)?		
Does it quote numbers and other data accurately?		

TIP Another good way to check your answer is to ask a friend to read it and recreate the original diagram.

Activity 2.14

Draw the diagram that this answer is talking about.

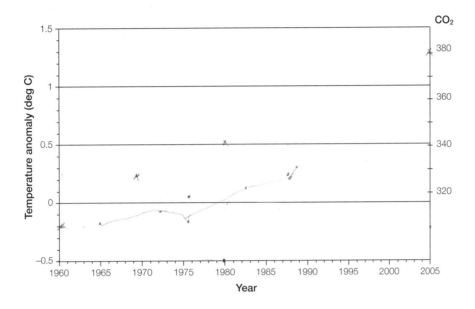

The graph shows that CO_2 levels increased steadily between 1960 and 2005, while average global temperatures also rose, but not as steeply and with some fluctuation. Despite a slow start at the beginning of the period, by the middle of the period, the temperature anomaly was rising fairly quickly, increasing by nearly 5°C in 20 years.

In 1960, CO_2 levels were at around 310 ppmv, but they increased steadily by around 15 ppmv per decade. Halfway through the period, in 1980, they had reached 340 ppmv and by the end of the period, in 2005, they had risen to around 380 ppmv.

Meanwhile, the increase in average global temperature also increased between 1960 and 2005, though not so smoothly. For almost the first 20 years (1960 to 1978) there was no net increase, and the temperature difference remained under 0, with troughs of nearly –2°C in 1965 and 1976 and a small peak, at nearly –1°C, in 1971. From around 1978, the average temperature anomaly began to increase, with small peaks in 1982 (at 1°C), 1989 (at 2°C) and 2000 (at 4°C). At the end of the period, the average temperature difference was 0.5°C.

When you use the practice answers at the back of this book, remember to check them with the checklist, and then ask a friend to recreate the diagram.

You can check all your answers to the activities in this unit in the Answer Key in Appendix 1.

respectively

UNIT 3

Coherence and Cohesion

When the examiner marks your writing, they are looking at the following things.

Coherence and cohesion	
Ideas are logically organised.	✓
Writing is organised into paragraphs.	✓
Each paragraph has one main topic.	✓
Uses a range of cohesive devices: • reference • substitution • linking words	✓ ✓ ✓

What does it mean? **Coherence** means:

– Is your answer logical?
– Does one idea connect to the next idea?
– Are sentences organised into paragraphs?

> **TIP** You must separate your paragraphs clearly. Leave a one-line space between them, or indent the first sentence of a new paragraph.
> If your paragraphing is not clear, you will not get a good mark for Coherence and Cohesion.

Cohesion means:

– Does one phrase connect to another phrase to make a sentence?
– Does each sentence connect to the next sentence?

> **TIP** The important thing is to use a **variety** of cohesive devices.

Activity 3.1

Here are some common coherence and cohesion problems. What is wrong with each answer?

1

x was the most popular in 2007 (at 70 per cent). x fell dramatically over the period, to 33 per cent. y showed a steady upward trend, from 23 per cent in 2007 to 33 per cent. By 2011, x and y were equally popular.

2

The population of developing countries increased slowly and then more quickly and then very rapidly. The population of industrialised countries increased gradually and then a little faster and then it plateaued and was much lower than the population of developing countries.

3

The survey results show that as people get older, particularly after age 45, they become better at paying their bills on time and become less worried about their debts. There seems to be a relationship between these things. Most people aged under 45 (65 per cent of under-30s and 58 per cent of 30- to 45-year-olds) don't pay their bills on time. Meanwhile, most people over 45 do pay their bills on time, with 30 per cent of 45- to 60-year-olds and only 15 per cent of the over-60s not paying. It seems that bill-paying behaviour splits the population into two groups: under 45 and over 45. This is the same with worrying about debt. In the two younger age groups, most people are worried about debt: 75 per cent of the under-30s and 66 per cent of the 30–45s. In contrast, only 33 per cent of 45- to 60-year-olds and 15 per cent of over-60-year-olds are concerned about debt. Overall, there seems to be a connection between not paying bills on time and being worried about debt. Where there is one, you also see the other.

Coherence

For logical writing, you *must* write an essay plan for Task 1. When we write an answer without planning it first, we tend to add ideas as we think of them. For example, we might forget to write about an important point and quickly add it at the end. This makes the Task 1 answer random, hard to read, and illogical.

You only need to spend one or two minutes on your plan: just write some short notes on the question booklet. A plan will make sure that:

1 your answer is logically ordered
2 each paragraph has one main idea
3 you don't miss any important points.

A Task 1 answer is only around 150 words, so you will probably write around three paragraphs. A simple and effective plan is:

Overview

Summarise the information and mention the most important trends and differences.

Data discussion 1

Describe one set of data: for example, one graph or one category.

Data discussion 2

Describe the other set of data.

> **TIP**   If you can't think of a good structure, just write about the data in the order they appear on the page.

Look at this example.

The chart below shows the percentage of men and women who participate in sport at different ages.

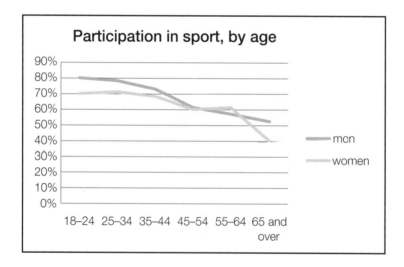

A good essay plan would look like this:

> ### Overview
> Men and women both ↘ with age
> Men generally do more sport than women, except at age 55–64.
> Women show more fluctuation than men.

Men
Steady ↘ 18 to 35.
Faster ↘ 35 to 54.
55 to 65+ steady ↘.

Women
Less than men.
18 to 34 stable.
35 to 44 ↘.
45 to 64 stable: overtakes men.
rapid ↘ for 65 and over.

This is your plan, so it doesn't show any data. When you write the full answer, you need to give the exact percentages.

TIP   Your essay plan is a good place to 'brainstorm' useful vocabulary and grammar.

Activity 3.2: Essay plan

Look at this task:

The chart below shows the population of developing and industrialised nations from 1750, with a prediction up to 2050.

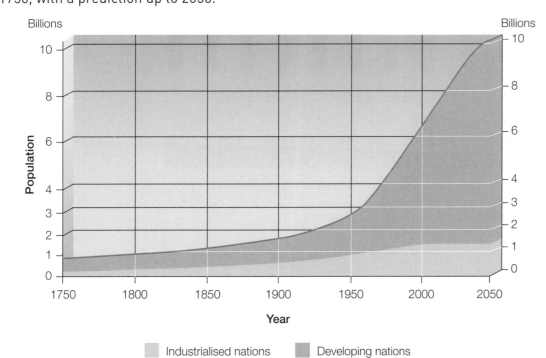

[continued from previous page]

Write the main points in the correct box below.

Overview

Data discussion 1

Data discussion 2

Activity 3.3

Choose the best essay plan for this task:

The charts below show the number of workplace injuries, per year, at a factory and the actions that were taken to reduce injuries, between 1985 and 1995.

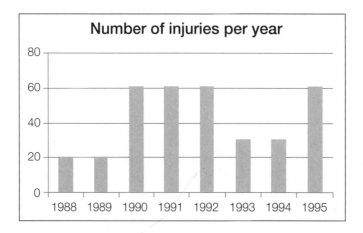

Year	Action
1990	New machines introduced
1991	Safety manager appointed
1993	Safety classes for all staff
1995	Training manual replaces classes

Plan 1

Overview: 4 actions in 8 years

Describe table of 'Actions'

Describe graph of 'Number of injuries per year'

Plan 2

Overview: Injury rate fluctuates

1990 action and injuries
1991 action and injuries
1993 action and injuries
1995 action and injuries

Plan 3

Overview: Safety classes had best effect

1988 and 1989 = low injuries 1990 = new machines = injuries ↑
1991 Tried to reduce injuries but didn't work

Good result
1993 safety classes = reduced injuries

Bad result
1995 = tried another thing = safety manual = injuries ↑
Overall, safety classes were best idea.

Activity 3.4: Process diagram

Some IELTS Task 1 diagrams show a process. To organise this data logically, you should summarise the main stages of the process.

The following diagram shows how essential oil is produced from leaves.

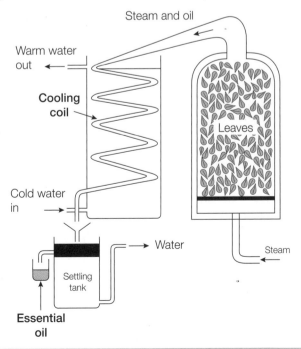

[continued from previous page]

There are two main stages:

1.   taking the oil out of the leaves
2.   taking the oil out of the water.

A good structure for this answer is:

Overview

Stage 1

Stage 2

Activity: Where should the information go?

Write 0 for overview, 1 for paragraph 1, and 2 for paragraph 2.

cold oil rises to top of water	
Hot: water and oil can mix. Cold: water and oil separate.	
steam and oil mixture cooled down	
steam and oil rise to top	
steam and oil go through cooling coil in cold water	
water extracts oil then oil needs to come out of water	
steam mixes with leaves	
Oil taken from top of tank. Water taken from bottom of tank.	

Activity 3.5: Process diagram (tea production)

Some Task 1 diagrams show processes with slight differences. You need to compare them to highlight the differences.

The following diagram shows how three different types of tea are made.

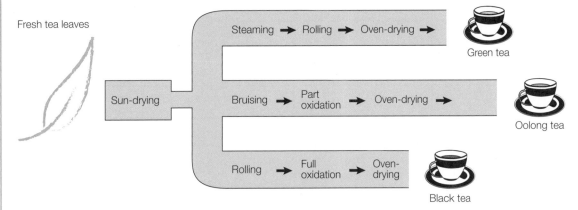

*Oxidation: a reaction with oxygen that changes the leaf colour to brown.

Activity: Identify the stages of the process

Look at the processes from the tea diagram. Which box do they belong in? One process does not fit a category. Which one?

drying	**oxidation**	**crushing**
sun-drying		

bruising	steaming	sun-drying
part oxidation	rolling	full oxidation
oven-drying		

[continued from previous page]

Activity: Which tea uses which process?

The first example has been done for you.

	Green tea	Oolong tea	Black tea
drying	✓	✓	✓
steaming			
crushing			
oxidation			

1. Which two types of tea have similar processes?

2. Which tea is different?

Activity: Structure the answer

This is a good structure for this type of process.

> Overview

> Similar processes

> Different processes

Which paragraph does each point belong in? Write the sentence number in the correct paragraph.

1. One ingredient → three different products

2. No oxidation, so not brown

3. Basically same processes: drying / crushing (but different kinds of crushing) / drying

4. Same process: oxidation, but different amounts

5. Unique: steaming

6. Basically the same: dry, crush, oxidation, dry

7. Use same process: drying at start and finish

Cohesion

To get a good mark, you must clearly show the link from one idea to another idea. There are four main ways to do this.

1   Linking words

For example: *and, however, therefore.*

2   Pronouns

For example: *it, they, ones, which.*

3   Substitution

Replace a chunk of a sentence with words like *ones, so, do so.*
Group specific things into a more general category. For example: replace [*cars and motorcycles and vans*] with [*these vehicles*].

4   Grammatical structures

You can use some grammar forms to link your sentences more fluently. This is discussed in Unit 5.

Linking words

> **TIP**   Imagine that the examiner can't see the Task 1 diagram and knows nothing about the topic. You need to carefully explain all your conclusions and generalisations to them.

Linking words are the basic way to show a relationship between ideas. They are like signposts on a road to show your reader where you are leading them. You shouldn't use too many of them because it looks clumsy. Make sure you use a range of other devices too.

pg 14, 157,

Types of links

Linking words fall into general categories a

Adding information	Comparing things		
and	however		
also	but		
in addition (to)	whereas		
furthermore	while		
moreover	as opposed to		
besides	on the other hand		
finally	despite	simultaneously	in short
	in spite of	at this point	in summary
	nevertheless	to begin with	to summarise
	yet	first, last	in conclusion
	similarly	first, second, third	as has been said
	likewise	afterwards	
		then	
		subsequently	

Illustrating a point	Conceding something	Showing cause and effect
for example	although	so
for instance	even though	therefore
such as	in spite of	consequently
in particular	of course	as a consequence
specifically	while it may be true that	thus
especially		as a result
including		in order to
that is		this is why
in other words		hence
in fact		for this reason
		accordingly

Note: *while* has two uses.

Using linking words

In IELTS Task 1, you need to interpret data from an image and put it into words. The simplest paragraph structure for this kind of writing is:

1 Make a general statement.
2 Explain what you mean.
3 Give some proof.

Activity 3.6

When do you use each type of linking word? Match the *type of linking word* from the table above (summarising, illustrating, etc.) to each function.

Making a general statement	summarising
Explaining what you mean	
Giving proof	

(Some types are useful for more than one step.)

Activity 3.7

Improve sentences 1 and 2 using the linking words in the box below.

furthermore	~~overall~~	although	for instance	whereas	such as

1. 20 per cent of younger students were quite satisfied with their course, and 25 per cent were satisfied with their course and 40 per cent were very satisfied with their course. Older students were quite unsatisfied, unsatisfied, or very unsatisfied (20 per cent, 30 per cent, and 15 per cent respectively).
    Overall, younger students were satisfied with their course, _____ most older students were unsatisfied with their course.

2. 40 per cent of waste is recycled. 70 per cent of glass is recycled. 25 per cent of plastic is recycled. 10 per cent of e-waste is recycled. 80 per cent of people in inner suburbs recycle and 50 per cent of people in outer suburbs recycle and 50 per cent of people in country areas recycle.
    _____ 40 per cent of waste is recycled, some materials, ~~_____~~ glass, are recycled more than others. _____, some people recycle more than others. _____, people in inner suburbs recycle more than people in other areas.

Improve sentences 3 and 4 using the linking words in the box below.

in fact	at this point	also	despite	but	specifically

3. In 2007, the average household income fell by 10 per cent. In 2007 the average household expenditure dropped by 5 per cent.
    In 2007, the average household income fell. _____ the average household expenditure _____ dropped _____ not by much.

4. The company tried several actions to reduce the number of accidents. Accidents didn't decrease. The accidents increased after they replaced the safety classes with a training manual.
    _____ trying several actions, the company did not reduce the number of accidents over the period. _____, they actually increased the accident rate with one action, _____, replacing the safety classes with a training manual.

Activity 3.8: Match the endings

Task: The following charts show the favourite colours for cars among men and women, and the proportion of actual car sales, in 2011.

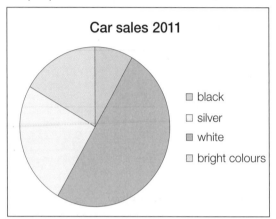

Car sales 2011

□ black
□ silver
■ white
□ bright colours

Survey results: favourite car colour

Colour	Men	Women
black	80%	10%
white	5%	10%
silver	10%	55%
bright colours	10%	25%

1. Most men claimed that black was their colour of choice, however ...

2. Most men preferred black cars, while ...

3. Although white was not rated very highly by either group, ...

4. Bright colours were not well liked overall and ...

5. The survey results show that bright colours were reasonably popular with women but ...

    a women favoured silver cars.

    b they were also not a big seller.

    c the sales figures suggest they didn't actually buy this colour.

    d it had the highest sales.

    e not with men.

Using linking expressions more skilfully

Linking expressions are often used at the beginning of a sentence. Good writers, however, use linking expressions more skilfully.

Some linking words can go after the subject of the sentence. If you do this, you must put a comma before and after the word. For example:

> The majority of men preferred black cars. Women, <u>however</u>, did not show this tendency.

> In every region, sales rose after an advertising campaign. Sales, <u>therefore</u>, showed an increase related to advertising.

This structure, with the linking word after the subject, highlights the subject, making it the focus of the sentence.

Linking expressions that can be used after the subject

however	in particular	in other words
therefore	especially	meanwhile
moreover	specifically	at this point
for example	on the other hand	as a consequence
for instance	of course	as a result

Activity 3.9: Using linking words after the subject

The chart below shows the number of people who had recently contacted family or friends.

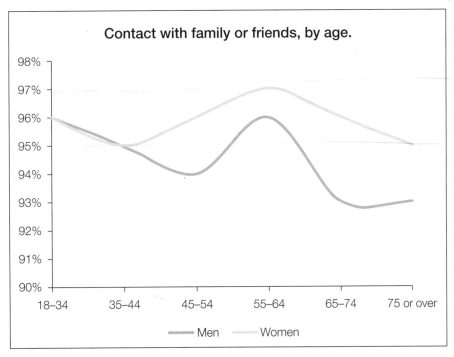

Write the second sentence to finish the idea. Put the words in the correct order and add the punctuation.

1. The overall trend for both groups is two periods of decline with a large increase in the middle.
    / show a slight decrease / men / in later years / however /
    Answer: Men, however, show a slight decrease in later years.

2. Although the amount of social contact changes over the lifespan, women show no net decrease overall.
    / in other words / as 18- to 34-year-olds (around 95 per cent) / have / a similar amount of contact with family and friends / 75-year-olds /

3. The oldest group of women have the same amount of social contact as the youngest group.
    / have / men / much less social contact / than at age 18–34 / on the other hand / at age 75 and over /

[continued from previous page]

4. For women, the first downward trend ends at age 35–44.
/ men / until age 45–54 / continue to show a decrease / meanwhile /

5. The second decline in social contact happens at age 55–64.
/ show a sharp drop / in particular / at this age / men /

6. For the older groups, there's a fair difference, except at age 55–64.
/ men / show a slight increase / from 94 per cent to 96 per cent / at this point /

Reference

Pronouns refer to something already mentioned. This can link your sentences together smoothly. Pronouns are words like:

they	that	them	it	these
one	this	those	ones	

For example:

1 Older workers were more likely to feel 'unskilled', yet they were least likely to take up formal training. [they = older workers]
2 Finally, the tea is dried in an oven and this stops the oxidation process. [this = dried in an oven]
3 Women had a lower literacy rate than men. This was most noticeable in developing nations. [this = Women had a lower literacy rate than men]

Pronouns can refer to a noun phrase, as in sentence 1; a verb phrase, as in sentence 2; or a whole sentence, as in sentence 3.

Activity 3.10

What does the pronoun refer to? Underline the phrase.

1. Japan has around 1700 mm of rain every year. Most of **this** falls between June and September.

2. A safety manager was appointed in 1999, but **this** had no effect on the accident rate.

3. As the steam passes through the cooling coil, **it** cools down.

4. The chart shows four recycling categories. **These** are glass, paper, metal and plastic.

5. As the steam rises through the leaves, it mixes with **their** moisture and oil.

6. At the start of the period, widgets were the biggest seller, but by the end of the period **they** were the lowest-selling product.

Of which/of whom

Improve your cohesion with these useful expressions for discussing data.

[proportion] of which/whom

some of which	most of whom	20 per cent of which
all of which	both of whom	

For example:

The country has four distinct seasons, <u>two of which</u> have some rainfall.
[= two out of the four seasons]

The council collects 30 kg of waste per household, <u>25 per cent of which</u> is recycled. [= 25 per cent of the waste]

The [property] of which

the size of which	the sales of which	the effect of which
the temperature of which	the cost of which	

For example:

The biggest selling items were widgets, <u>the cost of which</u> increased by $50 over the period. [= the cost of widgets]

The flapper is attached to a wheel, <u>the speed of which</u> is controlled by gears.
[= the speed of the wheel]

Activity 3.11

Rewrite the sentences with 'of which'/'of whom'.

1. The shop has two storage rooms. One storage room will be converted to a display area.
    Answer: The shop has two storage rooms, <u>one of which</u> will be converted to a display area.

2. The EU produced around 520 kg of waste per person. 20 per cent of the waste was recycled.
    The EU produced around 520 kg of waste per person, _____.

3. The diagram shows three processes for producing tea. Two processes involve oxidation.
    The diagram shows three processes for producing tea, _____.

4. The boiler produces steam. The steam's heat is controlled by a thermostat.
    The boiler produces steam, _____.

[continued from previous page]

5. In 2012, the theme park had 10,000 visitors. Half of the visitors were from Asia.

In 2012, the theme park had 10,000 visitors, _____.

6. There are two stages. The stages involve water.

There are two stages, _____.

7. The company employs 320 women. 30 per cent of the women who work for the company work part time.

The company employs 320 women, _____.

8. The storage tank holds hot water. Some water goes to the hot taps in the kitchen and bathroom.

The storage tank holds hot water, _____.

9. The graph shows global population growth. The global population growth rate is predicted to rise.

The graph shows global population growth, _____.

10. The graph compares two industries. Both industries require on-the-job training.

The graph compares two industries, _____.

Substitution

Substitution will help you get a good IELTS result. It helps you to avoid repetition and links your ideas smoothly. Use these words to replace parts of a sentence.

so	do so	one	be so	ones

For example:

The water needs to cool down. To do so, it passes through a cooling coil.

Activity 3.12

Join the ideas with substitution. Rewrite the second sentence using the words in brackets.

1. The graph compares four ways to deal with waste. The most popular ways to deal with waste were burying and recycling. [ONES]

Answer: The graph compares four ways to deal with waste. The most popular ones were burying and recycling.

2. The hot water passes around the house. After it has passed around the house, it is cool and needs to be heated again. [DO SO]

3. The second chart shows car sales by colour. Surprisingly, the highest-selling colour was white. [ONE]

4. There were two periods when imports exceeded exports. Imports exceeded exports in 2007, and again in 2011. [THIS + BE SO]

5. The first chart shows the salaries of five different industries. The highest-paid industries were health care and legal services. [ONES]

6. The satisfaction rate dropped in 1995 and 2000. It fell again in 2003, but only slightly. [DO SO]

Another kind of substitution is replacing a group of specific things with a more general word. This helps you summarise data, and can improve your IELTS band score. For example:

NOT SO GOOD

Black was the highest-rated by men (at 80 per cent), while women preferred silver (at 55 per cent). However, black and silver did not show very high sales.

GOOD

Black was the highest-rated by men (at 80 per cent), while women preferred silver (at 55 per cent). These colours, however, did not show very high sales.

Activity 3.13: Matching

Match the specific words (1 to 10) with the categories (A to J).

1 people in the workforce aged 45 to 55	**A** these changes
2 yellow, orange, pink	**B** these groups
3 cars, buses, vans, motorcycles	**C** teenagers
4 computers, MP3 players, mobile phones	**D** electrical goods
5 1 per cent increase, 3 per cent increase, 5 per cent increase	**E** vehicles
6 adding an exhibition space, adding a shop, reducing the size of the storage area	**F** electronics
7 students and unemployed people	**G** these forms of transportation
8 refrigerators, washing machines, microwave ovens	**H** these older workers
9 car, bus, train, walking	**I** these bright colours
10 14-year-old people, 15-year-old people, 16-year-old people	**J** these small increases

Activity 3.14

Use a substitution phrase from the table to make these sentences better.

1. At the beginning of the period, walking and taking the train were the most common ways to get to work. However, by the end of the period, walking and taking the train were the least common.

2. Around this time, social contact increased from 94 per cent to 96 per cent for men and from 95 per cent to 97 per cent for women. Due to the scale of the graph, the increases from 94 per cent to 96 per cent for men and from 95 per cent to 97 per cent for women look quite dramatic.

3. People aged 15 to 17 years old visited the cinema most frequently. Furthermore, people aged 15 to 17 years old also spent the most time in the cinema per visit.

4. The new swimming pool will have a larger café area and a larger gym area. The larger café area and a larger gym area will make the pool attractive to a wider range of people.

5. Staff aged between 45 and 55 took the fewest holidays, perhaps because staff aged between 45 and 55 tended to have management positions.

Assessment checklist

Look at this sample answer. How good are the coherence and cohesion? Write examples in the table.

Coherence and Cohesion	Yes/no	Example
Ideas are logically organised		
Writing is organised into paragraphs. Each paragraph has one main topic.		
Uses a range of cohesive devices: • reference • substitution • linking words.		

The chart below shows the number of people who had recently contacted family or friends.

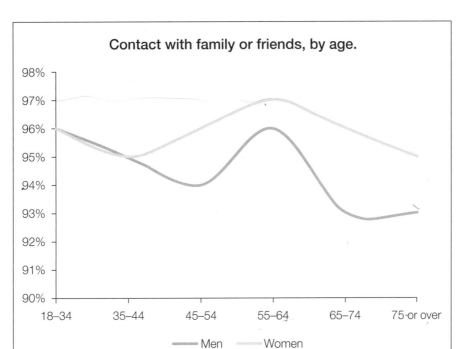

The table shows six age groups of adults and the percentage of whom had recently contacted family and friends. In general, women did so more than men, although it varies from age.

First, the persentage of women from 18–34 who had contact was 96 per cent then it decreased gradually until 95 per cent for females 35–44 years old. Then it rose steady up to 55 to 64 years old. They had contact 97 per cent and this was the peak of women who contacted family and friends. After that, the number of women who did so decreased slightly to 95 per cent for the 75 or over group.

Second, the picture for men was quite similar. Their peak number was 96 per cent. This was in 55–64 years old group. The lowest percentage, however, was for ages 65 to 74 and 75 and over. In these oldest groups, only 93 per cent contacted family and friends recently.

To sum up, the number of female contacts was more than male ones. The trend, however, was similar for both sexes.

You can check all your answers to the activities in this unit in the Answer Key in Appendix 1.

UNIT 4

Lexical Resource

Task 1 is very short, only 150 words. This makes it difficult to use a wide variety of language. Also, the topic might be something you don't know about, so you won't know a lot of vocabulary. The trick is to use a wide variety of words to describe the trends and differences and to summarise the information.

> **TIP** Lower-level writers use very strong, definite language. For example, 'the data <u>clearly</u> show …', 'it is <u>obvious</u> that …', '… there were <u>dramatic</u> changes'. Higher-level writers use milder language. For example, 'the data <u>seem</u> to show …', 'it <u>appears</u> that …', 'there was <u>some</u> fluctuation'.

Describing change

Some Task 1 diagrams show change over time. Learn some useful vocabulary for describing the shape of the graph.

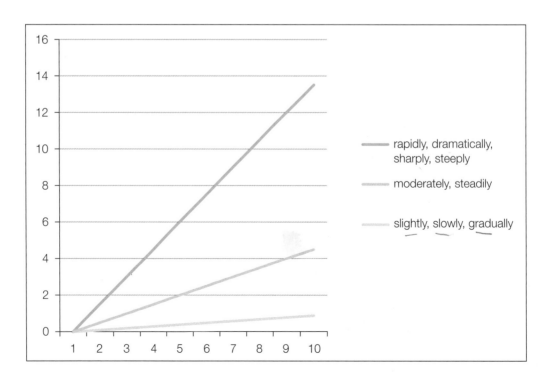

For example:

> The number of customers <u>increased slightly</u> in June and July.
>
> The cost of living is predicted to <u>rise steadily</u> over the period.
>
> Sales of tobacco products <u>fell dramatically</u> between 2000 and 2010.

Activity 4.1

The graph shows the number of widgets and gadgets that were sold by a company in one year.

Widgets vs gadgets: numbers sold

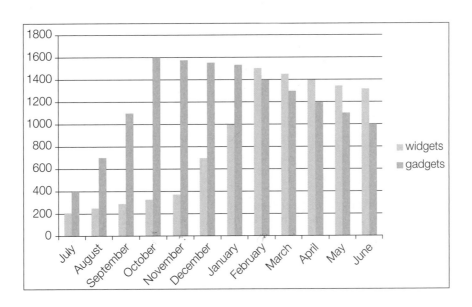

Complete the sentences about this graph, using:

a dramatically, rapidly, sharply, steeply

b moderately, steadily

c slightly, slowly, gradually

1. From July to November, sales of widgets increased <u>slightly</u>.

2. Between November and February, widget sales rose _dramatise_.

3. Widget sales dropped ___Slightly___ from February to June.

4. Sales of gadgets grew ___dramasic___ from July to October.

5. From October to February, gadget sales decreased ___Slier___.

6. Gadget sales fell ___Slightly___ between February and June.

Activity 4.2

The graph shows the average number of local and international visitors to a museum, per year, from 2001 to 2011.

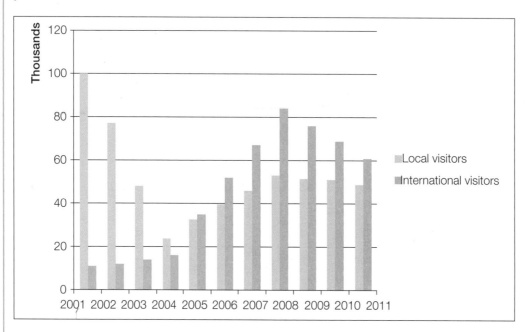

Complete the sentences about this graph, using:

[fell/dropped/decreased/declined] **AND** [dramatically/rapidly/sharply/steeply]
[rose/grew/increased]   [moderately/steadily]
                                          [slightly/slowly/gradually]

1. Between 2001 and 2004, the number of international visitors grew slowly.
2. The number of local visitors _____ _____ from 2001 to 2004.
3. Between 2004 and 2008, the number of local visitors _____ _____.
4. The number of international visitors _____ _____ between 2004 and 2008.
5. From 2008 to the end of the period, the number of local visitors _____ _____.
6. The number of international visitors _____ _____ from 2008 to 2011.

You can also use these words as an adjective plus noun. For example:

> Emigration decreased slightly over the period, while immigration showed a steady increase.
>
> A sharp decline **in** imports occurred between 2002 and 2004.
>
> There was a dramatic rise **in** sales from 1996 to 1998.
>
> For most of the twentieth century, the local economy experienced a gradual decline.

NOTE: When there is a noun after the phrase (like examples 2 and 3), you must use the preposition 'in'.

dramatically – dramatic	moderately – moderate	slightly – slight
rapidly – rapid	steadily – steady	slowly - slow
sharply – sharp		gradually – gradual
steeply – steep		

increased – an increase	fell – a fall
rose – a rise	decrease – a decrease
grew – growth	dropped – a drop
	declined – a decline

Activity 4.3

Complete the sentences.

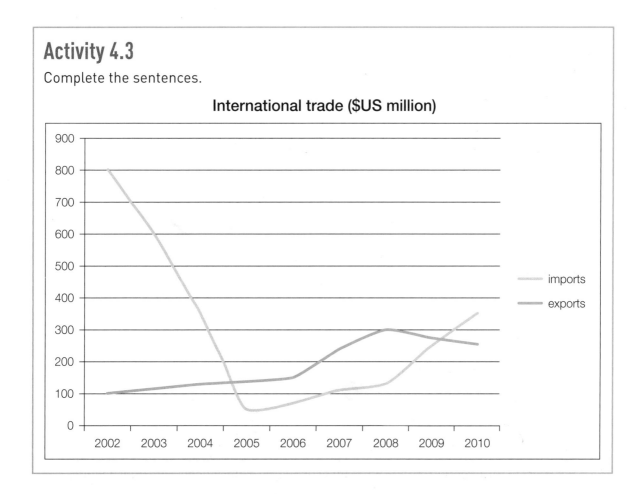

International trade ($US million)

[continued from previous page]

1. There was <u>a steep drop in</u> imports between 2008 and 2010.

2. Between 2002 and 2006, exports experienced _____.

3. There was _____ exports from 2008 to 2010.

4. From 2005 to 2008, imports showed _____.

5. The period 2006 to 2008 saw _____ exports.

6. Between 2008 and 2010, imports showed _____.

TIP   Don't use 'dramatic/dramatically' too often.

You can also use:

significant/significantly

noticeable/noticeably

marked/markedly

considerable/considerably.

These words don't describe the slope of the graph. They just mean 'big enough to see'. For example:

Although sales increased overall, there was <u>a marked decrease</u> between 1965 and 1967.

There is expected to be <u>a noticeable improvement</u> in sales from 2020, after the new model is released.

The popularity of landline telephones <u>decreased significantly</u> over the period.

Staff attendance showed <u>considerable variation</u>, depending on the time of year.

NOTE: 'Significant' can mean 'big', but it can also have a more technical meaning. In statistics, 'a significant change' means 'a change that is not normal variation'.

Comparing

In Academic Writing Task 1, you often need to say how much something has changed, compared to another thing. For example:

Although **widget** sales were quite <u>high</u>, **gadget** sales were generally <u>higher</u>.

Domestic sales showed <u>a smaller</u> improvement <u>than</u> **international** sales.

Although **all countries** showed a decline in imports, <u>the greatest</u> decrease was seen in **South America**.

Recycling was common in **each district**, but was <u>most common</u> in **South-Central**, where 97 per cent of residents recycled their rubbish regularly.

Yellow was generally <u>less popular</u> than any other colour, except for a 2-year period, when **white** was <u>the least popular</u> colour.

Note the pattern:

Adjective	Comparative	Superlative
high	higher (than)	(the) highest
small	smaller (than)	(the) smallest
great	greater (than)	(the) greatest
common	more common (than)	(the) most common
popular	less popular (than)	(the) least popular

Activity 4.4

Use the comparatives and superlatives to complete the sentences below.

Task: The following diagrams show how goods were transported in a European country, in three different periods.

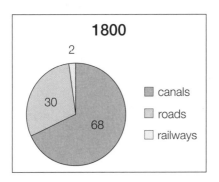

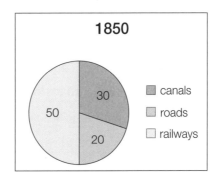

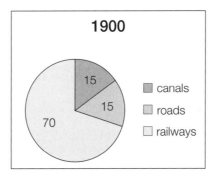

*canal: a straight, artificial river.

[continued from previous page]

1. Until 1900, canals were <u>more popular than</u> roads for transporting goods.

2. The use of railways showed <u>the greatest</u> change over the period.

3. Roads experienced _____ change in usage over the period.

4. In 1800, canals were _____ widespread method of transportation, but after that they became _____ .

5. Railways were _____ prevalent mode of transportation for goods in 1800, but _____ mode in the other periods.

6. _____ change was seen in the use of railways, between 1800 and 1850.

7. In 1800, goods were usually transported by canals, but by 1900 this method was one of _____ .

More language for comparing

When you compare things, you sometimes need to say that they are the same. Look at the task above. In 1900, canals and roads have the same share of the pie chart (around 15 per cent each). We can say:

> In 1900, roads were <u>as popular as</u> canals for transporting goods.
>
> By 1900, railways were <u>as common as</u> canals had been in 1800.

You may also want to highlight that things are **not** the same. You can do this with ['not as … as']. For example:

> The use of roads and canals declined over the period, but it was <u>not as dramatic</u> for roads <u>as</u> for canals.
>
> By 1850, canal transportation was <u>not as widespread as</u> it had been, because railway transportation became more common.

Notice that you can use the ['as … as'] structure to focus on different parts of the sentence.

Comparing the subject of the sentence:

> <u>Japan</u> produced as many smartphones as <u>Korea</u>.
>
> <u>Women</u> didn't earn as much money as <u>men</u>.
>
> <u>Natural materials</u> don't last as long as <u>artificial materials</u>.

Comparing the object of the sentence:

> Japan produced as many smartphones as laptops.
>
> By 2050, the company will produce as many motorbikes as cars.

Comparing the verb of the sentence:

> Japan imported as many smartphones as it exported.
>
> The country burned as much rubbish as it recycled.

Activity 4.5

Task: The following chart describes visitors to a theme park in the USA, over one year. It shows how long visitors from each region stayed and how much money they spent in the park.

Region	Average stay (hours)	Average spent ($US)
North America	6	200
South America	8	120
Asia	4	350
Europe	6	150

True or false

1. Asian visitors didn't stay as long as North American visitors.

2. North American visitors spent as much money as Asian visitors.

3. Asian visitors didn't stay as long as North American visitors, but they spent more money.

4. European visitors stayed as long as North American visitors, and spent as much money.

5. European visitors stayed as long as North American visitors, but didn't spend as much money.

6. Visitors from South America stayed the longest and spent the least.

7. No other visitors stayed as long as South American visitors, and nor did they spend as little.

More language for comparing

To get a good mark in Task 1, you also need to say how big a difference is. For example:

Shop	Apples	Bananas
Healthy Harvest	$4.99 per kilo	$5.99 per kilo
Farm Fresh	$4.99 per kilo	$8.99 per kilo

At both stores, bananas are **more expensive** than apples, but at Farm Fresh they are **considerably more expensive** (an extra $4 per kilo), while at Healthy Harvest they are only **slightly more expensive** (an additional $1 per kilo).

Small difference	Big difference
slightly	considerably
somewhat	far
	significantly
	much

For example:

Widget sales fell between 2007 and 2009, but gadget sales experienced a <u>far greater</u> decrease in the same period.

The new shopping mall will have a <u>much larger</u> car park.

Between 2000 and 2010 economic growth showed a <u>slightly sharper incline</u>.

Activity 4.6

Complete the sentences.

Task: The diagrams on the following pages show the planned changes to a public swimming pool.

1. The car park will be <u>considerably larger</u>. [LARGE]

2. The children's area will be _____. [BIG]

3. The free swimming area will be _____. [SMALL]

4. The cafeteria will be moved _____ to the entrance. [NEAR]

5. With the relocation of the cafeteria, there will be more room in the outside area, allowing the training lanes to be _____. [LONG]

6. The new change rooms will be _____. [SMALL]

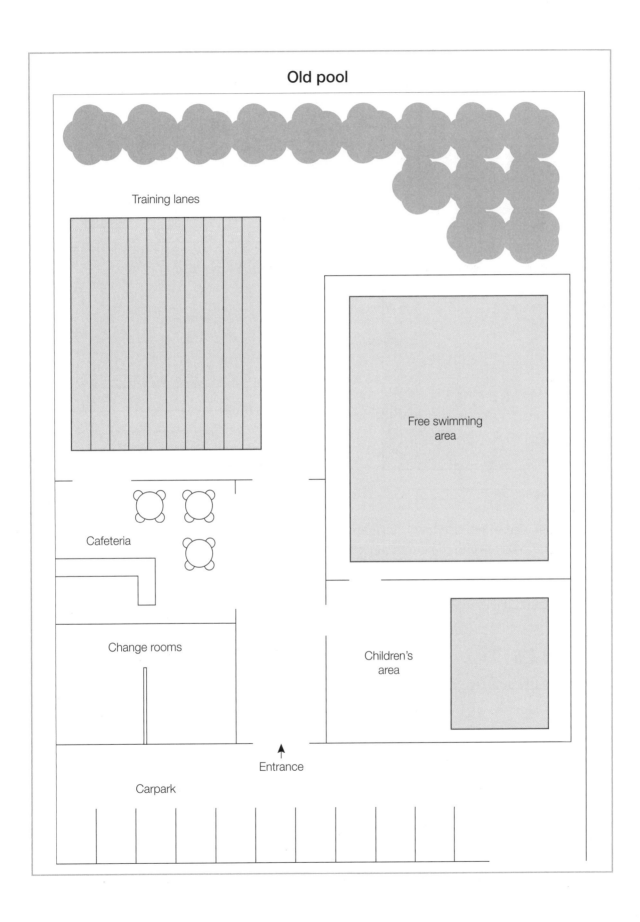

Old pool

Training lanes

Free swimming area

Cafeteria

Change rooms

Children's area

Entrance

Carpark

[continued from previous page]

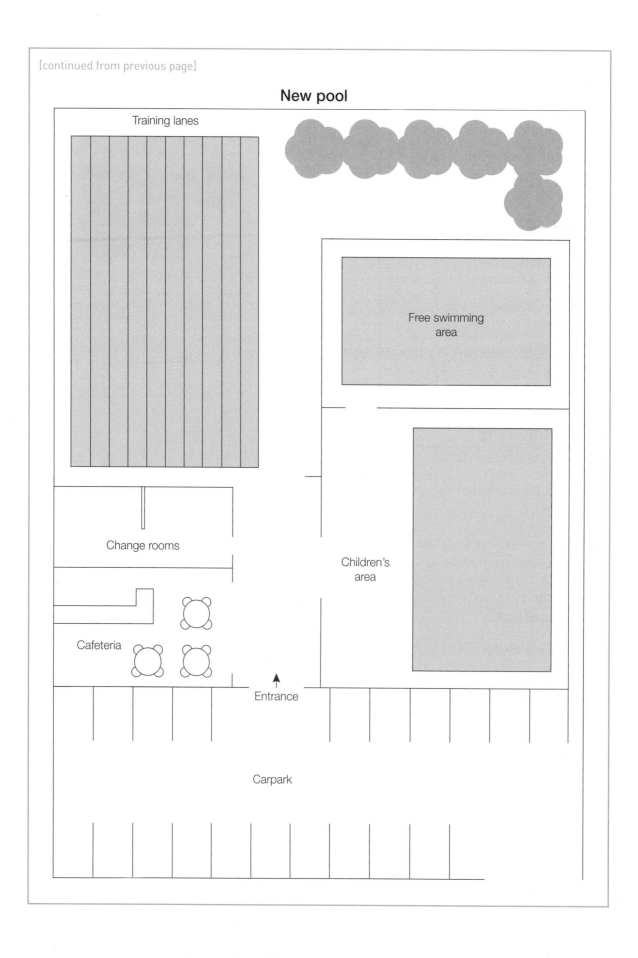

New pool

Rather and *fairly*

Another useful way to describe differences is to give your opinion about them. You can do this with the words 'rather' and 'fairly'. These words mean 'slightly', but they also have a faintly negative meaning. For example:

> Sales of widgets were low from 1990 to 1995. This could be because they were fairly expensive, compared to gadgets, during this period. [You are hinting that 'expensive' = 'bad'.]

> Although the literacy rate for men was close to the world average, the literacy rate for women was rather low. [You are hinting that 'low literacy rate' = bad.]

'Rather' can also have a faint meaning of 'unexpected'. For example:

> Sales of pink cars were almost zero for most of the period, but for a short period (1987 to 1989) the colour was rather popular.

> Although Sweden has the lowest birth rate, it has a rather high number of paediatricians per capita.

Review activity

Rewrite the sentence so it has the same meaning.

1. Imports were slightly smaller than exports. ➜ Exports were slightly bigger than imports.

2. The survey found that Australia has a lower-than-expected literacy rate. ➜ The survey found that Australia has a rather low literacy rate.

3. Compact cars are more economical than SUVs. ➜ SUVs are not _____ as compact cars.

4. The old model cost $20, and the new model will cost $20. ➜ The new model will cost _____ the old model.

5. Surprisingly, computers are somewhat expensive in China. ➜ Computers are _____ expensive in China.

6. China produces 24 per cent of the world's CO_2, Russia produces 6%. ➜ China produces _____ CO_2 than Russia.

7. The new kindergarten will be a little too close to a dangerous road. ➜ The new kindergarten will be _____ close to a dangerous road.

Phrases

Phrasal verbs and collocations will improve your score for Lexical Resource. The important thing is to memorise each phrase as a unit. If you get one part of the phrase wrong, it will sound bad or have a different meaning. For example, don't say 'imports made a peak': say 'imports reached a peak'.

show an upward trend

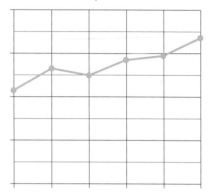

show a downward trend

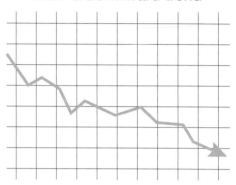

show some fluctuation

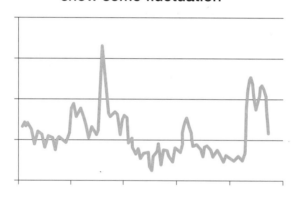

remain stable (remain static, remain constant)

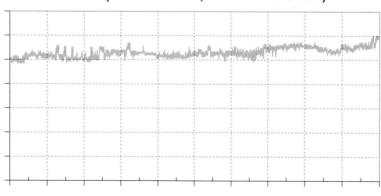

reach a peak (hit the highest point)

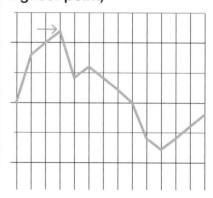

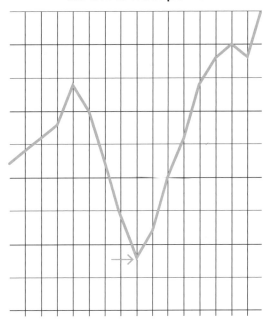

hit the lowest point

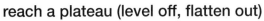
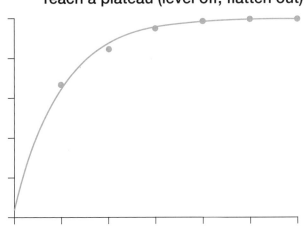

reach a plateau (level off, flatten out)

TIP   Don't say 'showed a fluctuating trend'. Fluctuation means there is no trend!

Activity 4.7

Replace the 'normal' word with a phrase.

1. After 1950, the grain yields increased steadily until in 1960 they stopped increasing.

2. Although the literacy rate saw both increases and decreases over the period, it fell overall by 5 per cent.

3. The number of noise-related complaints was smallest in January (at 15 complaints).

4. It is predicted that average commuting times will be the same from 2020 to 2030.

5. The average food basket cost rose from 2000 to 2002, then fell slightly from 2003 to 2004, then increased again between 2005 to 2008, going up from $30 to $40 overall.

Activity 4.8

Write your own description of this graph, using these useful phrases.

The following graph shows the average distance, in metres, that small and large dogs, aged 1 to 7 years old, walk per day with their owners.

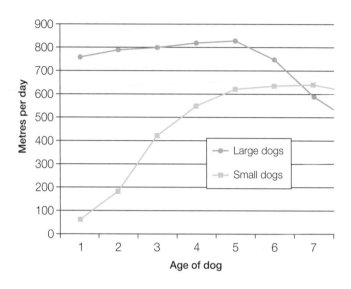

From ages 1 to 5, the distance that large dogs walk _____, at around 800 m per day, though increasing slightly (from around 760 m to 820 m). In contrast, the daily distance walked by small dogs increases significantly between ages 1 and 5 (from 50 m to 600 m) before _____. From ages 5 to 7, walking distances for smaller dogs _____ at around 600 m per day, whereas for large dogs, after _____ at age 5 (820 m), walks become increasingly shorter, falling to 500 m per day by age 7.

Idioms

Idioms will improve your score for Lexical Resource. The following examples are suitable for academic writing, and they show that you have a varied vocabulary—exactly what you need for a 'good' IELTS band.

> **TIP** To learn idioms for talking about data, look at popular science or economics websites and magazines. They tell interesting stories about data, using idiomatic language.

to skyrocket

a surge (in)

a boom (in)
(sales/exports)*

to plummet

to plunge

to dive

to dip

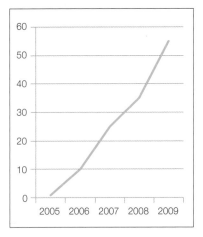

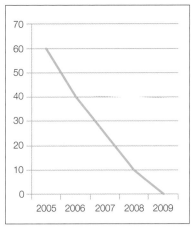

*Note that this is only used for positive things. Don't say 'there was a boom in the crime rate' or 'there was a pollution boom'. Also, it is mainly used for population or money-related things.

Activity 4.9

Replace the 'normal' words with these idiomatic words:

BOOM ~~SKYROCKET~~ SURGE DIP PLUNGE

1. Sales of smartphones increased rapidly after 2007. → Sales of smartphones skyrocketed after 2007.

2. There was a large population increase after the war. → There was a population _____ after the war.

3. House prices increased overall, but for 5 years in the middle of the period they were a little bit less. → House prices increased overall, except for a 5-year _____ in the middle of the period.

4. The injury rate fell dramatically, as soon as the new safety equipment was installed. → The injury rate _____, as soon as the new safety equipment was installed.

5. Swimwear retailers experience a huge increase in demand in summer. → Swimwear retailers experience a _____ in demand in summer.

Describing numbers

Some IELTS tasks show a chart or table. You don't need to describe change over time – you need to compare different amounts.

More	Less
twice	half
three times	a third
four times	a quarter
five times	a fifth
six times	a sixth
ten times	a tenth
twenty times	a twentieth

You can use these phrases with an adjective or adverb:

Onions (at $4 per kilo) are **four times as expensive as** potatoes ($1 per kilo).

Freight trains travel **half as fast as** passenger trains.

There were **three times as many** men **as** women admitted to hospital over the period.

The crime rate is **twice as high** in the city, compared to the countryside.

You can use these phrases with a noun:

Imports are increasing at **half** the rate **of** exports.

The UK has around **twice** the population **of** Canada.

The new shopping mall will be **three times** the size **of** the old one.

Activity 4.10

Fill in the missing words.

Task: The chart below shows the number of cars that one dealer sold in a year, by colour.

Colour	Number
white	1000
silver	500
red	250
black	50

1. The dealer sold half as many silver cars as white cars.

2. The dealer sold twice as many _____ cars as silver cars.

3. White cars were _____ times as popular as red cars.

4. _____ cars sold a quarter as many units as white cars.

5. Black cars were the lowest selling, with _____ of the sales of red cars (the other low performer), and only _____ of the sales of the most popular colour, white.

6. Silver cars saw _____ the sales of white cars, but _____ the sales of red cars.

Activity 4.11

Use the clues to label the chart. Write the regions in the table.

Task: The following chart shows the amount of widgets used worldwide, by region.

Region	Widgets (million)
	180
	240
North America	120
	40
	90
	60

[continued from previous page]

1. Europe uses **twice as many** widgets **as** North America.

2. South America uses **a third of** the widgets that North America uses.

3. Oceania shows **a quarter of** Europe's widget consumption.

4. Asia uses **three times as many** widgets **as** Oceania.

5. Africa uses **half as many** widgets **as** Asia.

Activity 4.12

Use the words in brackets to complete the sentences.

Task: The chart below shows the amount of waste that each person produced in one year, in several countries.

Country	Waste (kilograms)
USA	800
UK	600
Japan	400
Fiji	200

1. Per person, Fiji produced <u>half as much waste as</u> Japan. [MUCH]

2. Per person, the UK produced _____ Fiji. [MUCH]

3. The USA's per capita waste production was _____ Japan's, and
   _____ Fiji's. [HIGH]

4. Fiji produced _____ the UK per capita. [MUCH]

Numbers as verbs

You can improve your score for Lexical Resource by using words in different forms. For example, the following words are usually used as adjectives, but you can also use them as verbs.

Adjective	Verb
double	to double
half	to halve
triple	to triple

For example:

> It can be seen that, during the economic boom years (1980 to 1990), the average household income almost **doubled**.
>
> The new highway **will halve** the average commuting time.
>
> By 2000, the population **had tripled**.

Activity 4.13

Complete the sentences with 'halve', 'double', 'triple'.

Task: The charts below show the number of workplace injuries, per year, at a factory and the actions that were taken to reduce injuries, between 1985 and 1995.

Year	Action
1990	New machines introduced
1991	Safety manager appointed
1993	Safety classes for all staff
1995	Training manual replaces classes

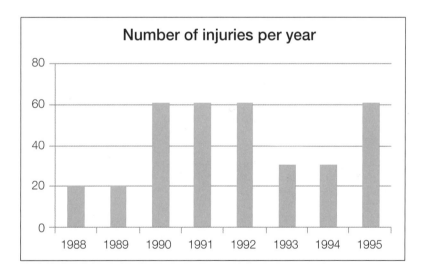

Number of injuries per year

1. In 1990, after the new machines were introduced, the injury rate _____.

2. In 1993, safety classes were introduced for all staff, and it seems that this _____ the injury rate.

3. When the safety classes were replaced by a safety manual in 1995, the injury rate _____.

4. In spite of the Health and Safety activities, the injury rate _____ between 1988 and 1995.

Activity 4.14

Mind map: Write synonyms for these words in the empty circles.

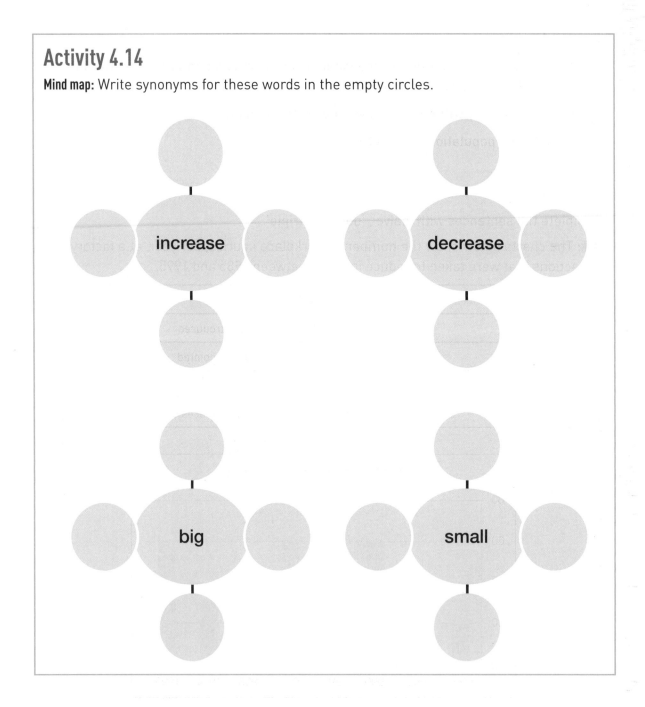

Activity 4.15

Replace the repeated words with synonyms.

1. First, add some synonyms to this mind map.

2. Now, use these synonyms to make this answer better. Replace the <u>repeated words</u> with synonyms.

    The diagram below shows how a central heating system in a house works.

    Summarise the information by selecting and reporting the main features, and make comparisons where relevant.

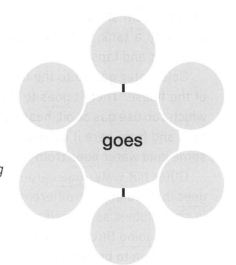

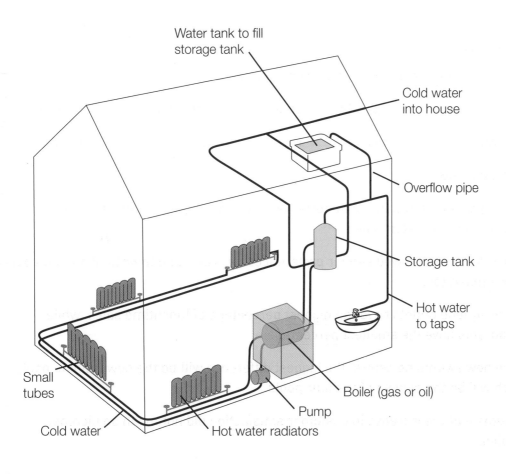

Water tank to fill storage tank

Cold water into house

Overflow pipe

Storage tank

Hot water to taps

Small tubes

Cold water

Hot water radiators

Pump

Boiler (gas or oil)

[continued from previous page]

This diagram shows a house's central heating system. It shows that cold water goes into a tank, and then goes into a boiler and then goes through pipes to radiators and taps.

Cold water goes into the house and goes into a water storage tank at the top of the house. Then it goes to the boiler, at the bottom of the house. This boiler, which can use gas or oil, heats the water. Some of the hot water goes to a storage tank and from here it can go to taps to provide the hot water for the house. Also some cold water goes from the tank to the taps.

Other hot water goes around the house by being pumped through pipes and goes into radiators in different rooms. The water goes through hot water radiators in small tubes, so the radiators get hot and this heats the house.

After going through the pipes and radiators the water is cold, so it goes to the boiler again to be heated again and then go around the house again.

Activity 4.16

Replace the repeated word with a synonym from the box.

roughly	comparable	share	most significant	greatest
proportion	around	rise	about	growth
almost the same				

1. While approximately half the imports were electronics, approximately a third of imports were also electronics.

2. Men and women showed similar preferences for travel and their total holiday costs were similar, too.

3. Takeaway food outlets have the highest percentage of lunchtime sales, while restaurants have the smallest percentage.

4. In the new swimming centre, the biggest difference will be the new training pool, which will be the biggest of the four pools.

5. It seems that the increase in customer satisfaction did not mean an increase in sales.

Spelling

Activity: Look → say → cover → write → check

Here are some words that are often spelled incorrectly in IELTS Task 1. Practise spelling them with this technique.

1. **Look** at the word.

2. **Say** the word.

3. **Cover** up the word with your hand.

4. **Write** the word.

5. **Check** your spelling.

Look at these words	Write the words here
diagram	
population	
increase	
proportion	
percentage	
information	
following	
slightly	
fluctuate	
thousand	

TIP   You can also improve your spelling by reading a lot of English. If you see words often, you will remember how they are spelled.

Word choice and word formation

Get to know the kind of errors you often make (for example, ie ↔ ei), and look out for them. When you have finished writing your Task 1 answer, go back and check for your common errors.

The next activity shows some common errors that candidates make.

Activity 4.17

Spot the common IELTS errors.

1. The chart shows the economical growth in a certain country.

2. There was an increase of unemployment between 2007 and 2008.

3. At first, the water goes into the channel.

4. Nearly twice many men as women bought widgets.

5. Despite the proportion of music sales decreased, this was still the biggest area of spending for teenagers.

6. Third world nations had lower literacy rates than first world nations.

7. The table shows the average rainfall in London, Berlin and Paris. Every city has its highest rainfall in winter.

8. The graph shows that news programs had the most viewers everyday.

Activity 4.18

Assess this sample answer.

Task: The following diagrams show how goods were transported in a European country, in three different periods.

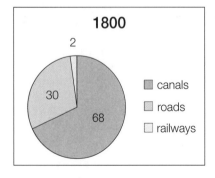

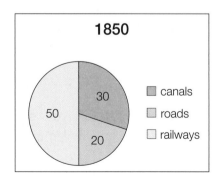

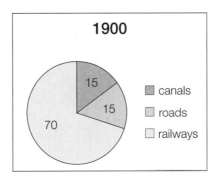

The given pie charts show the information about the amount of the goods transported in a European country in the three different time periods and shows that the cannals changed from most popular to unpopular. Railways changed from least popular to most popular, but roads did not very much change.

The level of goods transported by canals became very less very quickly, from 68 per cent in 1800, to 30 per cent in 1850, to 15 per cent in 1900. On the other hand, using railways increased a very much between 1800 (2 per cent) and 1850 (50 per cent), and then increased more to 70 per cent in 1900.

Roads showed a decerasing trend during the time period but not dramaticaly as the other transports. As can be seen from the infomation shown, roads were 30 per cent of transport in the beginning of 1800 and 20 per cent in 1850 and 15 per cent at the ending of 1900. To sum up, it is obvious that the most popular kind of goods transported it was canals and then railways.

Lexical resource	Yes/no	Examples
Does it use a wide variety of vocabulary, including phrasal verbs, academic words, and collocations?		
Are most words spelled correctly? *Not sure? Check by typing the answer on your computer and then using the spellcheck function.*		

You can check your answers to the activities in this unit in the Answer Key in Appendix 1.

UNIT 5

Grammatical Range and Accuracy

In Task 1 you only write 150 words, which is around 10 to 15 sentences. Such a short answer makes it difficult to use a wide variety of grammatical structures. However, you must do this to get a good mark.

When the IELTS examiner looks at your writing, they are looking for these things.

Grammatical Range and Accuracy
Does it use a variety of grammatical structures?
Are grammar and punctuation **mostly** correct?

Notice that you can make mistakes and still get a good mark. The important thing is the **variety** of your grammar.

Let's look at some grammar structures you can use.

Present simple

> 1 The graph compares the number of imports and exports from 2000 to 2010.
> 2 The tables show the proportion of students who live in dorms.
> 3 The water passes around the house in metal pipes.

These sentences use the **present simple** because they describe facts, and they describe things that are permanent.

When you describe a process, you are describing something that is a fact – it is always true. It was true in the past, it is true now, and it will be true in the future. For this situation, you can use the present simple, like sentence 3 above. For variety, you can combine this with the passive mood, like sentence b, below.

For example:

> a Steam goes in and mixes with the oil. [present simple]
> b The steam is cooled down in the cooling coil. [present simple passive]
> c The oil rises to the top. [present simple]

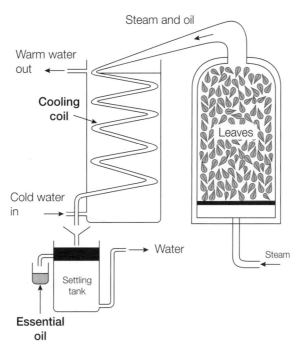

When you describe a graph, pie chart, or data table, it is a little more complicated. To describe the appearance of the diagram, you can use the present simple, like sentences 1 and 2 above. This is because you are describing something printed on paper. It can't change or move.

For example:

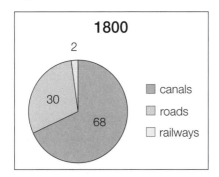

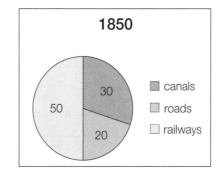

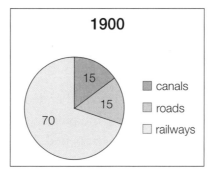

These are pie charts. [present simple]
The information highlights the changes in transportation methods over time. [present simple]
The charts compare three types of transportation. [present simple]

However, when you start describing the data in a graph, you usually can't use the present simple. This is because the data shows past results (e.g. sales in 2003) or is a prediction about the future (e.g. the world population in 2050).

For example, when you talk about the pie charts above, you can't use the present tense because the data is about the past. When you are describing the data you are talking about how things were 'back then'. For example:

> The chart <u>shows</u> [present simple] that in 1800, railways <u>were</u> [past simple] the least common method of transport, but by 1900 they <u>were</u> the most common method. [past simple]
>
> It <u>seems</u> [present simple] that in 1900, roads and canals <u>were</u> equally popular. [past simple]

Activity 5.1

Correct the errors in these sentences, or write 'OK' if they are correct.

1. In 1990, exports drop dramatically.

2. The graphs compared the increase in global temperatures and CO_2 production from 1910 to 2010.

3. The diagram shows the proposed changes to a public park.

4. The graph shows that people spend more money on household goods in 1980 than in 2000.

5. Water boils and produces steam, which rises up through the valve.

Past simple

> The ocean temperature <u>increased</u> slightly between 1950 and 2000.
>
> In 1900, fresh foods <u>showed</u> higher sales than processed foods.

Use the past simple to talk about things that started and ended in the past. If something started in the past but hasn't finished yet, you should use the present perfect (see page 195).

It doesn't matter how long ago something happened. Whether it finished long ago or recently, you should use the past simple. For example:

> In 1350, the world population <u>was</u> around 370 million. [past simple]
>
> In 2010, the world population <u>was</u> around 7 billion. [past simple]

Activity 5.2

Correct the errors in these sentences, or write 'OK' if they are correct.

1. The world population rose dramatically since 1900, and is predicted to keep rising.

2. The consumption of sugar was increasing between 1950 and 1960.

3. In 2010, production peaked (at 90 per cent of capacity), but dropped back down to around 80 per cent the following year.

4. For the first three centuries (from 1500 to 1800), the proportion of teenagers in the workforce did not change.

5. The graph showed that, before 1950, wages were the main factor affecting production costs.

Future simple

> The graph shows that sales of widgets <u>will</u> probably <u>decrease</u> to 2500 in 2030.
>
> The prediction is that CO_2 levels <u>will continue</u> to rise.

Task 1 graphs sometimes include predictions for the future—be careful! Use the future tense for any data that describes the future.

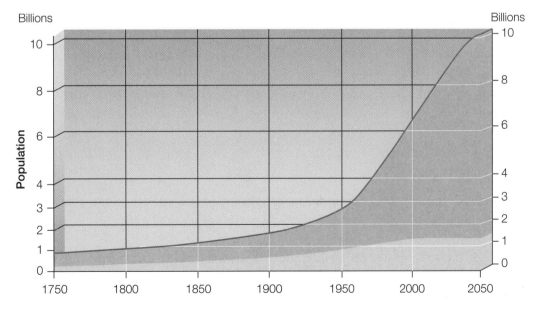

For example:

> Around 1950, the world population began <u>to rise more</u> rapidly and the graph suggests that it <u>will continue</u> this rapid rise until the end of the period.

Activity 5.3

Matching: Which tense goes with which?

1.	A time period from 2000 to 2010	[present simple]
2.	Changes between 2030 and 2040	[present simple]
3.	The temperature of boiling water	[past simple]
4.	An event in the year 1066	[past simple]
5.	Introducing a graph and pie chart that show data from 1950 to 2050	[future simple]

The perfect

The perfect is not a *tense*, it is an *aspect*. You combine the perfect with a tense (past, present, or future) to add detail about *how* the activity happened. For example, you can suggest that an activity isn't finished yet (present perfect).

Present perfect

> Since 1950, the population has grown exponentially.

This sentence says that something (the population growing very fast) started in 1950, but it doesn't say when the activity ends. It **hints** that the activity continues up to the reference time – which is right now, when we are speaking – and it may keep happening for a long time afterwards, too.

We are talking about a **past** activity, but our focus is on **right now**. Why do we do this? Often, we do this to hint that there is some connection between the past activity and now. For example:

> Global CO_2 levels have increased since 1960. [This implies '... *and now there is some effect from this*'.]

> From 1750 to 1950 the population increased by only 2 billion. Since 1950 it has grown much faster. [This implies '... *and we can see a result* **now**'.]

We also use the present perfect to talk about a time period that hasn't finished yet, such as this decade or this century. For example:

> There were around 80 major earthquakes in the twentieth century, and there have been 14 major earthquakes this century. [This century = from 2000 to 2099.]

> Although Comptronic started selling mobile phones after its rivals, it has earned around $5 billion this decade, and is expected to become the number-one company in the next decade. [This decade = from 2010 to 2019, next decade = 2020–29.]

Activity 5.4

Fill the blanks with the present perfect form of the verb.

1. Since 1997, the country _____ a severe-weather warning system. [have]

2. The country _____ 15 severe weather events this century. [experience]

3. There _____ fewer weather-related deaths since the warning system was introduced. [be]

4. So far, only 20 people _____, compared to 250 in the same time period last century. [die]

5. The severe-weather warning system seems to _____. [succeed]

Future perfect

> The graph shows that by 2050, the world population will have grown to 10 billion people.

With the future perfect, the focus is on a reference time in the future (2050), but you also hint about things happening before and after this time.

An activity (growing) started at some time before 2050. The activity is still happening in 2050. The future perfect *suggests* that the activity could continue after 2050.

In other words, the future perfect is used to focus on an interesting point in a story. This point is usually near the end of the story and a lot of interesting things have happened in the story before this interesting point.

Activity 5.5

Predict the future based on the information. Use the key words to write your sentence. The first one has been done for you.

1. News websites are becoming more and more popular, while print newspapers are becoming less popular. By 2030 / print newspapers / disappear / and / news websites / replace / them.

   Answer: By 2030, print newspapers will have disappeared and news websites will have replaced them.

2. Around 6000 square kilometres of the Amazon rainforest are destroyed every year. Within 40 years / the Amazon rainforest / disappear.

3. Startup.com competes aggressively with a rival company, Dinosaur.com. In ten years / Startup.com / crush / Dinosaur.com.

[continued from previous page]

4. A company is selling its assets and not creating new ones. In five years' time / the company / sell / all its assets / and / it / go bankrupt.

5. These days, Japanese car manufacturers tend to make their cars offshore (in other, cheaper countries). This trend will continue. By 2040 / all Japanese car manufacturers / move / offshore / and / all the car factories in Japan / close.

6. Country A has more oil reserves than country B, but it uses them faster. They will not last for a long time. By 2053 / Country A's oil reserves / run out.

Past perfect

CO_2 levels <u>had risen</u> significantly before there was an increase in global temperatures.

By 1970, exports <u>had increased</u> to 15 million cars per year.

You don't use the past perfect by itself. You must always use the past perfect with another past tense, or with a date in the past. It is used to show the sequence of events in the past.

The past perfect is a skilful way to show the order of events, without using words like 'first', 'second', 'next', 'then'. Let's try an example.

Activity 5.6

Use this information to complete the sentences on the next page, using the words given. The first one has been done for you.

Year	Action
1990	New machines introduced
1991	Safety manager appointed
1993	Safety classes for all staff
1995	Training manual replaces classes

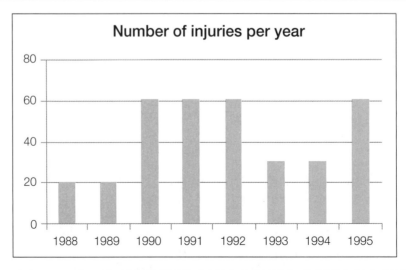
Number of injuries per year

1. The injury rate / be steady at around 20 per year / when the company / introduce / new machines.

    Answer: The injury rate had been steady at around 20 per year when the company introduced new machines.

2. The company / appoint / a safety manager / after the injury rate / triple.

3. By 1992, the injury rate / not / decrease.

4. Although the safety classes / halve / the injury rate, they were replaced with a safety manual in 1995.

5. It seems the safety classes / were / very successful. However in 1993 the injury rate / be / still higher than it / be / in 1988–89, before introducing the new machines.

Activity 5.7

Let's review. Use the correct form of the verb in brackets to fill the gaps.

1. The data show that by 2035, the proportion of manufacturing companies based offshore _____ 95 per cent. [reach]

2. By 1950, Unifood's income from milk products _____ all other income. [exceed]

3. From 1980 to 2010, trains experienced a drop in popularity, but in this decade they _____ popular again. [become]

4. Book sales boomed in 1960 and again in 1980. However, by 1990 they _____ back down to 1950 levels. [drop]

5. The conservative estimate is that that, by 2020, fish stocks _____ by 50 per cent. [deplete]

The passive

Academic writing uses more passives than normal writing. Try to use some passive sentences to get a better mark. For example:

> A dip in sales <u>can be seen</u> around 2010. [not 'we can see a dip in sales around 2010'.]

The passive is useful because we don't need to say the subject of the verb. This means we don't have to say *who* is doing the action. For example:

> The proportion of workers is predicted to rise between 2020 and 2030.

This can be useful for IELTS Task 1 because IELTS diagrams don't give a source for their information. For example, you can't say:

> The London School of Economics predicts that the proportion of workers will rise between 2020 and 2030.

If you don't know who said something, it sounds better to use the passive. Otherwise you have to say:

> Someone predicts that the proportion of workers will rise between 2020 and 2030.

This doesn't sound very academic, so use the passive instead.

Note: It is incorrect to say 'The graph predicts that …'. A graph can't predict anything. Only a human can 'predict'.

Another reason for using the passive is to highlight some information by putting it first. Here's an example:

> The company sold 500,000 cars in 1995. [Active voice]

The important news is '500,000 cars'. If you change this to a passive sentence, the important news is first. This makes the sentence more interesting.

> 500,000 cars were sold in 1995. [Passive voice]

Finally, sometimes the subject of the verb is so obvious that it sounds silly if you say it. For example:

> The police caught more criminals in 2003 than 2005.

Only police can catch criminals – it's obvious! It's better to say:

> More criminals were caught in 2003 than 2005.

Activity 5.8

Change these sentences into the passive. The first one has been done for you.

1. Computer shops sold 5,000,000 computers in 1997.

    Answer: 5,000,000 computers were sold in 1997.

2. The data predicts that average temperatures will rise by 5°C.

3. The police caught twice as many speeding drivers with the new camera.

4. People made more noise-related complaints on weekends.

5. The builders will build a new shop on the east side of the museum.

6. Amateur and professional biologists discovered 19,232 new species in 2011.

Qualifying language

Academic writing often uses language that is not definite or strong. For example:

> The results seem to show that women have lower literacy levels than men in most countries. (not 'The results clearly show')
>
> There appears to be a relationship between literacy level and income. (not 'There is an obvious relationship')
>
> Testimonials don't appear to influence customers. (not 'Testimonials don't influence customers')

   If you use this kind of language when summarising the information in your overview, you will improve your IELTS band.

Activity 5.9

Reword these sentences using the word in brackets. The first one has been done for you.

1. The new library obviously uses more space for computers and less space for books. [appear]

    Answer: The new library appears to use more space for computers and less space for books.

2. The new airlines clearly caused a drop in airfares. [seem]

3. There is a connection between the literacy rate and economic development. [appear]

4. The minimum wage isn't keeping up with the cost of living. [seem]

[continued from previous page]

5.   The process involves some inefficiency. [appear]

6.   Lowering the quality of the product obviously doesn't improve profits. [appear]

Grammar for process diagrams

A process diagram shows something that is generally true. For example, the diagram about home heating systems shows how most houses are heated in a certain country.

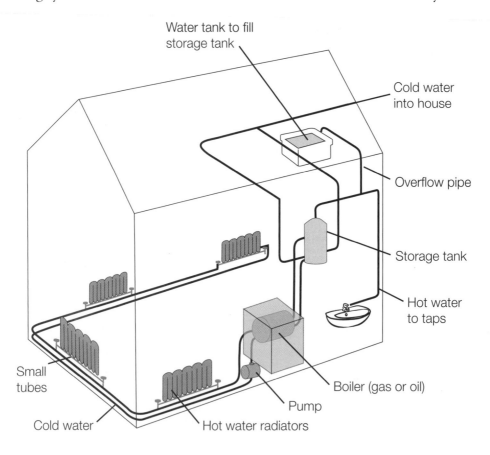

They were heated this way 10 years ago, they are heated this way now, and they will probably be heated this way 10 years into the future. The grammar for this kind of situation is the **present simple**. For example:

> The water passes into the house through underground pipes. [present simple active]
>
> Some of the hot water is sent to the bathroom taps. [present simple passive]
>
> The thermostat keeps the water at the right temperature. [present simple active]

Although the basic structure is present simple, you can use a variety of structures to show the sequence of steps, and the relationship between steps. Remember, variety is how you get a good score!

Participial structures with before/after

Simple version: The water is heated and then goes into the pipes.

Better version: <u>Before going</u> into the pipes, the water is heated.

Simple version: The beans are washed. Then they are processed.

Better version: <u>Before being</u> processed, the beans are washed.

Simple version: The leaves lie in the sun for two days. After that they go into a fermenting barrel.

Better version: <u>After lying</u> in the sun for two days, the leaves go into a fermenting barrel.

Simple version: The pulp is bleached and then the pulp is sieved.

Better version: <u>After being</u> bleached, the pulp is sieved.

Note that the sentence can be active (like sentence 3), passive (like sentences 2 and 4), or a mixture (like sentence 1). Let's try an example.

Activity 5.10

Change the sentences using participial structures. Use the word in brackets. The first one has been done for you.

1. The steam passes through the leaves and then escapes through a pipe at the top. [After]

   Answer: After passing through the leaves, the steam escapes through a pipe at the top.

2. The steam is cooled down in the cooling coil then flows into the settling tank. [Before]

3. The water is used to cool down the steam. Then it is pumped out of the top of the cooling-coil tank. [After]

4. The steam loses its heat in the coil and becomes water. [After]

5. The oil is left to separate from the water in the settling tank. After that it is bottled. [Before]

6. The apples are polished after they are waxed. [Before]

The perfect participle

1 <u>Having turned</u> the turbines, the water travels back down to the reaction chamber.

2 <u>Having turned</u> the flywheel, the steam is released through a vent.

3 <u>Having been roasted</u>, the coffee beans are crushed.

4 <u>Having been pressed</u>, the pulp goes into an airing chamber for 10 hours.

The perfect participle is another skilful way to show the sequence of events without using words like 'first', 'second', 'third' or 'next'. If you use it correctly, it will improve your IELTS band.

Notice that you can use this with active structures like sentence 1 or passive structures like sentence 3. You can also use it in mixed structures, like sentences 2 and 4.

Note: Be careful with the subject! The subject of the perfect participle phrase (e.g. 'having turned', 'having been pressed') must be the noun that comes straight after the comma (e.g. 'the steam', 'the pulp'). For example, in sentence 3, the subject is 'the coffee beans', so coffee beans are roasted *and* coffee beans are crushed. Don't get this wrong. If you say:

<u>Having been roasted</u>, the workers crush the coffee beans.

it means that the workers were roasted!

The perfect participle for cause and effect

The perfect participle can also imply that there is a cause and effect. This is a more skilful technique than using words like 'because' and 'therefore'. If you use the perfect participle correctly, it will improve your IELTS band. For example:

Simple version: The water has warmed up the radiators all over the house so it is no longer hot.

Better version: <u>Having warmed up</u> the radiators all over the house, the water is no longer hot.

Simple version: The potatoes are washed. This makes them damp.

Better version: <u>Having been washed</u>, the potatoes are damp.

Simple version: The steam passes through the cooling coil and this condenses the steam.

Better version: <u>Having passed</u> through the cooling coil, the steam has condensed.

Notice that you can use the perfect participle with the passive (sentence 2) or active (sentences 1 and 3).

Activity 5.11

Improve these sentences using the perfect participle. The first one has been done for you.

1. The water absorbs the heat from the steam so it is warm.

    Answer: Having absorbed the heat from the steam, the water is warm.

2. There is now room for more cars because the hotel converted its basement to an underground carpark.

3. The leaves are brown because they have been oxidised.

4. The tea leaves are sun dried so they still contain moisture.

5. When it has delivered its parcels, the truck is empty.

6. The water washes the potatoes so it is dirty.

Present continuous

As the hot air <u>is escaping</u>, ...

Note: The present continuous is often used incorrectly in IELTS task 1. People often use it instead of the present simple (see page 190).

When you are describing two things that happen at the same time, you can use the **present continuous** for part of the sentence. Use the present continuous for the activity that lasts longer. For example, in sentence 1 below, the water passes around the house for a long time. For some of that time it is cool: 'pass around' lasts longer than 'cool down'. In sentence 2, 'gas released through vent' starts before 'intake valve opens'.

Simple version: The water passes around the house. It cools down.

Better version: The water gradually <u>cools</u> down as it <u>is passing</u> around the house.

Simple version: The spent gas is released through the vent. This is where the intake valve opens to let in fresh air.

Better version: As the spent gas <u>is being released</u> through the vent, the intake valve <u>opens</u> to let in fresh air.

Activity 5.12

Combine the two sentences into one, using the present continuous tense for one of the verbs. Use the word in brackets. The first one has been done for you.

1. The dough passes through the oven. It is sprayed with oil. [As]

   Answer: As the dough is passing through the oven, it is sprayed with oil.

2. The van returns to the store. It collects returned items. [While]

3. The super-hot steam pushes the piston. Meanwhile, the cooled steam is released through a valve at the top. [As]

4. The fruit is sprayed with wax and polished. This happens while the fruit rolls along the conveyor belt. [When]

5. The biscuits harden. This is when they are stamped with a picture. [While]

6. The leaves dry in the sun. They oxidise. [As]

Punctuation

Good punctuation is important for good writing because it helps the reader to understand your ideas. You need to use punctuation well to get a good IELTS mark.

> TIP   Do pay attention to the punctuation in English novels and non-fiction books. Don't copy the punctuation used on websites: they often have incorrect punctuation.

The most important punctuation marks are the full stop (.) and the comma (,).

Full stop

A full stop is a dot that marks the end of a sentence. It shows that the sentence describes a whole idea. The next word after a full stop is the start of a new sentence: it must start with a capital (or 'upper case') letter. For example:

The diagram shows that the process for extracting essential oil relies on water in two ways. Steam removes the oil from the leaves and then cold water cools the steam so that it separates from the oil.

Activity 5.13

Add the full stops and capital letters in these sentences. The first one has been done for you.

1. the steam passes into the chamber and mixes with the leaves the oil from the leaves mixes with the steam and rises out the top of the chamber

    Answer: The steam passes into the chamber and mixes with the leaves. The oil from the leaves mixes with the steam and rises out the top of the chamber.

2. the first and last stages of the process are the same for all three types of tea they are all sun dried and oven dried

3. the graph compares the amount of social contact that men and women have at different ages it seems that older women generally have more contact with their family and friends than older men

4. men of all ages generally participate in more sport than women the only age when this is not true is 45 to 55

5. the survey results show that people are less likely to worry about debts as they get older this could be because they get better at paying bills on time

6. company A sold more widgets than gadgets between 2000 and 2005 company B's sales were the complete opposite of this

Comma

A comma is a dot with a tail that marks a break within a sentence. Your handwriting should clearly show which one you are using: a full stop or a comma. Basically, commas help to break a sentence into chunks so that it is easier to read.

Commas to break up long sentences

Commas are used when a sentence is made of long clauses. This helps the reader to understand a long sentence.

> The average maximum temperature in European countries was generally lower than in other regions, although Spain's average was as high as in some African countries.
>
> Although the national average wage increased over the period, the average wage for rural workers did not change.
>
> Women's literacy rates were generally lower than men's, especially in developing nations.

Commas for sentence modifiers

Adverbs usually modify one word. For example, 'Sales rose rapidly'. The adverb 'rapidly' tells us something about the verb 'rose'. However, some adverbs and adverbial phrases modify a whole sentence. These are words like: firstly, secondly, at first, however, to start with, sometimes, on the other hand, in spite of this, meanwhile, for this reason.

These sentence modifiers should be followed by a comma. For example:

> Firstly, the leaf is sun dried to remove most of the moisture.

> A safety manager was appointed in 1991. However, this did not reduce the number of workplace injuries.

Commas for lists

Commas are used to separate items in a list, so that the reader knows straight away he/she is reading a list. This helps the reader to understand. For example:

> Los Angeles, Beijing, Mexico City and Guangzhou had the worst air pollution in 2010.

> The rainfall was highest in June, July, August and September with 300 mm, 500 mm, 900 mm and 700 mm respectively.

Commas for extra information

Commas are used to separate one phrase from the rest of the sentence. This is useful in Task 1 to add detail (e.g. sentence 1) or to add some evidence (e.g. sentence 2).

> The capital city of Japan, Tokyo, has the largest metropolitan area.

> The average number of complaints was lowest in March, at 5 per day, and highest in November, at 42 per day.

> **TIP**   This is an easy way to improve your answer after you have finished writing.
> If you realise that you haven't included enough data, go back and add these
> clauses. For example:
> Average summer temperatures were highest in Seville, at 32 degrees, and
> lowest in Vladivostok, at 22 degrees.

Activity 5.14

Add commas to these sentences.

1.   The diagram shows that three different processes can make one ingredient tea leaves into three different products.

2. Green tea oolong tea and black tea are all produced by slightly different processes.

3. In Europe where recycling taxes were highest about 50 per cent of people recycled often.

4. International exports of raw materials increased steadily from 1995 to 2005 but this gain was lost when exports plummeted between 2005 and 2010.

5. On the other hand international exports of manufactured materials showed no change over the period.

Activity 5.15

Add the full stops, commas and capital letters to this Task 1 answer.

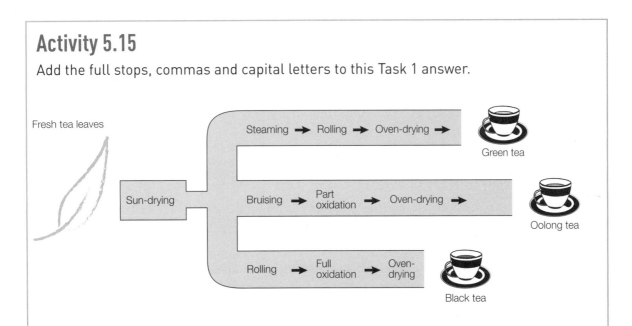

the diagram shows that slightly different processes can make three different kinds of tea from the same raw ingredient tea leaves the common stages in the process sun-drying and oven-drying are the first and last steps it is the steps in the middle that make the final products different

green tea is unlike the other types of tea while oolong tea and black tea are oxidised green tea isn't the leaves are simply sun dried steamed rolled and then oven dried

meanwhile black tea and oolong tea are sun dried and then squashed in some way oolong tea is bruised and black tea is rolled these two teas are also different in how much oxidation they get with part oxidation for oolong tea and full oxidation for black tea after the oxidation process both types of tea are oven dried as noted earlier this step is the same for all types of tea

Common grammar mistakes

1   'Each' and 'every' describe plural things, but they are grammatically singular.

> Every item was more expensive in 2010. [NOT every items were ...]

> Each box is sealed and labelled. [NOT each boxes are ...]

2   'A machine for making something' NOT 'A machine to make something'.
Remember this structure:
A tool/device/machine/gadget for DOING something.
'The diagrams illustrate two different types of factories for packing fruit.'

3   'Sales of computers' NOT 'Computers' sales'.

For nouns that relate to people, you can use 's. This includes countries, cities or companies. For example, 'New York's population'; 'the company's new factory'; 'the government's budget'.

For other nouns, you cannot use 's. For example, you can *not* say 'The item's cost increased'. You should say 'The cost of the item increased'.

For example:

> The population of London has increased. OR London's population has increased. [Both are OK]

> The new government's taxes are higher. OR The taxes of the new government are higher. [Both are OK]

> The volume of imports fell noticeably over the period. [There is no other way to say this. Don't say 'Import's volume fell ...'.]

Activity 5.16

Let's review. Correct the mistakes. If the sentence is correct, write 'OK'.

1.   Most visitors to London's museums are local people.

2.   The diagram shows a machine to manufacture chocolate biscuits.

3.   Each biscuit is scanned for imperfections.

4.   From about 1970, books' popularity started to decrease.

5.   Every years showed a dip in profits around January to February.

Activity 5.17

Check this answer using the check box below. Focus on the grammar and punctuation only.

Task: **The chart at right shows the number of visitors arriving in a particular country for a short trip, and the number of residents leaving that country for a short trip, with a prediction for the future.**

Summarise the information by selecting and reporting the main features, and make comparisons where relevant.

Write at least 150 words.

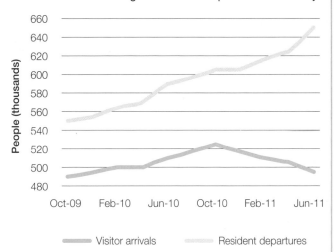

Visitor arrivals   Resident departures

Sample answer

The chart shows the number of visitor arrivals and resident departures in a particular country. Both go up over the period but at some point activity is change and visitor arrivals go down.

The number of visitor arrivals increases every year gradually till 2010, from 490,000 to about 520,000. Then the number decreases to the future till 2020 it is about 500 thousand. This category's start figure and end result is almost same.

The number of resident departures goes up every year gradually from 550,000 to about 600,000 in 2010. From 2010 to maybe 2013 there is a plateau then it increases again and in a future it will reach 650,000 in 2020.

Between 1995 to 2010, both go up in similar rate, but in 2010, something happened and visitor arrival will go down. On the other hand, resident departures will go up.

Grammatical range and accuracy	Yes/no	Example
Does it use a variety of grammatical structures? For example:		
Does it use 'seem' or 'appear'?		
Does it use a passive structure?		
Does it use the future prefect?		
Does it use the past perfect?		
Does it use any participle structures?		
Are grammar and punctuation mostly correct?		

You can check your answers in the Answer Key in Appendix 1.

UNIT 6

Practice Questions

How to use these practice questions

1 Write your answer. Take 20 minutes and don't use a dictionary.
2 Wait a day or so.
3 Use the checklist to check your answer. Also use a dictionary, your computer's spellchecker, and a grammar book.
4 Ask a friend to check your answer, too. Ask them to use the checklist, and ask them to draw the diagram based on your answer.
5 Write the answer again. It should be much better!
6 Keep a list of your common mistakes.

Example

A student (Tomo) wrote an answer and assessed it himself. He then asked a friend (Naomi) to assess it.

The charts below show the number of visitors arriving in a particular country for a short trip, and the number of residents leaving that country for a short trip.

Summarise the information by selecting and reporting the main features, and make comparisons where relevant.

Write at least 150 words.

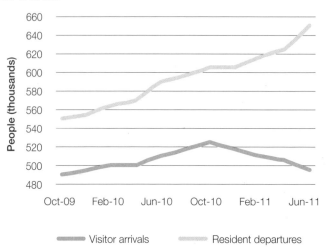

Tomo's answer

Thease charts shows number of people for visitor and residents departures for short trip in one country. There are some charactoristic datas in charts.

Firstly, The number of visitor arrivals from overseas was glowing up. from Oct, 2009 to Oct, 2010, for one year. Then from the peak of Oct 2010, the number of people was going down rapidly within one year.

Secondy, number of resident departures was growing up from Oct, 2009 to Jun; 2011. It has grown about 100,000 people per year:

To summarise for thease charts, I guss that this country's economy was growing and growing, and in Oct 2010, There was big event in this country. In this time the charts show the peak of visitor and stay of number of departure. Then there was rapid going up of resident departures.

Tomo's self-assessment

Feature		Example
Task Achievement (Unit 2)		
Does it give an overview of main patterns?	yes	Visitors growing and then going down. Residents just growing.
Does it talk about the most important details?	yes	
Does it have any irrelevant information (for example, personal experience or opinions)?	no	
Does it quote numbers and other data accurately?	yes	Actually, not so much numbers.
Coherence and Cohesion (Unit 3)		
Is it well organised? Is it easy to understand how one idea flows to the next one?	yes	First paragraph is about visitor. Second is resident. Third is comparison.
Does it use a variety of linking words and linking structures?	no	Lots of same vocabulary.
Lexical Resource (Unit 4)		
Does it use a wide variety of vocabulary, including phrasal verbs, academic words, and collocations?	no	A lots of same phrases. 'Grow' a lot. 'Stay' should be 'plateau'. 'Go down' should be 'fall' or 'decline'.
Are most words spelled correctly?	yes	mistake: growing/glowing characteristic/ charactoristic.

Grammatical Range and Accuracy (Unit 5)		
Does it use a variety of grammatical structures?	no	
Are grammar and punctuation mostly correct?	yes	

Naomi's assessment

Feature		Example
Task Achievement (Unit 2)		
Does it give an overview of main patterns?	no	The first paragraph copies the question. It doesn't say going up or going down.
Does it talk about the most important details?	no	NO numbers!! Should say '500,000' and '660,000'.
Does it have any irrelevant information (for example, personal experience or opinions)?		Don't 'guess' about a 'big event'.
Does it quote numbers and other data accurately?	no	No! There aren't any numbers.
Coherence and Cohesion (Unit 3)		
Is it well organised? Is it easy to understand how one idea flows to the next one?	yes	
Does it use a variety of linking words and linking structures?	OK	'Firstly', 'secondly', 'then'. Maybe use something like 'however', 'furthermore'.
Lexical Resource (Unit 4)		
Does it use a wide variety of vocabulary, including phrasal verbs, academic words, and collocations?	OK	Some good words: 'rapidly', 'peak'.
Are most words spelled correctly?	OK	Mistakes: Thease, charactoristic, guss
Grammatical Range and Accuracy (Unit 5)		
Does it use a variety of grammatical structures?	no	'was growing … was going … was growing … was going'
Are grammar and punctuation mostly correct?	yes	's' is wrong sometimes 'these charts shows'.

Tomo used Naomi's comments and his own checklist to improve his answer:

Tomo's answer, version 2

These charts show that number of visitors and residents departures for short trip were increasing the same from 2009 to 2010 but after the peak of 2010, visitors numbers fell and resident departures grew.

Firstly, The number of visitor arrivals from overseas improved from 490,000 in Oct 2009 to 530,000 in Oct 2010. Then from the peak of Oct 2010, the number of people was decreasing rapidly within one year to 490,000. This is the same as starting figure in Oct 2009.

Secondly, number of resident departures had risen from 550,000 in Oct, 2009 to 650,000 in June 2011. It had grown steadily but it has a plateau for maybe 2 months in Oct 2009. This is same time visitor arrivals started to decline.

To sum up, there was a peak in visitor arrivals and a short time of plateau in October 2010 for number of departures. Then there was rapid increase of resident departures and decline of visitor arrivals.

Checklist for Tomo's version 2

Feature		Example
Task Achievement (Unit 2)		
Does it give an overview of main patterns?	yes	1. Both things go up at first. 2. In 2010 visitor arrivals started to go down while resident departures went up.
Does it talk about the most important details?	yes	
Does it have any irrelevant information (for example, personal experience or opinions)?	no	
Does it quote numbers and other data accurately?	yes	
Coherence and Cohesion (Unit 3)		
Is it well organised? Is it easy to understand how one idea flows to the next one?	yes	
Does it use a variety of linking words and linking structures?	some	'then', 'this', 'but', 'firstly', 'secondly'.
Lexical Resource (Unit 4)		
Does it use a wide variety of vocabulary, including phrasal verbs, academic words, and collocations?	some	Better. More variety.
Are most words spelled correctly?	yes	

Grammatical Range and Accuracy (Unit 5)		
Does it use a variety of grammatical structures?	no	Better. 'Was decreasing', 'had risen', 'started to go'.
Are grammar and punctuation mostly correct?	no	Most sentences have errors with articles (a, an, the). However, punctuation is better.

Activity 6.1

Complete the checklist for this answer.

The charts below show the main reason for study by age and the proportion of students who received support from their employers.

Summarise the information by selecting and reporting the main features, and make comparisons where relevant.

Write at least 150 words

Students receiving study support from their employer, by age
* support: time off work and financial assistance

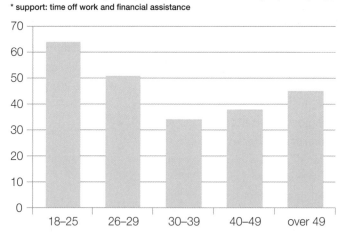

Main reason for study, by age

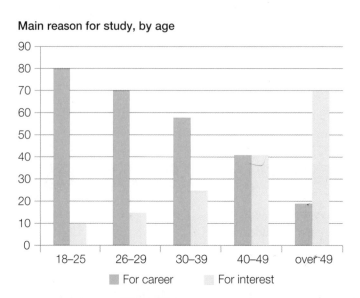

■ For career   ▢ For interest

Sample answer

The two graphs show the reasons why people study at different ages and the amount that their employers support them.

The first graph shows there a gradual decerase in study for career reasons with age. Nearly 80 per cent of students under 26 years, study for their career. This percentage gradually declines by 10–20 per cent every decade. Only 40 per cent of 40–49 yr olds and 18 per cent of over 49 yr olds studing for carreer reasons in late adulthood. Conversely, the first graph also shows that study stemming from intrest increases with age. There only 10 per cent of under 26 yr olds studing out of interest. The percentage increases slowly till the beginning of the fourth decade, and increases dramatically in late adulthood. Nearly same number of 40–49 yr olds study for career and intrest. However 70 per cent of over 49 yr olds study for interest in comparison to 18 per cent studing for career reasons in that age group.

The second graph shows that employer suport is approximately 60 per cent for the under 26 yr students. It drops rapidly to 32 per cent up to the third decade of life, and then increses in late adulthood up to about 38 per cent for 40 to 49 yr students and then about 44 per cent for over 49 yr students.

Self-study checklist

Feature		Example
Task Achievement (Unit 2)		
Does it give an overview of main patterns?		
Does it talk about the most important details? Does it have any irrelevant information (for example, personal experience or opinions)?		
Does it quote numbers and other data accurately?		
Coherence and Cohesion (Unit 3)		
Is it well organised? Is it easy to understand how one idea flows to the next one?		
Does it use a variety of linking words and linking structures?		
Lexical Resource (Unit 4)		
Does it use a wide variety of vocabulary, including phrasal verbs, academic words, and collocations?		
Are most words spelled correctly?		

[continued from previous page]

Grammatical Range and Accuracy (Unit 5)		
Does it use a variety of grammatical structures?		
Are grammar and punctuation mostly correct?		

Over to you

When you have used the checklist a few times, look for common problems. What do other people often say about your writing? What do you need to improve?

Task Achievement: common problems

Coherence and Cohesion: common problems

Lexical Resource: common problems

Grammatical Range and Accuracy: common problems

Practice questions

The following practice questions are based on the data you have already worked with in Part 1 of the Academic Writing. Use them to write your own answers.

Use the self-study checklist to evaluate your answer and ask a friend to do the same.

1

The charts below show the number of visitors arriving in a particular country for a short trip, and the number of residents leaving that country for a short trip, from 2009 to 2011.
Summarise the information by selecting and reporting the main features, and make comparisons where relevant.
Write at least 150 words.

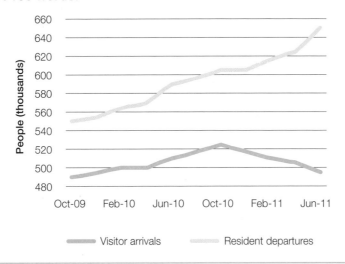

2

The following graph shows the population growth in developing countries and industrialised countries, with a prediction to 2050.
Summarise the information by selecting and reporting the main features, and make comparisons where relevant.
Write at least 150 words.

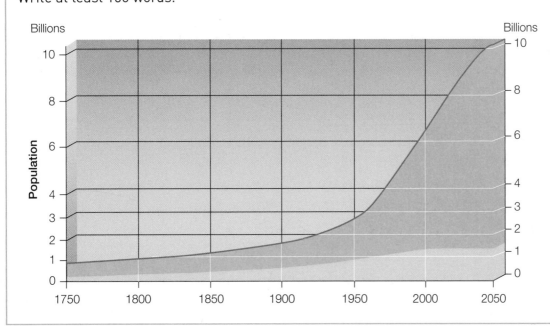

3

The following tables show the average age of students at a college, and how happy the students were with their courses.
Summarise the information by selecting and reporting the main features, and make comparisons where relevant.
Write at least 150 words.

How happy students were with their courses

	Certificate	Diploma
very happy	73%	5%
happy	16%	12%
unhappy	10%	42%
very unhappy	1%	41%

Average age of students

	Certificate	Diploma
15 to 25	79%	17%
25 to 35	18%	62%
35 to 45	1%	20%
45 and over	2%	1%

4

The following diagrams show changes to a museum from 2010 to 2012.
Summarise the information by selecting and reporting the main features, and make comparisons where relevant.
Write at least 150 words.

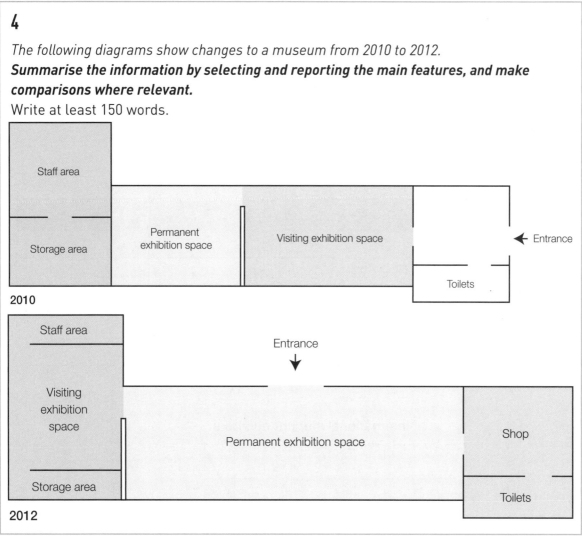

5

The graph shows the percentage of people who recycle their rubbish, in five countries, over 12 years.
Summarise the information by selecting and reporting the main features, and make comparisons where relevant.
Write at least 150 words.

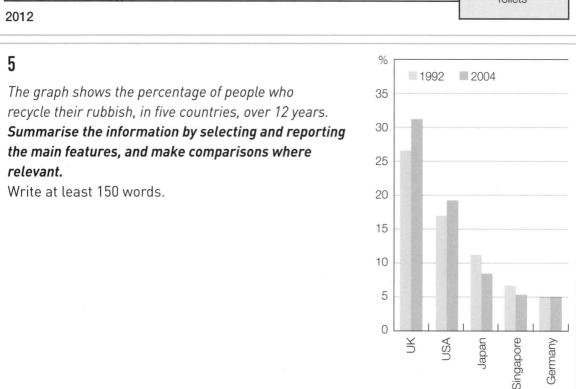

6

The following diagrams show international student enrolments at a university from 1975 to 2009.
Summarise the information by selecting and reporting the main features, and make comparisons where relevant.
Write at least 150 words.

Students' home region

	1975	2009
Asia	20%	65%
Europe	20%	20%
Africa	15%	10%
North America	15%	10%
South America	30%	0%

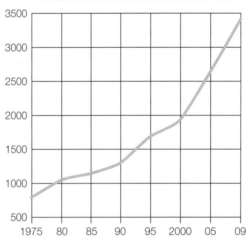

International student numbers

7

The chart below shows the percentage of men and women who participate in sport at different ages.

Summarise the information by selecting and reporting the main features, and make comparisons where relevant.

Write at least 150 words.

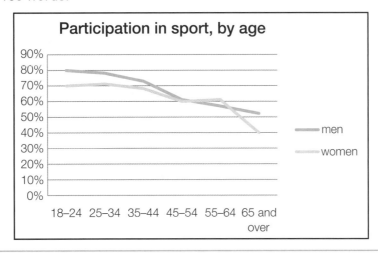

8

The charts below show the number of workplace injuries per year at a factory, and the actions that were taken to reduce injuries, between 1985 and 1995.

Summarise the information by selecting and reporting the main features, and make comparisons where relevant.

Write at least 150 words.

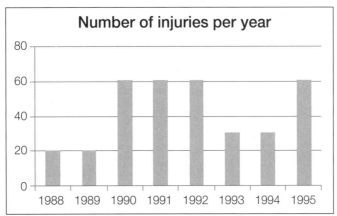

Year	Action
1990	New machines introduced
1991	Safety manager appointed
1993	Safety classes for all staff
1995	Training manual replaces classes

9

The following diagram shows how essential oil is produced from leaves.
Summarise the information by selecting and reporting the main features, and make comparisons where relevant.
Write at least 150 words.

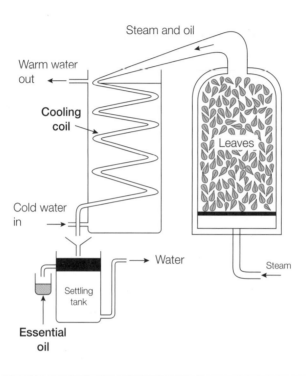

10

The following tables show the average commuting time for employees at five companies and the average number of employee absences at each company per year.
Summarise the information by selecting and reporting the main features, and make comparisons where relevant.
Write at least 150 words

Company	Commuting time (minutes)	Company	Absences (per employee)
E and B	60	E and B	16
Futureform	15	Futureform	10
Haleston	45	Haleston	16
King and Co.	75	King and Co.	18
New Look	30	New Look	10

11

The chart below shows the number of people who had recently contacted family or friends.
Summarise the information by selecting and reporting the main features, and make comparisons where relevant.
Write at least 150 words.

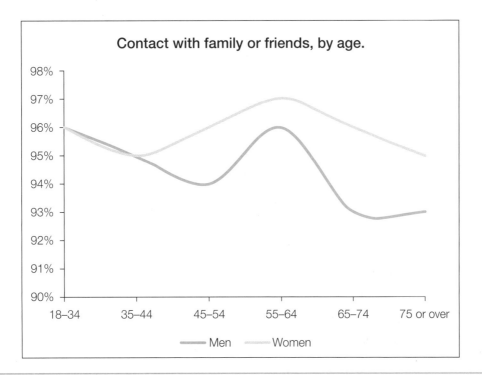

Contact with family or friends, by age.

12

The following diagram shows how three different types of tea are made.
Summarise the information by selecting and reporting the main features, and make comparisons where relevant.

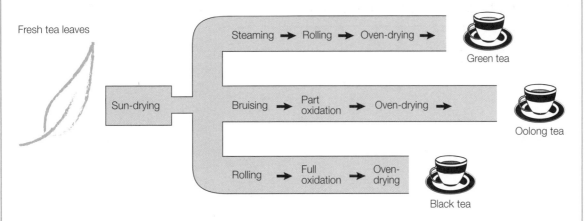

*oxidation: a reaction with oxygen that changes the leaf colour to brown.
Write at least 150 words.

13

The following charts show the favourite colours for cars among men and women, and the proportion of actual car sales, in 2011.
Summarise the information by selecting and reporting the main features, and make comparisons where relevant.
Write at least 150 words.

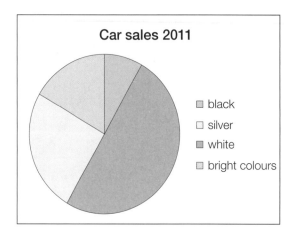

Survey results: favourite car colour

Colour	Men	Women
black	80%	10%
white	5%	10%
silver	10%	55%
bright colours	10%	25%

14

The graph shows the number of widgets and gadgets that were sold by a company in one year.
Summarise the information by selecting and reporting the main features, and make comparisons where relevant.

Write at least 150 words.

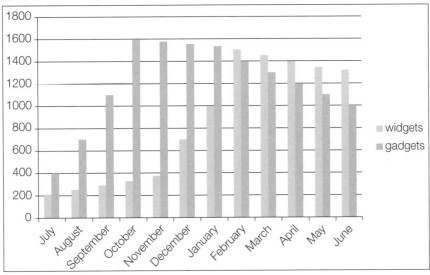

Widgets vs gadgets: numbers sold

15

The graph shows the average number of local and international visitors to a museum, per year, from 2001 to 2011.
Summarise the information by selecting and reporting the main features, and make comparisons where relevant.

Write at least 150 words.

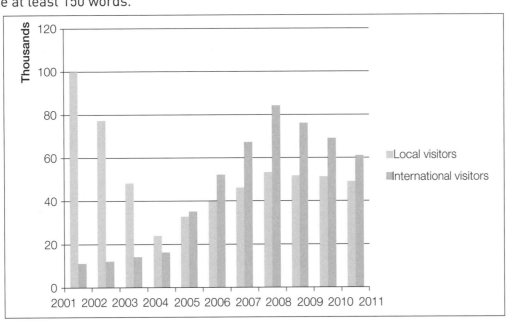

16

The following diagrams show how goods were transported in a European country, in three different periods.

Summarise the information by selecting and reporting the main features, and make comparisons where relevant.

Write at least 150 words.

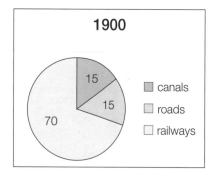

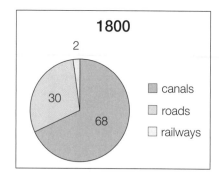

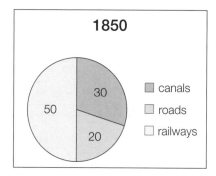

*canal: a straight, artificial river.

17

The following chart describes visitors to a theme park in the USA, over one year. It shows how long visitors from each region stayed and how much money they spent in the park.

Summarise the information by selecting and reporting the main features, and make comparisons where relevant.

Write at least 150 words.

Region	Average stay (hours)	Average spent ($US)
North America	6	200
South America	8	120
Asia	4	350
Europe	6	150

18

The following diagram shows the paper manufacturing cycle.
Summarise the information by selecting and reporting the main features, and make comparisons where relevant.
Write at least 150 words.

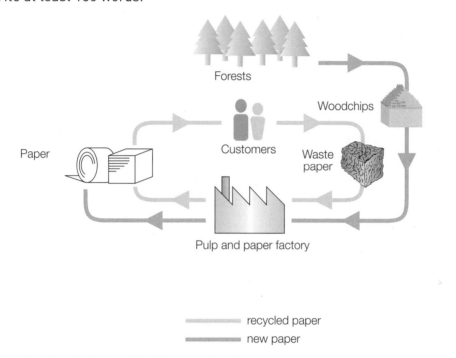

recycled paper
new paper

19

The following chart shows the percentage of workers, by age, in four different industries.
Summarise the information by selecting and reporting the main features, and make comparisons where relevant.
Write at least 150 words

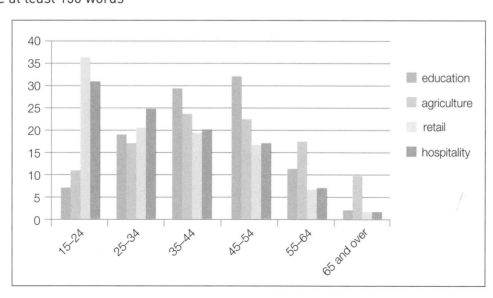

PART 3

ACADEMIC WRITING TASK 2

UNIT 1

About Task 2

Task 2 in the Academic Writing Module is different from Task 1 in the following ways:

- Task 2 should take about 40 minutes.
- In Task 2, you need to write an essay giving your opinion.
- In Task 2, you need to write at least 250 words.

Example of Task 2 question

Here is a typical Task 2 question. The instructions for the task are always the same and include the three points mentioned above. The task itself is written in bold and varies in type: *opinion*, *argument*, or *problem solving*. These are discussed in Unit 2.

> You should spend about 40 minutes on this task.
>
> Write about the following topic:
>
> **Fast-food companies should not be allowed to give away free toys with their food.**
>
> **To what extent do you agree or disagree?**
>
> Give reasons for your answer and include any relevant examples from your own knowledge or experience.
>
> Write at least 250 words.

Timing

You should spend 40 minutes on Task 2. Always try to do practice tests for 40 minutes so you get used to the timing.

Number of words

You need to write at least 250 words. You will be penalised if you write fewer than 250 words but not if you write more. However, if you write too many more words, you will take time that could be used for editing your work and making it better.

Understanding the assessment criteria

Understanding the way that Academic Writing Task 2 is assessed can help you achieve a better result and focus your studies. The following table shows the type of assessment criteria used for marking writing, plus some skills that may help you to achieve a GOOD score in Task 2, along with the relevant units focusing on those skills. Further information on IELTS assessment is available in a public version on www.ielts.org.

Task Response	Coherence and Cohesion	Lexical Resource	Grammatical Range and Accuracy
For a GOOD band score you need to: address all parts of the task show your opinion clearly through the essay extend your main ideas with support	organise your essay well use suitable linking words make sure each paragraph has one main idea	have accurate use of academic vocabulary, including less common words have good control of spelling and word form	use a good variety of complex sentence structures accurately most of the time have very few punctuation problems
To achieve these, you should: analyse the task and use brainstorming techniques (see Units 2 and 3) plan your essay (see Unit 4)	organise your essay using introduction, body paragraphs, and conclusion (see Unit 5) use linking words/phrases, especially at the beginning of each paragraph and to join sentences with a common idea (see Unit 5) start each body paragraph with a topic sentence and follow it with supporting ideas (see Unit 5)	include academic vocabulary throughout your essay (see Unit 6) check your spelling (see Unit 6)	have accurate use of grammar (see Unit 7) use a variety of sentence structures (see Unit 7) check your punctuation (see Unit 7)

The following units are designed to help you improve your result in each of the above assessment criteria.

UNIT 2

Analysing the Task

To analyse the task, it helps to understand the three main task or question types that are typically presented in Academic Writing Task 2. These can be categorised as:

- opinion
- argument
- problem-solving.

Opinion

What is it?

This task generally gives an opinion on a topic, usually a problem or issue in society, and then asks for your opinion.

Examples

- **Fast-food companies should not be allowed to give away free toys with their food. To what extent do you agree or disagree?**
- **Governments alone cannot be expected to solve environmental problems. It is also the responsibility of businesses and individuals to help. To what extent do you agree or disagree?**

What needs to be done?

This task requires you to evaluate the given opinion and say whether or not you agree with it. You do not need to write about both sides of the problem, although you can write a concession paragraph (see Unit 5).

Argument

What is it?

This question type gives two sides of an argument or two differing opinions on an issue, and then asks you to discuss and give your opinion.

Examples

- **Some people think that boys and girls should be educated in the same schools. Others, however, believe that girls achieve better results when educated in single-sex schools. Discuss both these views and give your opinion.**
- **Many governments spend millions of dollars in space exploration and research, as they feel it is an important investment; however, many citizens feel that it is a waste of money. Discuss both these opinions and include your own.**

What needs to be done?

You need to evaluate both sides of the argument. You should also give your own opinion on the argument.

Problem-solving

What is it?

Generally, in this task type you are given a problem, again often based on issues in society, and you are usually asked one or two questions regarding the problem or issue, such as why it occurs or what causes it, and what can be done to solve it.

Examples

- **Traffic congestion is a growing problem in many cities today. What are some of the causes of traffic congestion and what measures can be taken to help reduce it?**
- **Working from home has become more common with technological advances; however, it has many challenges associated with it. What are some of the challenges that someone working from home may face? What are some of the influences on society of more people working from home? What is your opinion?**

What needs to be done?

You need to answer all the questions asked. If the question asks for reasons or causes then you need to outline these. Effects or solutions may be asked for; again, you need to outline these. You also need to include your opinion.

Activity 2.1

Look at the following tasks and decide whether the task type is opinion, argument or problem-solving. Check your answers in the Answer Key.

a   Many lesser-known languages are disappearing. Young people should be forced to learn these languages so they are not lost forever. To what extent do you agree or disagree with this statement?

b   Mobile phones are considered essential by most people nowadays. Discuss the advantages and disadvantages of mobile phones and state your own opinion.

c   Childhood obesity is increasing at rapid rates in developed countries. What are some of the causes of this problem? What are some ways in which childhood obesity rates can be reduced?

d   An ageing society provides challenges to the whole society. To what extent do you agree or disagree?

e   Computers are widely used for communication nowadays. How have computers changed the way we communicate? Are these changes positive or negative?

f   Many people feel that all children should be immunised against childhood diseases in order to control these diseases. Some people, however, feel that they should be given a choice of whether or not to immunise their children. Discuss both these views and give your opinion.

Strategy for analysing the task

To analyse the task, first read the task, then ask yourself the following questions:

*   What are the key topic words? (Underline them.)
*   What are the question words? (**Highlight** or circle them.)
*   What do you need to include in your answer?

    Read the following task and consider the above questions.

You should spend about 40 minutes on this task.

Write about the following topic:

Some people think that boys and girls should be educated in the same schools. Others, however, believe that girls achieve better results when educated in single-sex schools.

Discuss both these views and give your opinion.

Give reasons for your answer and include any relevant examples from your own knowledge or experience.

Write at least 250 words.

a   What are the key topic words? Underline them.
You should have underlined:
boys and girls educated same schools
girls educated single-sex schools

b What are the question words? Highlight or circle them.

You should have highlighted or circled:

Discuss both these views   give your opinion

c What do you need to include in your answer?

In this Task 2, you need to include:

- why boys and girls should be educated together
- why girls should be educated in single-sex schools
- your opinion on which is better.

> **TIP**   Remember you need to answer ALL parts of the question.

Activity 2.2

Read the following task and answer the questions below to analyse the task. Check your answers in the Answer Key.

You should spend about 40 minutes on this task.

Write about the following topic:

Traffic congestion is a growing problem in many cities today. What are some of the causes of traffic congestion, and what measures can be taken to help reduce it?

Give reasons for your answer and include any relevant examples from your own knowledge or experience.

Write at least 250 words.

a   What are the key topic words? Underline them.

b   What are the question words? Highlight them.

c   What do you need to include in your answer?

UNIT 3

Brainstorming Ideas

The next step in the essay-writing process is to brainstorm ideas or think of the ideas that you would like to use in your essay.

Brainstorming means that you write down everything you know on a topic. There are many different ways to brainstorm; however, the most commonly used techniques are **listing**, **mind mapping** and **tabling**.

You need to choose a technique that suits both you and the time constraints of Task 2. Remember, you have 40 minutes, with only a few minutes to brainstorm.

Look at the task below.

> You should spend about 40 minutes on this task.
>
> Write about the following topic:
>
> **Mobile phones are considered essential by most people nowadays.**
>
> **Discuss the advantages and disadvantages of mobile phones and state your opinion.**
>
> Give reasons for your answer and include any relevant examples from your own knowledge or experience.
>
> Write at least 250 words.

Note: this is an **argument**-style task in which you need to discuss both sides of the argument, so in this case you should write about the advantages of mobile phones and the disadvantages of mobile phones and also give your opinion.

Brainstorming for this task could look like this:

Listing

Advantages

- small, portable
- cheaper than landlines
- can SMS rather than call – cheaper, more convenient

Disadvantages

- expensive, especially in poorer countries
- addictive
- may cause cancer – unknown but suggested

Mind mapping

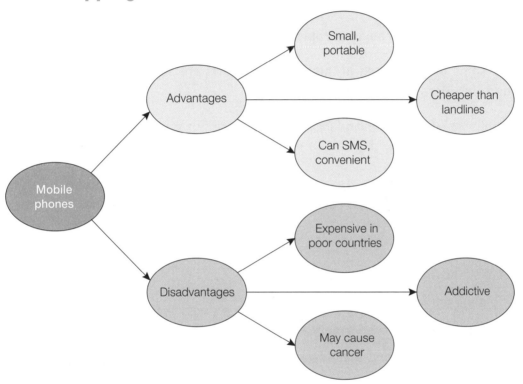

Tabling

Advantages	Disadvantages
small, portable	expensive, especially in poorer countries
cheaper than landlines	addictive
can SMS rather than call, more convenient	may cause cancer – unknown but suggested

Activity 3.1

Using the technique that you prefer, brainstorm the following task. If you are not sure which technique suits you best, try completing all three outlines below. Compare your ideas with a classmate or look at the suggested answers in the Answer Key.

You should spend about 40 minutes on this task.

Write about the following topic:

Childhood obesity is increasing at rapid rates in developed countries.

What are some of the causes of this problem? What are some ways in which childhood obesity rates can be reduced?

Give reasons for your answer and include any relevant examples from your own knowledge or experience.

Write at least 250 words.

a Listing

Causes of childhood obesity

_____

_____

_____

_____

_____

Ways to reduce childhood obesity

_____

_____

_____

_____

_____

_____

b Mind mapping

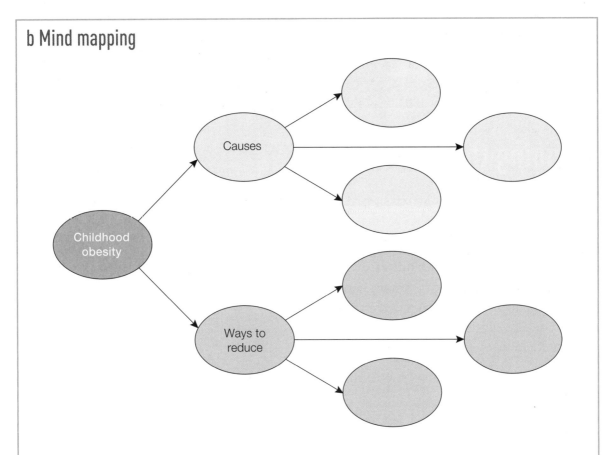

c Tabling

Causes	Ways to reduce

UNIT 4

Planning the Essay

Once you have brainstormed ideas, you need to plan how your essay will be organised. Most essays have **three** parts – **introduction**, **body**, and **conclusion** – and an Academic Writing Task 2 essay usually needs two or three body paragraphs, depending on which task type you are writing. The essay can be structured as follows:

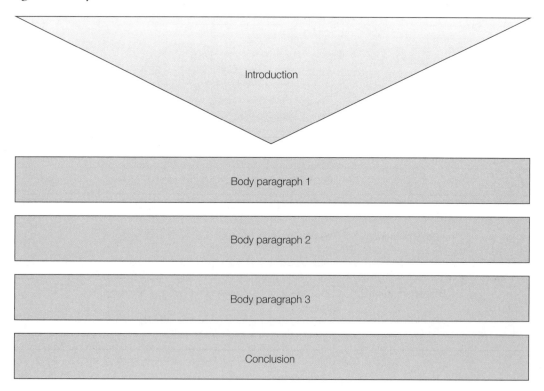

Introduction

Body paragraph 1

Body paragraph 2

Body paragraph 3

Conclusion

Try to think about your essay plan while you are brainstorming, as this will use less time. You should aim to spend 3–4 minutes in total analysing, brainstorming and planning your essay. The main idea of the plan is to organise your argument to make sure that you include your opinion, have a thesis statement in your introduction, and that your main ideas are logically organised in body paragraphs with support and examples.

Here is a task followed by a sample plan. Look at how the essay is planned.

You should spend about 40 minutes on this task.

Write about the following topic:

Governments alone cannot be expected to solve environmental problems. It is also the responsibility of businesses and individuals to help.

To what extent do you agree or disagree?

Give reasons for your answer and include any relevant examples from your own knowledge or experience.

Write at least 250 words.

Introduction:
Broad statement – env problems need to be solved
Thesis/my opinion: needs joint effort from
govt/bus/individuals

| Body paragraph 1: | Expensive to solve, govts alone can't afford it
Businesses cause some probs so they should help pay
Example: systems to stop more pollution/pay taxes |

| Body paragraph 2: | Needs a lot of effort – everyone needs to put effort in |

| Body paragraph 3: | Opposing – govt very powerful/without govt no change
will happen
Example: carbon tax |

| Conclusion: | ... |

In this plan, abbreviations and shortened words (such as *govt* instead of *government*) have been used to save time. You can see the writer's opinion is noted and in this case is included in the introduction. There are three body paragraphs with supporting ideas. Examples have been noted in two of the paragraphs. There are no planned ideas for the conclusion as the conclusion is a rephrasing of the main ideas. It is not always necessary to plan the conclusion. Unit 5 covers each part of the essay in more detail.

Activity 4.1

Here is a sample Task 2 and brainstorming for the task. Organise the ideas into an essay plan, using the essay structure diagram.

You should spend about 40 minutes on this task.

Write about the following topic:

Childhood obesity is increasing at rapid rates in developed countries.

What are some of the causes of this problem? What are some ways in which childhood obesity rates can be reduced?

Give reasons for your answer and include any relevant examples from your own knowledge or experience.

Write at least 250 words.

Brainstorming

Causes of childhood obesity

- too much fast food
- too much time playing computer games
- not enough sport/exercise

Ways to reduce childhood obesity

- parents cook meals, not buy takeaway
- limit time on computer
- more sport at and after school

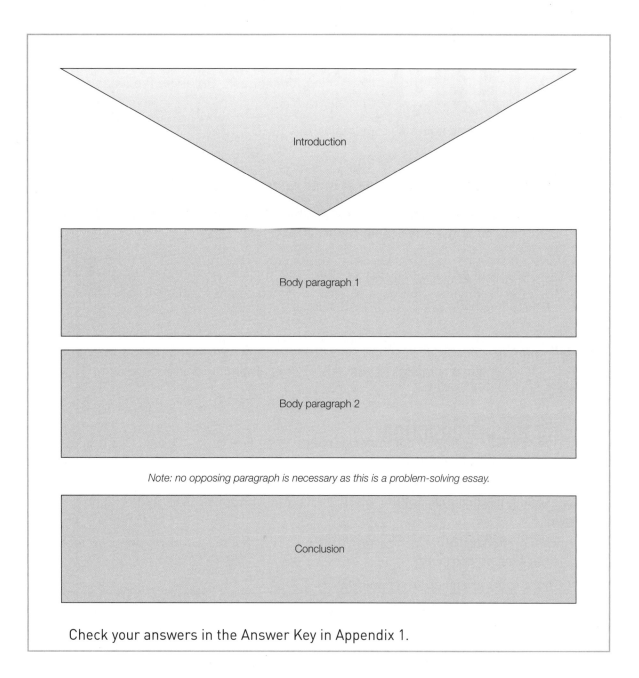

Introduction

Body paragraph 1

Body paragraph 2

Note: no opposing paragraph is necessary as this is a problem-solving essay.

Conclusion

Check your answers in the Answer Key in Appendix 1.

UNIT 5

Writing the Essay

Writing the essay will take the majority of your time. You should aim to spend 30–32 minutes writing the essay. Remember you need to write 4–5 paragraphs totalling at least 250 words.

> **TIP**   Don't write a draft or rough copy of your essay – write your essay only once. If you make any mistakes, just rub or cross them out and keep writing!

Writing the introduction

An introduction should contain two or three sentences starting with a **broad, general statement** about the topic and ending with a **thesis statement** (the main sentence of the essay containing the main idea of the whole essay). Your introduction should be approximately 50 words.

Writing an effective introduction for Academic IELTS Task 2 can be done by following three easy steps:

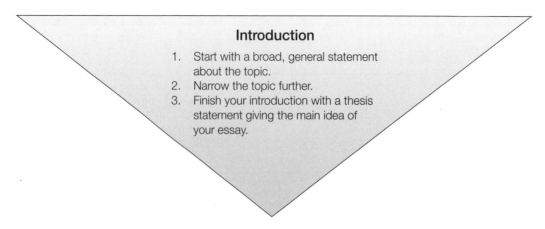

Introduction

1.   Start with a broad, general statement about the topic.
2.   Narrow the topic further.
3.   Finish your introduction with a thesis statement giving the main idea of your essay.

Look at the following sample of an introduction to the task below:

You should spend about 40 minutes on this task.

Write about the following topic:

Government alone cannot be expected to solve environmental problems. It is also the responsibility of businesses and individuals to help.

To what extent do you agree or disagree?

Give reasons for your answer and include any relevant examples from your own knowledge or experience.

Write at least 250 words.

It is agreed that our environmental problems need to be solved; however, there is argument over who should solve them. Some people feel that only the government should be responsible for finding solutions to these issues, but the problems that exist are so large and, therefore, overcoming them requires joint efforts from government, as well as businesses and individuals.

You can see that the introduction begins with a **broad, general statement** about the topic of solving environmental problems. It then goes on to **narrow the topic** down towards the argument over who in particular should solve these problems before giving **a thesis statement** that tells us the main idea of the essay, which in this case is that solving environmental problems requires efforts by government and businesses and individuals. Interestingly, in this sample introduction the thesis statement is in the final part of the second sentence, rather than a whole sentence in itself.

Activity 5.1

Look at the next sample paragraph. The sentences are not in the correct order. Rewrite the paragraph in the correct order, and then underline the thesis statement. Check your answers in the Answer Key.

There are both positive and negative changes; however, the majority of these changes have negatively affected the way people communicate today. Over the last twenty years, computers have become an important part of our lives and many people use a computer to communicate with others. This has meant that the way in which we communicate has changed dramatically.

Activity 5.2

Write a thesis statement for each of the following tasks:

a   Traffic congestion is a growing problem in many cities today. What are some of the causes of traffic congestion, and what measures can be taken to help reduce it?

b   Mobile phones are considered essential by most people nowadays. Discuss the advantages and disadvantages of mobile phones and state your own opinion.

[continued from previous page]

c   Working from home has become more common with technological advances; however, it has many challenges associated with it. What are some of the challenges that someone working from home may face? What are some of the effects on society of more people working from home? What is your opinion of this?

Suggested answers are given in the Answer Key.

Activity 5.3

Now, look at the notes in the sample plan below to help you write an introduction for the following task. Remember to use the three steps to guide you.

You should spend about 40 minutes on this task.

Write about the following topic:

Childhood obesity is increasing at rapid rates in developed countries.

What are some of the causes of this problem? What are some ways in which childhood obesity rates can be reduced?

Give reasons for your answer and include any relevant examples from your own knowledge or experience.

Write at least 250 words.

Introduction

Broad statement: Childhood obesity is rising all over the world …
Thesis: Many causes and many ways to overcome …

There are no 'right' or 'wrong' answers to this activity; however, suggested answers are given in the Answer Key.

TIP   Don't copy the exact words from the task itself – use your own words!

Writing the body

The body will generally contain two or three paragraphs. Each paragraph needs to begin with a **topic sentence** (the main idea of that paragraph) followed by **supporting ideas** and relevant **examples**. You could have either two longer paragraphs (approximately 75 words each) or three shorter paragraphs (50 words each) if you are going to write an **opposing argument** or a **concession paragraph.**

These three steps can help you write each body paragraph:

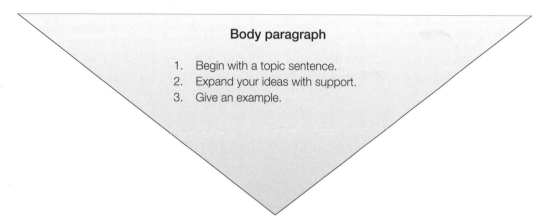

Body paragraph

1. Begin with a topic sentence.
2. Expand your ideas with support.
3. Give an example.

Here is the body for the task on environmental problems. This sample includes three short body paragraphs as this writer has included a paragraph containing an opposing argument. Read the sample paragraphs and underline the topic sentence in each body paragraph. Then highlight the **supporting ideas** and any **examples** that may have been included.

> Solving environmental problems is expensive and the financial burden on governments alone is too high. As businesses are often responsible for causing some of the environmental problems, they should help with the cost of solving the problems. This could be done by contributing funds or by implementing new systems to minimise further pollution.
>
> A second reason that solving our environmental problems requires joint contribution is that action and effort are needed. The government can spend money on campaigns or introduce taxes; however, slowing or stopping the problems requires effort from all. If businesses do not stop polluting and individuals do not minimise their waste, no advertising campaign will be effective.
>
> Admittedly, the government does have the power to make an enormous impact on the environment and without government intervention change would probably not happen. The introduction of the carbon tax in Australia is an example of government action helping solve environmental problems. However, without all parties contributing this change would not be effective.

You should have underlined the first sentence of each paragraph. The **topic sentence** is almost always the **first** sentence of a paragraph and contains the main idea of the paragraph.

The **supporting ideas** are usually written in the second and maybe third sentences of a paragraph and the **examples** generally follow the supporting ideas.

TIP   You don't need to include examples in every paragraph; however, you should use at least one example in your essay.

Activity 5.4

Look at the sentences below and decide which are (i) topic sentences, (ii) supporting ideas and (iii) examples. Then decide which sentences belong in the same paragraph and rewrite the sentences as full paragraphs. Check your answers in the Answer Key.

a   In Australia, for example, some people in remote areas still have limited access to medical facilities, and money should be spent on this rather than on space exploration.

b   It is very social at an office.

c   This is particularly important in senior years when students are preparing for university entrance.

d   Girls should be working on their studies rather than deciding which boy they like or whom they want to date, for instance.

e   Research into space exploration is very expensive.

f   For example, many companies have staff parties and other activities for people to talk and make friends.

g   By spending millions of dollars on space research, governments are not using extra funds to help improve the lives of their citizens.

h   Firstly, in single-sex schools, girls can focus solely on their academic tasks without being distracted by boys.

i   Although many people think that it is better to work at home rather than go to an office, it can be quite lonely.

Activity 5.5

Look again at the task on childhood obesity in Activity 5.3 and, using the ideas in the plan below, write two body paragraphs for the task. Remember to start each of your paragraphs with a topic sentence and then follow with supporting ideas and examples if possible. Suggested answers are included in the Answer Key, or alternatively you could ask a teacher or classmate to check your answers for you.

Body Paragraph 1: Causes – too much fast food, too much time playing computer games, not enough sport/exercise

Example ...

Body Paragraph 2: Ways to reduce – parents cook meals not buy takeaway, limit time on computers, more sport at and after school

Example ...

Writing an opposing argument (concession paragraph)

An **opposing argument** (or a concession paragraph) usually belongs in an **opinion task** (you are given an opinion and you need to evaluate it). In an opinion task, you do not necessarily need to discuss both sides of the argument; however, many writers like to give concession to the opposite side of the argument.

Reread these three body paragraphs from the previous section and decide what the two sides of the argument are and which paragraph contains the opposing argument.

> Solving environmental problems is expensive and the financial burden on governments alone is too high. As businesses are often responsible for causing some of the environmental problems, they should help with the cost of solving the problems. This could be done by contributing funds or by implementing new systems to minimise further pollution.
>
> A second reason that solving our environmental problems requires joint contribution is that action and effort are needed. The government can spend money on campaigns or introduce taxes; however, slowing or stopping the problems requires effort from all. If businesses do not stop polluting and individuals do not minimise their waste, no advertising campaign will be effective.
>
> Admittedly, the government does have the power to make an enormous impact on the environment and without government intervention change would probably not happen. The introduction of the carbon tax in Australia is an example of government action helping solve environmental problems. However, without all parties contributing this change would not be effective.

You should have decided that the **writer's argument** is that governments alone cannot solve environmental problems, and that the **opposing argument** is that the government has a lot of power and can make large changes. The opposing argument is in the third body paragraph.

The structure of a concession paragraph is the same as other body paragraphs in that it has a topic sentence followed by supporting ideas and examples; however, this paragraph usually uses **concession words,** such as:

despite this	however	admittedly	nevertheless
even though	although	in spite of	

Activity 5.6

Look again at the opposing argument above and underline the concession words that have been used. Check the answers in the Answer Key.

Writing the conclusion

The conclusion should **restate the main ideas** of the essay using new words and needs to have your **opinion** included. To reach the 250-word count, aim to write 50 words in your conclusion.

Conclusions usually begin with:

In conclusion   finally   to sum up   to summarise   overall

To write a conclusion, follow these easy steps:

Conclusion
1. Begin with concluding words. 2. Restate your main ideas. 3. Give your own opinion.

Look at the following example of a conclusion. It begins with the **concluding words** *in conclusion*, then **restates the writer's main idea** (that the government should not be the only group to solve the environmental problems), and then finishes by expressing **the writer's opinion** that all groups can work together to make effective changes.

> In conclusion, the government does need to be the leader in solving our environmental problems, but it needs the financial assistance and the efforts of businesses and individuals to make any long-term, effective change to the problems that exist.

TIP   Don't include any new ideas in your conclusion.

Activity 5.7

Write a conclusion to follow your body paragraphs from Activity 5.5. Follow the three steps for writing conclusions. Remember that it is not necessary to write a plan for a conclusion, as you are restating main ideas; however, one is included in this activity to help guide you.

Conclusion – restate plus my opinion – big problem but can be overcome if parents take action.

There are no 'right' or 'wrong' answers for this activity. You could ask a teacher or classmate to check your writing, or you could look at the suggested answers in the Answer Key.

Using linking words

A well-written essay should have a variety of **linking words** to give it cohesion or flow. There are many different kinds of linking words.

Here are some **examples** that you could use in your essay:

in addition	although	despite	furthermore
firstly/secondly	consequently	however	next
lastly	on the other hand	finally	moreover
whereas	to conclude	as a result of	in conclusion

Activity 5.8

Look again at the sample essay for the task on environmental problems printed in full below. Underline the linking words that have been used. Check your answers in the Answer Key.

It is agreed that our environmental problems need to be solved; however, there is argument over who should solve them. Some people feel that only the government should be responsible for finding solutions to these issues, but the problems that exist are so large and, therefore, overcoming them requires joint efforts from government, as well as business and individuals.

Solving environmental problems is expensive and the financial burden on governments alone is too high. As businesses are often responsible for causing some of the environmental problems, they should help with the cost of solving the problems. This could be done by contributing funds or by implementing new systems to minimise further pollution.

A second reason that solving our environmental problems requires joint contribution is that action and effort are needed. The government can spend money on campaigns or introduce taxes; however, slowing or stopping the problems requires effort from all. If businesses do not stop polluting and individuals do not minimise their waste, no advertising campaign will be effective.

Admittedly, the government does have the power to make an enormous impact on the environment and without government intervention change would probably not happen. The introduction of the carbon tax in Australia is an example of government action helping solve environmental problems. However, without all parties contributing this change would not be effective.

In conclusion, the government does need to be the leader in solving our environmental problems, but it needs the financial assistance and the efforts of businesses and individuals to make any long-term, effective change to the problems that exist.

Activity 5.9

1. The paragraph below has no linking words included. Use linking words to fill in the gaps and make the paragraph more cohesive. Note that there could be more than one suitable answer for each. Check possible answers in the Answer Key.

    a _____, immunising against childhood diseases stops children from suffering illnesses and spreading them to other youngsters. **b** _____, by ensuring their children are immunised, parents can send their children to school knowing they will not be exposed to such diseases, and, **c** _____, schools will be a healthier place.

2. Write a second paragraph to follow the paragraph above. You could either add to the argument or oppose the argument above, but make sure you use appropriate linking words to show which side of the argument you have taken.

There are no 'right' or 'wrong' answers for this activity; however, suggested answers are given in the Answer Key.

UNIT 6

Lexical Resource

Once you have mastered the skills required to achieve a GOOD band score for Task Response and Cohesion & Coherence, you can focus on improving your Lexical Resource and Grammatical Range & Accuracy. If you look back to Unit 1 at the assessment criteria used for Academic Writing Task 2, you will see that to improve your band score for Lexical Resource, it is important to include academic vocabulary in your essay and have accurate spelling.

Academic Vocabulary

In Academic Writing Task 2, you are expected to use **complex** or **academic vocabulary**; however, you do not need to know any specific technical words.

Look at some examples of everyday language and academic language – you can see that academic language is more advanced or complex.

Everyday	Academic
brother	sibling
but	however
plants	vegetation
car	vehicle
boss	employer
help	aid
about	approximately

Activity 6.1

Look at the following sentences and choose the academic word to help make the sentence better. Questions **d** and **e** require you to think of a more academic word.

a   The benefits/good points of working from home are many.

b   Continual use of/talking on mobile phones may cause cancer.

c   Traffic jams are common/abundant nowadays.

d   Old people/_____ have much to offer to both workers and society in general, and so/_____ they should keep/_____ working as long as possible.

e   Making/_____ young people (to) learn uncommon languages may lead to rebellion as young people usually fight/_____ against their mother and father/_____.

Avoiding informal vocabulary also helps make your essay better. In order to avoid using informal vocabulary, follow these simple rules:

- Avoid contractions (use *do not*, not *don't*).
- Avoid question forms (use *There are many advantages to working from home*, not *What are some of the advantages of working from home?*).
- Write numbers in words if below one hundred, beginning a sentence, or rounded numbers (use *eighty-five* not *85*).
- Do not use abbreviations (use *that is*, not *i.e.*).
- Avoid slang words or phrases (use *in my opinion*, not *I reckon*).
- Avoid personalised language (use *It is commonly thought that* …, not *I think that* …).

Activity 6.2

Read the two paragraphs below, containing mostly informal or mostly academic language. Find examples of vocabulary and phrases with similar meanings.

Informal

I think that computers have changed the way we communicate with each other a lot nowadays. We don't chat with friends face to face as much as we used to. Now, we chat online or email 2 or 3 times a day instead. I reckon that it's not a good form of communication as it's easy to get the person's meaning wrong cos you can't see their face or hear their tone.

Academic

In my opinion, computers have dramatically changed the way we communicate with each other nowadays. People do not talk with friends face to face as much as in the past; instead they chat online or email two or three times per day. This is not an effective form of communication as it is easy to misinterpret the person's meaning as you cannot see their face or hear their tone.

There are many ways to **improve your academic vocabulary** before taking the IELTS examination. Reading quality newspapers and academic articles either online or in journals is a very good way to improve your vocabulary. While reading, take note of or underline examples of vocabulary that you would like to use; look at how the words or phrases are used and try to reproduce these in your own writing.

Spelling

In Academic Writing Task 2, your **spelling** should not cause any problems for the person reading it. Look at the following two examples: both have spelling errors; however, one is difficult to read.

Paragraph 1	**Paragraph 2**
Mobile phones are very usefull and a convenient way to contact frends. Also, mobiles phones have become a lot cheaper in recent years. For example, some mobile phones have unlimited calls for $40 a month.	*Meny man and wiman hav mobile and dey tink there fone is good dey carnt slip becos fone is fun to chek email.*

The best way to solve your spelling problems is to learn to **recognise your spelling errors**. Ask yourself if the word looks right and sound it out. Learning the general spelling rules and common letter patterns (*-ious, -tion*), as well as memorising difficult spellings, are other strategies that can help you.

Activity 6.3

a   Reread the paragraphs above and correct the spelling errors.

b   Look at this list of common academic words and correct the spelling errors:

goverment	fisical	polution	spatious
conection	debateable	meazure	beleive
significent	abstrakt	freqent	demonstrait
skilful	apropriate	annuel	arguement

Check your answers to the activities in this unit in the Answer Key in Appendix 1.

UNIT 7

Grammatical Range and Accuracy

In the assessment criteria shown in Unit 1, you can see that in order to improve your result in Grammatical Range and Accuracy, you need to have accurate grammar, use complex sentence structures and have control of punctuation.

Accurate grammar

Most second-language learners find it difficult to see their grammar mistakes; after all, if you knew the correct structure you would have used it in the first place. So, working on grammar activities before taking IELTS is the best way to improve your grammar. However, in the exam itself, you can make some improvements by checking both basic grammar and the grammar you often get wrong. For example, if you often have problems with articles (*a/an/the*) when you use English, look specifically for these when editing your essay.

Common grammar problems include:

- problems with subject–verb agreement (*she go* instead of *she goes*)
- articles (*a/an/the*)
- singular and plural
- wrong tense choice
- wrong preposition choice.

Activity 7.1

Read the following paragraph. This writer often makes mistakes with tenses and some articles. Correct the mistakes.

Secondly, the education in single-sex schools is helping students to get better results for their university entrance. Students can be concentrating on the examination and not worrying about the play with other boys and girls. Example of this is my school. My friend always thinking about opinions of girls and he not studying hard then he fail examination. After that he study hard and get the better results.

If you are not sure which areas of grammar are a common problem for you, ask your teacher, a classmate or a native speaker to check your work with you. Grammar practice materials are readily available on the internet.

Complex sentence structures

You will need to use a variety of **complex sentences** to achieve well in Academic Writing Task 2. **Complex sentences** are used more in academic writing than **simple sentences** and **compound sentences**, and using them well shows a higher level of English skill.

A **simple sentence** is made up of a **subject** and **verb**, for example:

> *I study.*
> Subject + verb.

A **compound sentence** is **two simple sentences** joined with a **coordinating conjunction** (*and/but/so/or*), for example:

> *I studied hard but I didn't pass my exam.*
> Simple sentence + coordinating conjunction + simple sentence.

A **complex sentence** is a sentence made up of an **independent clause** and one or more **dependent clauses**, joined by a **subordinating conjunction** (such as *because/although/after*) or a **relative pronoun** (such as *who/what/which*).

Look at two examples of complex sentences:

> *Although I studied hard, I failed my exam.*
> *The people will elect a new prime minister after the government sets an election date.*

Looking at these examples, decide which is the independent clause and which is the dependent clause. What do you think makes them different?

You should have noted the independent clauses were:

> *I failed my exam.*

AND

> *The people will elect a new prime minister.*

and the dependent clauses were:

> *Although I studied hard*

AND

after the government sets an election date.

An **independent clause** has a meaning on its own whereas a **dependent clause** needs to be joined to an independent clause to make sense. By adding a **subordinating conjunction** to a clause, it becomes dependent.

Look at the examples again and highlight the subordinating conjunctions.

> ***Although** I studied hard, I failed my exam.*

AND

> *The people will elect a new prime minister **after** the government sets an election date.*

TIP   Commas are used to separate the clauses when the subordinating conjunction is at the beginning of the sentence.

Activity 7.2

Look at the following complex sentences taken from sample essays. Underline the independent clause and the dependent clause, and highlight the **conjunction**.

a   There are both positive and negative changes; however, the majority of these changes have negatively affected the way people communicate today.

b   Because we do not yet know the long-term effects of mobile phone use, the use of phones should be limited.

c   Childhood obesity is a problem that is difficult to solve because it affects both children and their parents.

d   Even though some languages are already dead, young people should be forced to learn some less common languages to keep them alive.

Activity 7.3

Read the following task and sample essay and underline the complex sentences.

You should spend about 40 minutes on this task.

Write about the following topic:

Many people feel that all children should be immunised against childhood diseases in order to control these diseases. Some people, however, feel that they should be given a choice of whether or not to immunise their children.

Discuss both these views and give your opinion.

Give reasons for your answer and include any relevant examples from your own knowledge or experience.

Write at least 250 words.

Nowadays, there is much controversy over regulating immunisations for children. Some people believe that vaccinations should be compulsory for all children, while others think that it should be the choice of parents. I believe that, while immunisations have many benefits, parents should be allowed to choose for themselves if they would like to give these vaccinations to their children.

On the one hand, vaccinations should be mandatory for all children as they help to prevent the spread of diseases and prevent children dying. Furthermore, there are many viruses that can modify very quickly in different forms. For this reason it is vitally important to give injections in childhood to strengthen children's immune systems. For example, many children in Africa die from diseases such as smallpox, although this could be avoided if children were vaccinated.

On the other hand, there is not enough knowledge and research about the side effects of some vaccines. Moreover, pharmaceutical companies are usually responsible for research but they also sell the vaccinations. This may be a conflict of interest as the pharmaceutical companies could change the research results to hide possible problems so that they could sell more medicines.

In conclusion, I am sure that it is important to immunise our children; however, I believe that parents should have a choice of whether or not to vaccinate their children as the consequences could be dangerous.

Activity 7.4

Using the same essay task as the sample above, use your own ideas to finish the complex sentences below. Compare your answers with a classmate or get a teacher to check your ideas. Suggested answers are given in the Answer Key.

1. I agree with this point of view because _____

    _____.

2. Although some people may agree that immunisations should be compulsory, _____

    _____.

3. Until immunisations are made compulsory, _____

    _____.

4. In conclusion, I am certain that _____

    _____.

Punctuation

In Academic Writing Task 2, you are required to have **good understanding of punctuation**. However, punctuation in English is complicated and often difficult to master. Learning some of the basic punctuation rules can help you achieve mastery. The most important forms of punctuation in Task 2 are the full stop, the comma, the semicolon, and apostrophes for ownership. Using capital letters appropriately is also important. Question marks, apostrophes for contractions, quotation marks for direct speech, exclamation marks and abbreviations do not usually present in Task 2. The use of dashes, colons, semicolons and brackets is more advanced and generally shows expert use of English punctuation.

Good understanding of punctuation helps your essay be better understood. Look at the following example paragraph, which has had all the punctuation removed. Read through it and notice how difficult it is to understand.

> young people are an easy target for fast food companies so parents have to check the quality of the food that their children are eating unfortunately it is not easy to resist an advertising campaign moreover children like toys and the atmosphere of fast food restaurants is often fun and friendly this gives a false idea about the quality of the food that the fast food companies serve

Activity 7.5

Rewrite the paragraph above and add the missing punctuation.

Check your answers for the activities in this unit in the Answer Key in Appendix 1.

UNIT 8

Editing

Now that you have worked through each of the skills required to write an Academic Writing Task 2, it is time to look at one final skill that will help enhance your writing ability. **Editing**, or checking your work for errors, is a very important part of the essay-writing process. Editing can help you fine-tune your writing and this gives you the best chance to achieve well. As time is limited in Task 2 (40 minutes), you should spend only 3–4 minutes editing your work. It takes practice to learn to edit quickly and well.

The best technique for editing your work is to **use a checklist** and **read your essay twice**!

EDITING CHECKLIST

1 Read the essay through the first time and check:

TASK RESPONSE

Have you addressed the task?
Have you supported your ideas?
Have you given your opinion?

COHERENCE AND COHESION

Have you used an Introduction–Body Paragraphs–Conclusion structure?
Have you used topic sentences for each paragraph?
Have you used linking words?

2 Read the essay through again and check:

LEXICAL RESOURCE

Have you used a variety of academic vocabulary?
Is your spelling correct?

GRAMMATICAL RANGE AND ACCURACY

Have you used accurate grammar?
Have you used complex sentence structures?
Is your punctuation correct?

Look at a sample answer written for the following task:

> You should spend about 40 minutes on this task.
>
> Write about the following topic:
>
> **It is argued that art galleries and museums should not be funded by governments, and that government money is better spent on necessities such as health care. Discuss and give your opinion.**
>
> Give reasons for your answer and include any relevant examples from your own knowledge or experience.
>
> Write at least 250 words.

Nowadays, there are many discussions between people and the goverment over the issue of how art galleries and museums should be funded. Some individuals believe that money can be spent more efficiently, while others think that it is our responsibility to maintain the hystorical and cultural heritage for our society. I believe that goverments should invest in museums and galleries for two reasons.

The first and the most important reason to support the funding of museums and art galleries is that it is financially reasonable. Moreover, art galleries and museums were built as public organisations and they should be available for all society. If the goverment does not support these institutions, people will have to pay for the opportunity to admire them and it will be unaffordable for many people. For example, all the hystorical and art organisations in Russia is funded by the goverment and the rate of visiting galleries and museums has increased every year because they are not expensive.

The second reason to support the funding of art galleries and museums is that it is vital to have knowledge about the past. Furthermore, it is important to educate people and the younger generations about our hystory and culture. Museums and art galleries not only have entertainment purpose, they also play an educational role in our life.

In conclusion, there is no doubt that we have many problems in our society and goverments should solve them by making investments in these areas. However, I believe that it is vitally important, in terms of the education of people and the appreciation of culture, to keep these national institutions funded by goverments.

Activity 8.1

Imagine that you wrote this essay. Now, edit it using the editing checklist. Read the essay through **once**, focusing on the **first** set of editing questions, which check Task Response and Coherence & Cohesion. Check the answers to the first set of editing questions in the Answer Key.

TIP   Just rub out or cross out your errors and rewrite the words neatly.

Activity 8.2

Read the essay **again** and focus on the **second** set of editing questions, which check Lexical Resource and Grammatical Range and Accuracy, and then check your answers in the Answer Key.

Remember: editing your own essay is quite difficult as it is often hard to see the mistakes you have made. Regular practice helps you become aware of your common mistakes and can help you improve your score in Academic Writing Task 2.

UNIT 9

Common Problems

The table below outlines some of the common problems students often have when practising for Academic Writing Task 2. Helpful ways to overcome these problems are given.

Common Problem	Solutions
Not enough words	When doing practice tests at home, always check the word count. Put a timer on and time how long it takes you to write 250 words. Know what 250 words of your handwriting looks like on paper. Remember: Introduction – 50 words Body Paragraphs – 2 × 75 words OR 3 × 50 words Conclusion – 50 words
Running out of time to write a conclusion	It is important to conclude your essay. Keep an eye on the time, and if you get to the last five minutes and you feel you have not quite finished, write a short conclusion – one sentence will do! Again, do some practice tests at home using a timer.
No paragraphs	Some people write a very good essay with interesting ideas and good language, but fail to use paragraphs. A good essay has clear paragraphs, so leave a line between your paragraphs or indent at the beginning of a new paragraph.
Off the topic	Sometimes it is easy to misunderstand the task and write an essay about a slightly different topic from the one in the task, or start off on the right topic but then write about something different. Analysing the task and planning the essay help you keep your essay on the right topic.

UNIT 10

Practice Tests

To get the greatest benefit from these practice tests you should write your own response before looking at the model answers in the Answer Key. Give yourself a maximum time of 40 minutes. Try to get a friend or teacher to look at your answer and give you feedback.

Practice Test 1

You should spend about 40 minutes on this task.

Write about the following topic:

Fast-food companies should not be allowed to give away free toys with their food.

To what extent do you agree or disagree?

Give reasons for your answer and include any relevant examples from your own knowledge or experience.

Write at least 250 words.

Practice Test 2

You should spend about 40 minutes on this task.

Write about the following topic:

Many lesser-known languages are disappearing. Young people should be forced to learn these languages so they are not lost forever.

To what extent do you agree or disagree with this statement?

Give reasons for your answer and include any relevant examples from your own knowledge or experience.

Write at least 250 words.

Practice Test 3

You should spend about 40 minutes on this task.

Write about the following topic:

Some people think that boys and girls should be educated in the same schools. Others, however, believe that girls achieve better results when educated in single-sex schools.

Discuss both these views and give your opinion.

Give reasons for your answer and include any relevant examples from your own knowledge or experience.

Write at least 250 words.

Practice Test 4

You should spend about 40 minutes on this task.

Write about the following topic:

Work is more important than leisure. Discuss and give your opinion.

Give reasons for your answer and include any relevant examples from your own knowledge or experience.

Write at least 250 words.

APPENDIX 1

ANSWER KEY

Part 1: Academic Reading

Unit 1: About the Academic Reading Module

Activity 1.1
Answers will vary.

Activity 1.2

1. pressure
2. activities
3. combat
4. seawater
5. NG
6. T
7. F
8. v
9. ii
10. i
11. iii
12. [shire of] Harvey
13. groundwater
14. waste heat
15. lower temperatures
16. c
17. GL
18. TP

Unit 2: The Skills You Need

Activity 2.1

NAMES

1. Andre Ash
2. Paul Gamblin

3.   Colin Yates   **4.**   Jim Dodds

5.   The National Climate Change Adaptation Research Facility

NUMBERS

1.   0.6–1.5°C   **2.**   2.2–5°C

3.   More than 100   **4.**   By 2070

5.   28   **6.**   67

7.   More than 12,000   **8.**   Nearly 50 per cent

9.   8 per cent   **10.** 12 per cent

11. 10–20 per cent   **12.** 80 per cent

Activity 2.2

1.   b. (solar energy), a. (to explain a   **2.**   c. (the Internet and privacy), c. (to give
         problem)   an opinion)

3.   a. (in a magazine about business), c. (why people buy)

Activity 2.3

A.   *eminent*
         Part of speech: adjective
         Approximate meaning: successful, well known, well regarded

B.   *exacerbate*
         Part of speech: verb
         Approximate meaning: make something worse

C.   *nocturnal*
         Part of speech: adjective
         Approximate meaning: active at night

D.   *aroma*
         Part of speech: noun
         Approximate meaning: smell, scent

E. *jeopardy*
Part of speech: noun
Approximate meaning: danger, risk

F. *revere*
Part of speech: verb
Approximate meaning: worship, look up to a great deal

Unit 3: Multiple-choice Questions

Activity 3.1

1. Paragraph 3

2. Paragraph 1

3. Paragraph 5

4. Paragraph 2

5. C

6. B

7. A

8. B

Activity 3.2

1. D

2. A

3. A

4. C

5. A

6. D

Unit 4: True/False/Not Given Questions

Activity 4.1

1. True [220 million years ago; yes]

2. False [freshwater turtles; there are none]

3. True [critically endangered; yes]

4. False [motor vehicles; yes; new habitat]

5. False [at the bottom of lakes and rivers; yes; no]

6. Not given [hundreds; we don't know]

7. False [yes; no]

8. Not given [no; no; no]

Activity 4.2

1. Not given (we know the Magdalen Islands are in Quebec, but we don't know where Cape Breton Island is)

2. False (the six largest are connected)

3. True

4. False (they noticed the decrease **since** the 1990s)

5. Not given (we know it was less than a full year, but not exactly how long)

6. True

7. False (it's an average – some islands would lose more or less)

8. False (only one was swept away)

Unit 5: Yes/No/Not Given Questions

Activity 5.1

1. **a** No
   b Not given
   c Yes

2. **a** Yes
   b No
   c Not given

3. **a** No
   b Yes
   c Not given

4. **a** Yes
   b Not given
   c No

Activity 5.2

1. Yes

2. Yes

3. No

4. Not given

5. Not given

6. Not given

7. Yes

8. No

Unit 6: Short Answer Questions

Activity 6.1

Text outline (b)

Short answer question	Answer located in paragraph no.	Relevant text in the paragraph	Two or three word answer
1 What is incorrectly believed about the sleeping needs of an elderly person?	1	... that sleep needs decline with age.	**decline with age**
2 What happens to total sleep time when sleep pattern changes?	2	... total sleep time tends to remain constant	**remain constant**
3 What conditions increase sleep disorders among the elderly?	4	... can be attributed to physical and psychiatric illnesses	**physical and psychiatric**
4 People may suffer with one of the two types of conditions of sleeplessness. What are they?	5	Insomnia may be chronic or acute and is ...	**chronic, acute**
5 In general, what conditions cause people to suffer with more sleep problems?	6	... people with poor health or chronic medical conditions have more sleep problems.	**poor health/chronic medical conditions**

Activity 6.2

1. sunrise and sunset

2. summer

3. winter solstice

4. twice

5. South Pole

Unit 7: Sentence Completion Questions

Activity 7.1

(Predictions for missing information will vary.)

1. Paragraph 1; geophysical imaging technology

2. Paragraph 2; three metres

3. Paragraph 2; farmers and small-holders

4. Paragraphs 2 and 3; ground-penetrating radar

5. Paragraph 4; monuments

6. Paragraph 5; excavation data

7. Paragraph 6; data-processing systems

8. Paragraph 7; funding

Activity 7.2

1. a Mars-sized body

2. orbit

3. thicker

4. global magma ocean

5. asteroids and comets

6. subsurface magma

7. potassium and phosphorus

8. rock samples

Unit 8: Diagram/Flow Chart Completion Questions

Activity 8.1

The description is in one paragraph (paragraph E).

Questions

1. sunlight

2. negative

3. positive

4. pairs

5. positively doped silicon

6. the depletion zone or space-charge region

Gaps

1. sunlight

2. negatively charged electrons

3. electron-hole pairs

4. depletion zone/space-charge region

5. positively charged holes

6. positively doped silicon

Activity 8.2

1. rubber and polyester

2. iron ore

3. wood pulp

4. vulcanised

5. 50,000 km

6. option

7. energy

8. outweighed

9. recycling

Unit 9: Table/Note Completion Questions

Activity 9.1

1. 10

2. year

3. how many people died; no

4. the cause of the shipwreck (noun only); verb + noun

5. noun

6. adjective

7. type of ship

8. the name of the ship (then read surrounding information)

TABLE ANSWERS

1. 1945

2. more than 4000

3. Soviet torpedoes

4. oil tanker

5. hit [an] iceberg

6. lifeboats

7. evacuation

8. passengers

9. poorly mapped

10. hospital ship

Activity 9.2

1. thyroid

2. metabolic process

3. hormones

4. 7 per cent

5. identify

6. treatable

7. [small] dose

8. women

9. men

10. 50

Unit 10: Summary Completion Questions

Activity 10.1

1. past participle verb

2. noun

3. adjective

4. noun

5. noun

6. noun

7. past tense verb

8. adjective

9. noun

10. noun

Noun	Adjective	Verb
majority	new	forced
bush	most	gave
end	Aboriginal	appeared
viewpoints	past (can be an adjective)	enabled
past	European	introduced
cinema	traditional	
mining	(past participle verbs can often	
camera	also be adjectives)	
Aborigines		
beginning		

1. introduced

2. end

3. Aboriginal

4. majority

5. camera

6. viewpoints

7. enabled

8. traditional

9. mining

10. past

Activity 10.2

1. rebel

2. gangs

3. proportion

4. business

5. buying

6. commute

7. gene

8. liberating

9. bond

Unit 11: Matching Headings Questions

Activity 11.1

Section A

A report reveals an inequity: MAIN IDEA
WA's growing population: DETAIL

Section B:

Only a third of revenue returned: DETAIL
A breakdown of the numbers: MAIN IDEA

Section C:

Why the government should invest more: MAIN IDEA
How much Canberra receives in taxes and fees: DETAIL

Section D:

Projected changes in funding and expenditure: MAIN IDEA
The end of a key program: DETAIL

Section E:

Funding affected by political relations: DETAIL
Sources of funding: MAIN IDEA

Section F:

The proportion of funding WA receives: DETAIL
An engine of economic growth now and in the future: MAIN IDEA

Activity 11.2

A. vi (Language and Health)

B. ix (Words of Meaning and Style)

C. x (A Few Words Used Often)

D. vii (Neurological Differences)

E. i (How Different Kinds of People Use Language)

F. viii (Ways of Writing)

G. iii (Potential Uses of this Knowledge)

Unit 12: Matching Features Questions

Activity 12.1

1.	E	**2.**	A
3.	C	**4.**	B
5.	A	**6.**	D
7.	F		

Activity 12.2

1.	D	**2.**	A
3.	D	**4.**	C
5.	C	**6.**	B
7.	D	**8.**	A

Unit 13: Matching Sentence Endings Questions

Activity 13.1

Keywords

1.	Amnesty	**2.**	court/ten million
3.	police officer/Douglas Turner	**4.**	demonstrations
5.	tased/multiple	**6.**	Taser manual
7.	Taser/ argued		

Sentence endings

1.	D	**2.**	F
3.	A	**4.**	G
5.	C	**6.**	H
7.	E		

Activity 13.2

1.	D	**2.**	J
3.	G	**4.**	A
5.	E	**6.**	I
7.	H	**8.**	B

Unit 14: Academic Reading Practice Tests

IELTS Academic Reading Practice Test 1

1.	D	**2.**	C
3.	A	**4.**	B
5.	E	**6.**	crystalline matter
7.	(yearly) pilgrimages	**8.**	chemical composition
9.	high speed	**10.**	sophisticated equipment
11.	True	**12.**	Not given
13.	False	**14.**	D
15.	C	**16.**	B
17.	D	**18.**	D
19.	C	**20.**	D
21.	B	**22.**	double-edged sword
23.	a clean feed	**24.**	illegal and inappropriate
25.	law enforcement agencies	**26.**	a blank cheque
27.	ii	**28.**	i
29.	vii	**30.**	vi
31.	iv	**32.**	D
33.	A	**34.**	B
35.	A	**36.**	D

37. True

38. False

39. False

40. Not given

IELTS Academic Reading Practice Test 2

1. E

2. C

3. G

4. B

5. D

6. endorsed [the] conclusion

7. commercial purposes

8. [the] temperature dropped

9. vapour and clouds

10. F

11. B

12. E

13. D

14. True

15. Not given

16. Not given

17. False

18. B

19. D

20. E

21. C

22. A

23. G

24. D

25. A

26. E

27. G

28. C

29. B

30. D

31. E

32. A

33. C

34. D

35. B

36. B

37. E

38. D

39. C

40. A

IELTS Academic Reading Practice Test 3

1. B

2. C

3. D

4. D

5. D	**6.** Yes
7. No	**8.** Not given
9. scientific ways	**10.** population pressure
11. social institutions	**12.** modern weapons
13. towards society	**14.** D
15. A	**16.** G
17. F	**18.** B
19. we all live	**20.** small minority of
21. profits high	**22.** wages low
23. run more smoothly	**24.** more privileged background
25. survive and flourish	**26.** compete for necessities
27. vi	**28.** i
29. viii	**30.** iii
31. v	**32.** vii
33. External influences / External factors / External reasons	**34.** Consumer connectivity
35. Safety concerns	**36.** Congestion
37. Market types	**38.** Internal influences / Internal factors / Internal reasons
39. Economics	**40.** Energy issues

IELTS Academic Reading Practice Test 4

1. E	**2.** A
3. D	**4.** B
5. C	**6.** B (in any order)
7. C (in any order)	**8.** E (in any order)
9. Yes	**10.** Not given
11. Yes	**12.** False

13. Not given

14. x

15. vii

16. vi

17. i

18. ii

19. iv

20. ix

21. B

22. H

23. I

24. E

25. F

26. A

27. altruism

28. their mother / the queen

29. temporal polyethism

30. nectar (and) pollen

31. nectar

32. eggs

33. protein

34. low, dark

35. lays

36. False

37. False

38. True

39. False

40. Not given

Part 2: Academic Writing Task 1

Unit 1: About Academic Writing Task 1

Quiz 1

1. **False**. Examiners focus on the good points of your work, not the bad points. If you can use a wide range of grammar to clearly explain yourself, you can get a good mark, even if you make some mistakes.

2. **True**. Punctuation counts towards your mark for Grammatical Range and Accuracy.

3. **False**. You must write in connected sentences that are organised into paragraphs.

4. **False**. It is better to use a wide range of vocabulary and make some mistakes.
5. **True**. If you write less than 150 words, you will lose marks.

Quiz 2

1. You will lose marks.

2. Nothing. You don't gain marks. You don't lose marks.

3. No. Any copied language is ignored by the examiner. You are just wasting your time.

4. It means you must find information in an image and convert it to words.

5. No. Task 1 does not ask you to do that. You will not get a good mark.

6. 20 minutes.

7. No. Only mention the **important** data, such as a minimum and a maximum, or a date when an important change happened.

8. No. You need to write in connected sentences, to describe the relationships in the data. For example, the sequence of events, or cause and effect relationships.

Unit 2: Task achievement

Activity 2.1

1. d	**2.** c
3. a	**4.** b

Activity 2.2

1. True	**2.** True
3. True	**4.** True
5. False	**6.** True
7. True	**8.** True
9. Not given	

Activity 2.3

a–E

b–F

c–D

Activity 2.4

A–2

B–2

C–1

D–2

E–4

F–2

G–3

Activity 2.5

1. B

2. D

3. A

4. C

Activity 2.6

Main features

1. Most certificate students were very happy with their course.

2. Most diploma students were unhappy or very unhappy with their course, with almost the same proportion in each category.

3. Certificate students tend to be younger than diploma students.

Overview: Answers will vary.

Activity 2.7

Main features

1. The permanent exhibition space is much bigger.

2. The visiting exhibition space is slightly smaller and has moved.

3. The entrance has moved and the old entrance room has been replaced by a shop.

4. The staff area and storage area are now much smaller, to make room for the visiting exhibition space.

Overview: Answers will vary.

Activity 2.8

Main features

1. Two ways to make paper.

2. Trees are made into woodchips then paper.

3. Paper is used and then recycled at the same factory that makes new paper.

Overview: Answers will vary.

Activity 2.9

1. Should be 110 thousand and 130 thousand.

2. The graph doesn't show change over time; it compares different types of items.

3. Should be 'Berlin', not 'London'.

4. The increase was not 'dramatic'. It only increased from 26 per cent to 31 per cent. Don't overuse the word 'dramatic'!

Activity 2.10

There were three stages of growth: a period of slow growth between 1975 and 1990; a period of faster growth between 1990 and 2000 and a period of rapid increase between 2000 and 2009.
It seems the increase came mainly from higher numbers of Asian students (up from 20 per cent in 1975 to 65 per cent in 2009). Proportions of students from other regions stayed roughly the same, or fell slightly, except for students from South America. These students accounted for 30 per cent of all international students in 1975, but by 2009 there were no students from this region.

Activity 2.11

There is no overview, no summary and no selecting. The answer just copies the task prompt and then lists the information in the charts, one by one.

Activity 2.12

There is no mention of the 'over 60' category. This means that the key points are missing and the answer will not get a good mark.

Activity 2.13

Task achievement	Yes/no	Example
Does it give an overview of main patterns?	yes	Germany and France – GDP is similar. USA has highest GDP and highest CO_2 per person.
Does it talk about the most important details?	yes	Describes all five countries. Describes changes in GDP. Describes CO_2 per person.
Does it have any irrelevant information (for example, personal experience or opinions)?	no	
Does it quote numbers and other data accurately?	no	The actual amounts of CO_2 per person are not mentioned, except for one time.

Activity 2.14

Average global temperature (°C) and CO_2 levels (ppmv).

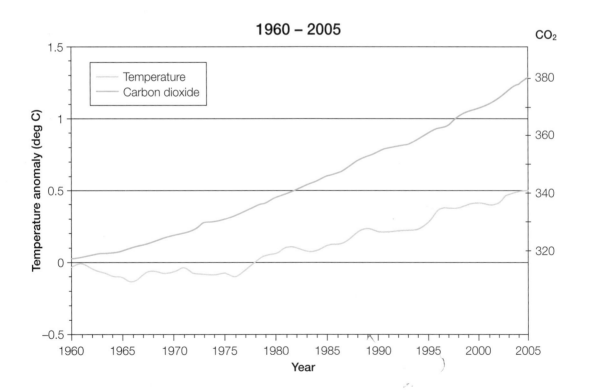

Unit 3: Coherence and Cohesion

Activity 3.1

1. There are no cohesive devices. Ideas are not connected. Compare it to this version:

    By 2011, x and y were equally popular, at 33 per cent, **but** they showed very different trends prior to this. y showed a steady upward trend, from 23 per cent in 2007 to 33 per cent, **whereas** x started as the most popular widget, at 70 per cent, **then** fell quite dramatically to 33 per cent.

2. This answer only uses one linking word: 'and'. There is little logical connection between ideas, making it sound like a list.

3. There are no paragraphs. The answer is just one block of text, so the reader can't see where one idea ends and another one starts. Even though the answer uses a variety of cohesive devices, it cannot get a good mark for coherence and cohesion, because there are no paragraphs.

Activity 3.2

Overview
both populations ↗ overall. Population of developing nations is much larger than industrialised nations. Industrialised nations ↗ slowly then predicted to plateau. Developing nations ↗ slowly then very rapidly.
Data discussion 1
Industrialised nations Small compared to developing nations. 1750 to 1900 gradual ↗ 1900 to 2000 a slightly faster ↗. 2000 to 2050 plateau.
Data discussion 2
Developing nations Larger population than industrialised nations Similar slow ↗1750 to 1900. 1900 to 1950 ↗getting faster. 1950 to 2050 ↗ rapidly.

(Note: This order would also be OK: 'data discussion 1: developing nations', then 'data discussion 2: industrialised nations'.)

Activity 3.3

Plan 1. Not good. It doesn't make a clear connection between the actions and their effect on the number of injuries.

Plan 2. Not good. The second paragraph is too long and contains too many different ideas. Remember, to get a good mark, each paragraph must have one 'main' idea.

Plan 3. Good. The information focuses on cause and effect. Paragraph 2 describes the problem and the first attempt to fix the problem, which didn't work. Paragraph 3 discusses the only action that reduced the number of injuries. Paragraph 4 discusses the final action, which had a bad effect.

Activity 3.4

cold oil rises to top of water	2
Hot: water and oil can mix. Cold: water and oil separate	0
steam and oil mixture cooled down	2
steam and oil rise to top	1
steam and oil go through cooling coil in cold water	2
water extracts oil then oil needs to come out of water	0
steam mixes with leaves	1
oil taken from top of tank. Water taken from bottom of tank	2

Activity 3.5

drying	oxidation	crushing
sun-drying oven-drying	part oxidation full oxidation	bruising rolling

Steaming does not fit a category.

Activity: Which tea uses which process?

	Green tea	Oolong tea	Black tea
drying	✓	✓	✓
steaming	✓		
crushing	✓	✓	✓
oxidation		✓	✓

1. Oolong tea and black tea.

2. Green tea.

Activity: Structure the answer

Overview 1, 3
Similar processes 4, 6, 7
Different process 2, 5

Activity 3.6

making a general statement	**summarising** **comparing things**
explaining what you mean	**showing cause and effect** **comparing things** **comparing time** **conceding something**
giving proof	**illustrating a point** **adding information** **showing cause and effect** **comparing things** **comparing time**

Activity 3.7

1. Overall, younger students were satisfied with their course, whereas most older students were unsatisfied with their course.

2. Although 40 per cent of waste is recycled, some materials, such as glass, are recycled more than others. Furthermore, some people recycle more than others. For instance, people in inner suburbs recycle more than people in other areas.

3. In 2007, the average household income fell. At this point the average household expenditure also dropped, but not by much.

4. <u>Despite</u> trying several actions, the company did not reduce the number of accidents over the period. <u>In fact</u>, they actually increased the accident rate with one action, <u>specifically</u>, replacing the safety classes with a training manual.

Activity 3.8

1. c

2. a

3. d

4. b

5. e

Activity 3.9

2. 75-year-olds, in other words, have a similar amount of contact with family and friends as 18–34-year-olds (around 95 per cent).

3. Men, on the other hand, have much less social contact by age 75 and over than at age 18–34.

4. Men, meanwhile, continue to show a decrease until age 45–54.

5. Men, in particular, show a sharp drop at this age.

6. Men, at this point, show a slight increase from 94 per cent to 96 per cent.

Activity 3.10

2. <u>A safety manager was appointed</u> in 1999, but **this** had no effect on the accident rate.

3. As <u>the steam</u> passes through the cooling coil, **it** cools down.

4. The chart shows <u>four recycling categories</u>. **These** are glass, paper, metal and plastic.

5. As the steam rises through <u>the leaves</u>, it mixes with **their** moisture and oil.

6. At the start of the period, <u>widgets</u> were the biggest seller, but by the end of the period **they** were the lowest-selling product.

Activity 3.11

2. The EU produced around 520 kg of waste per person, 20 per cent of which was recycled.

3. The diagram shows three processes for producing tea, two of which involve oxidation.

4. The boiler produces steam, the heat of which is controlled by a thermostat.

5. In 2012, the theme park had 10,000 visitors, half of whom were from Asia.

6. There are two stages, both of which involve water.

7. The company employs 320 women, 30 per cent of whom work part time.

8. The storage tank holds hot water, some of which goes to the hot taps in the kitchen and bathroom.

9. The graph shows global population growth, the rate of which is predicted to rise.

10. The graph compares two industries, both of which require on-the-job training.

Activity 3.12

2. The hot water passes around the house. After it has done so, it is cool and needs to be heated again.

3. The second chart shows car sales by colour. Surprisingly, the highest-selling one was white.

4. There were two periods when imports exceeded exports. This was so in 2007, and again in 2011.

5. The first chart shows the salaries of five different industries. The highest-paid ones were health care and legal services.

6. The satisfaction rate dropped in 1995 and 2000. It did so again in 2003, but only slightly.

Activity 3.13

1. H	2. I
3. E	4. F
5. J	6. A
7. B	8. D
9. G	10. C

Activity 3.14

1. At the beginning of the period, walking and taking the train were the most common ways to get to work. However, by the end of the period, these forms of transportation were the least common.

2. Around this time, social contact increased from 94 per cent to 96 per cent for men and from 95 per cent to 97 per cent for women. Due to the scale of the graph, these small increases look quite dramatic.

3. People aged 15 to 17 years old visited the cinema most frequently. Furthermore, teenagers also spent the most time in the cinema per visit.

4. The new swimming pool will have a larger café area and a larger gym area. These changes will make the pool attractive to a wider range of people.

5. Staff aged between 45 to 55 took the fewest holidays, perhaps because these older workers tended to have management positions.

Assessment checklist

Coherence and Cohesion	Yes / No	Example
Ideas are logically organised	yes	1: overview 2: women (from young to old) 3: men (from young to old) 4: overview
Writing is organised into paragraphs. Each paragraph has one main topic.	yes yes	There is a space between each paragraph. Each paragraph has one main topic (see previous box).
Uses a range of cohesive devices: • reference • substitution • linking words.	yes yes yes	They (women 55 to 64 years old) Their (men's) it (women's social contact) ones did so these oldest groups the percentage of whom this (97 per cent) In general however after that Starting the paragraphs with 'first' (women) and 'second' (men) is not good. There isn't actually any sequence to the data: men and women are doing things at the same time.

Overall, the coherence and cohesion of this Task 1 response are good.

Unit 4: Lexical Resource

Activity 4.1

2. a

3. c

4. a

5. c

6. b

Activity 4.2

2. fell/dropped/decreased/declined dramatically/rapidly/sharply/steeply

3. rose/grew/increased moderately/steadily

4. rose/grew/increased dramatically/rapidly/sharply/steeply

5. fell/dropped/decreased/declined slightly/slowly/gradually

6. fell/dropped/decreased/declined moderately/steadily

Activity 4.3

2. a slight/slow/gradual increase/rise/growth.

3. a slight/slow/gradual decrease/fall/drop/decline in

4. a slight/slow/gradual increase/rise/growth

5. a moderate/steady increase/rise/growth in

6. a moderate/steady increase/rise/growth

Activity 4.4

3. the smallest

4. the most; less popular/common/widespread/prevalent

5. the least; the most popular/common/widespread/prevalent

6. The largest

7. the least popular/common/widespread/prevalent

Activity 4.5

1. T   **2.** F

3. T   **4.** F

5. T   **6.** T

7. T

Activity 4.6

2. much/considerably/far/significantly bigger

3. much/considerably/far/significantly smaller

4. slightly/somewhat nearer

5. much/considerably/far/significantly longer

6. slightly/somewhat smaller

Review activity

3. SUVs are not <u>as economical</u> as compact cars.

4. The new model will cost <u>as much as</u> the old model.

5. Computers are <u>rather</u> expensive in China.

6. China produces [<u>much/considerably/far/significantly</u>] more CO_2 than Russia

7. The new kindergarten will be <u>rather</u> close to a dangerous road.

Activity 4.7

1. reached a plateau, levelled off, flattened out

2. showed some fluctuation

3. hit the lowest point

4. remain static/stable/constant

5. showed an upward trend

Activity 4.8

1. remains stable/static/constant

2. reaching a plateau, levelling off, flattening out

3. remain stable/static/constant

4. reaching a peak, hitting the highest point

Activity 4.9

2. boom

3. dip

4. plunged

5. surge

Activity 4.10

2. white

3. four

4. Red

5. a fifth; a twentieth

6. half; twice

Activity 4.11

Region	Widgets (million)
Asia	180
Europe	240
North America	120
South America	40
Africa	90
Oceania	60

Activity 4.12

2. three times as much waste as

3. twice as high as; four times as high as

4. a third as much waste as

Activity 4.13

1. tripled

2. halved

3. doubled

4. tripled

Activity 4.14

1. INCREASE: improve, rise, grow, show an upward trend

2. DECREASE: drop, fall, decline, show a downward trend

3. BIG: large, significant, sizeable, great, vast

4. SMALL: insignificant, little, tiny, slight

Activity 4.15

The following verbs can be used here: passes, is conducted, travels, flows, progresses, moves, courses, runs, proceeds, is pumped. The answer below is only one possibility.

This diagram shows a house's central heating system. It shows that cold water **goes** into a tank, and then **flows** into a boiler and then **travels** through pipes to radiators and taps.

Cold water **is conducted** into the house and **is pumped** into a water storage tank at the top of the house. Then it **progresses** to the boiler, at the bottom of the house. This boiler, which can use gas or oil, heats the water. Some of the hot water **moves** to a storage tank and from here it can **pass** to taps to provide the hot water for the house. Also some cold water **proceeds** from the tank to the taps.

Other hot water **courses** around the house by being pumped through pipes and **flows** into radiators in different rooms. The water **moves** through hot water radiators in small tubes, so the radiators get hot and this heats the house.

After **passing** through the pipes and radiators the water is cold, so it **returns** to the boiler to be heated again and then **travels** around the house again

Activity 4.16

1. roughly/around/about
2. comparable / almost the same
3. proportion/share
4. greatest / most significant
5. rise/growth

Activity 4.17

1. economical > [economic]
2. increase of > [increase in]
3. At first > ['first']. 'At first' means 'used to, but not any more'.
4. twice many > [twice as many]
5. Despite > ['Although']. 'Despite' is used with a noun phrase: 'Despite the decrease in the proportion of music sales …'.
6. Third world nations … first world nations > [It is more common to say 'developing' and 'developed/industrialised'.]
7. Every city > [For small numbers, use 'each'.]
8. everyday > ['every day']. 'Everyday' means 'normal' or 'boring'.

Activity 4.18

Lexical Resource	Yes/No	
Does it use a wide variety of vocabulary, including phrasal verbs, academic words, and collocations?	no	Make it better by: 1. Replacing a repeated word with a synonym (2 words) 2. Replacing a normal word with a useful phrase or idiom (2 words)
Are most words spelled correctly? *Not sure? Check by typing the answer on your computer and then using the spellcheck function.*	yes	but there are some spelling mistakes. Make it better by: 3. correcting the spelling (4 words)

1. Popular > prominent, widespread, prevalent

   Increased > grew, rose

2. became very less very quickly > plummeted, dove, plunged

   increased a lot > surged, skyrocketed, boomed

3. cannals > canals

   decerasing > decreasing

   dramaticaly > dramatically

   infomation > information

Unit 5: Grammatical Range and Accuracy

Activity 5.1

1. In 1990, exports <u>dropped</u> dramatically.

2. The graphs <u>compare</u> the increase in global temperatures and CO_2 production from 1910 to 2010.

3. OK

4. The graph shows that people <u>spent</u> more money on household goods in 1980 than in 2000.

5. OK

Activity 5.2

1. The world population <u>has risen</u> dramatically since 1900, and is predicted to keep rising. [The 'rise' hasn't finished yet.]

2. The consumption of sugar <u>increased</u> between 1950 and 1960. [The 'increase' started and finished in the past.]

3. OK

4. OK

5. The graph <u>shows</u> that, before 1950, wages were the main factor affecting production costs. [The graph is an unchanging fact.]

Activity 5.3

1. From 2000 to 2010 [past simple: the time period finishes in the past].

2. Between 2030 and 2040 [future simple: the time period starts and finishes in the future].

3. The temperature of boiling water [present simple: it is always true in the past, present and future].

4. An event in the year 1066 [past simple: it finished in the past].

5. Introducing a graph and pie chart that show data from 1950 to 2050 [present simple: the diagrams are unchanging].

Activity 5.4

1. Since 1997, the country <u>has had</u> a severe-weather warning system.

2. The country <u>has experienced</u> 15 severe-weather events this century.

3. There <u>have been</u> fewer weather-related deaths since the warning system was introduced.

4. So far, only 20 people <u>have died</u>, compared to 250 in the same time period last century.

5. The severe-weather warning system seems to <u>have succeeded</u>.

Activity 5.5

2. Within 40 years, the Amazon rainforest will have disappeared.

3. In 10 years, Startup.com will have crushed Dinosaur.com.

4. In 5 years' time, the company will have sold all its assets and gone bankrupt.

5. By 2040, all Japanese car manufacturers will have moved offshore and all the car factories in Japan will have closed.

6. By 2053 country A's oil reserves will have run out.

Activity 5.6

2. A safety manager was appointed after the injury rate had tripled.

3. By 1992, the injury rate had not decreased.

4. Although the safety classes had halved the injury rate, they were replaced by a safety manual in 1995.

5. It seems the safety classes were very successful. However, in 1993 the injury rate was still higher than it had been in 1998-99 before introducing the new machines.

Activity 5.7

1. The data show that by 2035, the proportion of manufacturing companies based offshore will have reached 95 per cent.

2. By 1950, Unifood's income from milk products had exceeded all other income.

3. From 1980 to 2010, trains experienced a drop in popularity, but in this decade they have become popular again.

4. Book sales boomed in 1960 and again in 1980. However, by 1990 they had dropped back down to 1950 levels.

5. The conservative estimate is that, by 2020, fish stocks will have been depleted by 50 per cent.

Activity 5.8

2. Average temperatures are predicted to rise by 5°C.

3. Twice as many speeding drivers were caught with the new camera.

4. More noise-related complaints were made at weekends.

5. A new shop will be built on the east side of the museum.

6. 19,232 new species were discovered in 2011.

Activity 5.9

2. The new airlines seem to have caused a drop in airfares.

3. There appears to be a connection between the literacy rate and economic development.

4. The minimum wage doesn't seem to be keeping up with the cost of living.

5. The process <u>appears to involve</u> some inefficiency.

6. Lowering the cost of the product <u>doesn't appear to</u> improve profits.

Activity 5.10

2. Before flowing into the settling tank, the steam is cooled down in the cooling coil

3. After being used to cool down the steam, the water is pumped out of the top of the cooling coil tank.

4. After losing its heat in the coil, the steam becomes water

5. Before being bottled, the oil is left to separate from the water in the settling tank.

6. Before being polished, the apples are waxed.

Activity 5.11

2. Having converted the basement to an underground carpark, the hotel now has room for more cars.

3. Having been oxidised, the leaves are brown.

4. Having been sun dried, the leaves still contain moisture.

5. Having delivered its parcels, the truck is empty.

6. Having washed the potatoes, the water is dirty.

Activity 5.12

2. As the van is returning to the store, it collects returned items.

3. As the super-hot steam is pushing the piston, the cooled steam is released through a valve at the top.

4. The fruit is sprayed with wax and polished as it rolls along the conveyor belt.

5. The cookies are stamped with a picture as they are hardening.

6. As the leaves are drying in the sun, they oxidise.

Activity 5.13

2. The first and last stages of the process are the same for all three types of tea. They are all sun dried and oven dried.

3. The graph compares the amount of social contact that men and women have at different ages. It seems that older women generally have more contact with their family and friends than older men.

4. Men of all ages generally participate in more sport than women. The only age when this is not true is 45 to 55.

5. The survey results show that people are less likely to worry about debts as they get older. This could be because they get better at paying bills on time.

6. Company A sold more widgets than gadgets between 2000 and 2005. Company B's sales were the complete opposite of this.

Activity 5.14

1. The diagram shows that three different processes can make one ingredient, tea leaves, into three different products.

2. Green tea, oolong tea and black tea are all produced by slightly different processes.

3. In Europe, where recycling taxes were highest, about 50 per cent of people recycled often.

4. International exports of raw materials increased steadily from 1995 to 2005, but this gain was lost when exports plummeted between 2005 and 2010.

5. On the other hand, international exports of manufactured materials showed no change over the period.

Activity 5.15

The diagram shows that slightly different processes can make three different kinds of tea from the same raw ingredient, tea leaves. The common stages in the process, sun-drying and oven-drying, are the first and last steps. It is the steps in the middle that make the final products different.

Green tea is unlike the other types of tea. While oolong tea and black tea are oxidised, green tea isn't. The leaves are simply sun dried, steamed, rolled and then oven dried.

Meanwhile, black tea and oolong tea are sun dried and then squashed in some way. Oolong tea is bruised and black tea is rolled. These two teas are also different in how much oxidation they get, with part oxidation for oolong tea and full oxidation for black tea. After the oxidation, both types of tea are oven dried. As noted earlier, this step is the same for all types of tea.

Activity 5.16

1. OK

2. The diagram shows a machine <u>for manufacturing</u> chocolate biscuits.

3. OK

4. From about 1970, <u>the popularity of books</u> started to decrease.

5. Every year showed a dip in profits around January to February.

Activity 5.17

Grammatical Range and Accuracy	Yes/ no	Example
Does it use a variety of grammatical structures?	no	Most structures are present simple, except one future simple ('*it will reach*'), and one past simple ('*but in 2010, something happened*').
Does it use 'seem' or 'appear'?	no	
Does it use a passive structure?	no	
Does it use the future perfect?	no	
Does it use the past perfect?	no	
Does it use any participle structures?	no	
Are grammar and punctuation mostly correct?	yes	There are only a few errors ('*activity is change*' / '*in a future*').

The answer only uses simple sentences, so it would not get a good mark.

Unit 6: Practice questions

Activity 6.1

Feature		Example
Task Achievement (Unit 2)		
Does it give an overview of main patterns?	no	The first sentence just copies what is said on the question paper. It is not an overview. The second sentence gives a good overview of one chart, but there is no overview of the other chart.
		It doesn't say anything that compares the two charts with each other. In the final paragraph, there are just a lot of numbers. There is no summary or description.
Does it talk about the most important details?	yes	
Does it have any irrelevant information (for example, personal experience or opinions)?	no	
Does it quote numbers and other data accurately?	yes	

Coherence and Cohesion (Unit 3)		
Is it well organised? It is easy to understand how one idea flows to the next one?	yes yes	The answer describes one chart, then the other, and describes them from left to right. This is easy to follow
Does it use a variety of linking words and linking structures?	yes	
Lexical Resource (Unit 4)		
Does it use a wide variety of vocabulary, including phrasal verbs, academic words, and collocations?	yes	
Are most words spelled correctly?	**no**	studing, increses, carreer, intrest
Grammatical Range and Accuracy (Unit 5)		
Does it use a variety of grammatical structures?	yes	For example: … the first graph also shows that study stemming from intrest increases with age. This percentage gradually declines by 10–20 per cent every decade.
Are grammar and punctuation mostly correct?	yes	

This is the answer after these points have been corrected:

The two graphs show that people study for different reasons at different ages, and that employers are most likely to support younger workers for their study.

The first graph shows that there is a gradual decrease in study for career reasons with age. Nearly 80 per cent of students under 26 years study for their career. This percentage gradually declines by 10–20 per cent every decade. Only 40 per cent of 40–49-year-olds and 18 per cent of over-49-year-olds study for career reasons in late adulthood. Conversely, the first graph also shows that study stemming from interest increases with age. There are only 10 per cent of under-26-year-olds study out of interest. The percentage increases slowly till the beginning of the fourth decade, and increases dramatically in late adulthood. Nearly same number of 40–49-year-olds study for career and interest. However 70 per cent of over-49-year-olds study for interest in comparison to 18 per cent study for career reasons in that age group.

The second graph shows that employer support is approximately 60 per cent for the under-26-year-old students. It drops rapidly to 32 per cent up to the third decade of life, and then increases in late adulthood up to about 38 per cent for 40- to 49-year-old students and then about 44 per cent for over-49-year-old students.

Part 3: Academic Writing Task 2

Unit 2: Analysing the Task

Activity 2.1

a. opinion

b. argument

c. problem-solving

d. opinion

e. problem-solving

f. argument

Activity 2.2

a. traffic congestion, growing problem

b. what are causes, what measures to reduce

c. You need to include some of the causes and some of the ways to reduce the problems of traffic congestion, plus give your own opinion of the problem.

Unit 3: Brainstorming Ideas

Activity 3.1

a. Listing

Causes of childhood obesity

– too much fast food

– too much time playing computer games

– not enough sport/exercise

Ways to reduce childhood obesity

– parents cook meals, not buy takeaway

– limit time on computer

– more sport at and after school

b.   Mind mapping

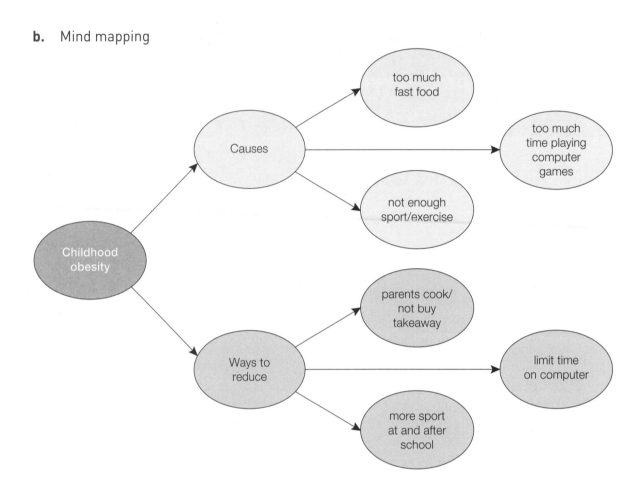

c.   Tabling

Causes	Ways to reduce
– *too much fast food* – *too much time playing computer games* – *not enough sport/exercise*	– *parents cook meals, not buy takeaway* – *limit time on computer* – *more sport at and after school*

Unit 4: Planning the Essay

Activity 4.1

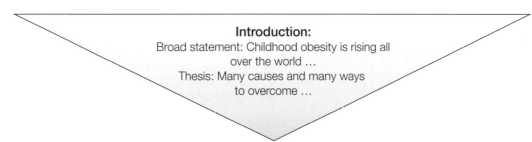

Introduction:
Broad statement: Childhood obesity is rising all
over the world …
Thesis: Many causes and many ways
to overcome …

Body paragraph 1: Causes: too much fast food, too much time playing computer games,
not enough sport/exercise.
Example: …

Body paragraph 2: Ways to reduce: parents cook meals not buy takeaway, limit time on
computers, more sport at and after school.
Example: …

Conclusion: Restate plus my opinion: big problem but can be overcome if parents
take action.

Unit 5: Writing the Essay

Activity 5.1

The correct order is sentence b, sentence c, sentence a.

Over the last twenty years, computers have become an important part of our lives and many people use a computer to communicate with others. This has meant that the way in which we communicate has changed dramatically. <u>There are both positive and negative changes, however, the majority of these changes have negatively affected the way people communicate today.</u>

Activity 5.2

a. There are many causes of this congestion; however, traffic problems can be reduced if the government introduces some measures to help.

b. Mobile phone use comes with both benefits and costs, and in my opinion the benefits far outweigh the costs for a variety of reasons.

c. Challenges exist for an individual who works from home and this may cause problems in society.

Activity 5.3

As nations become wealthier, starvation or hunger is less common and new challenges are created. Childhood obesity is one such challenge and it has started to become a problem all over the world, particularly in developed countries. There are many causes of obesity in children; however, with action we have the ability to reduce the incidence of this childhood problem.

Activity 5.4

i.   Topic sentences – e, h, i

ii.   Supporting sentences – b, c, g

iii. Examples – a, d, f

Research into space exploration is very expensive. By spending millions of dollars on space research, governments are not using extra funds to help improve the lives of their citizens. In Australia, for example, some people in remote areas still have limited access to medical facilities, and money should be spent on this rather than on space exploration.

Although many people think that it is better to work at home rather than go to an office, it can be quite lonely. It is very social at an office. For example, many companies have staff parties and other activities for people to talk and make friends.

Firstly, in single-sex schools, girls can focus solely on their academic tasks without being distracted by boys. This is particularly important in senior years when students are preparing for university entrance. Girls should be working on their studies rather than deciding which boy they like or whom they want to date, for instance.

Activity 5.5

Obesity in children may be caused by several factors, the most obvious being too much fast food. Nowadays, parents often work long hours and are too busy to cook so they buy their children takeaway food. This food is much higher in fat than home-cooked meals and as a result youngsters put on weight. Another cause of childhood obesity is that children are spending more time on computers and less time doing exercise than in the past. Children used to come home from school and play outside; however, since computers have become commonplace, they prefer to play computer games.

There are many ways to reduce the rate of childhood obesity. Firstly, parents should cook more meals for their children, and if they have to eat at McDonalds, for example, they could choose the healthier meals that are now on the menu. In addition, parents need to limit the time that children are allowed to play on computers and they should enrol their children in after-school sports or go together to a park and exercise.

Activity 5.6

The writer has emphasised a different opinion by using 'admittedly' at the beginning of the paragraph and also used 'however' to argue their own point.

Activity 5.7

Overall, childhood obesity is a growing problem in today's busy world, and although the causes are many, I feel that this issue is easily overcome. Parents need to help their children eat better and exercise more.

Activity 5.8

It is agreed that our environmental problems need to be solved; however, there is argument over who should solve them. Some people feel that only the government should be responsible for finding solutions to these issues, but the problems that exist are so large and, therefore, overcoming them requires joint efforts from government, as well as business and individuals.

Solving environmental problems is expensive and the financial burden on governments alone is too high. As businesses are often responsible for causing some of the environmental problems, they should help with the cost of solving the problems. This could be done by contributing funds or by implementing new systems to minimize further pollution.

A second reason that solving our environmental problems requires joint contribution is that action and effort are needed. The government can spend money on campaigns or introduce taxes; however, slowing or stopping the problems requires effort from all. If businesses do not stop polluting and individuals do not minimize their waste, no advertising campaign will be effective.

Admittedly, the government does have the power to make an enormous impact on the environment and without government intervention change would probably not happen. The introduction of the carbon tax in Australia is an example of government action helping solve environmental problems. However, without all parties contributing this change would not be effective.

In conclusion, the government does need to be the leader in solving our environmental problems, but it needs the financial assistance and the efforts of businesses and individuals to make any long-term, effective change to the problems that exist.

Activity 5.9

1. **a** Firstly
   b Moreover/Furthermore/Secondly
   c Consequently/As a result
2. On the other hand, immunisations themselves have been known to have side effects that may cause other health problems. Furthermore, immunisations are not always completely able to prevent diseases spreading throughout the community, for example, children are commonly given chicken pox vaccinations when young, but they may still catch the disease.

Unit 6: Lexical Resource

Activity 6.1

a. benefits

b. continual use of

c. abundant

d. elderly, therefore, continue

e. forcing (to), rebel, parents.

Activity 6.2

Informal	Academic
I think	In my opinion
a lot	dramatically
we don't chat	people do not talk
as we used to	in the past
2 or 3	two or three
I reckon it's not	this is not
it's	it is
cos	as
can't	cannot

Activity 6.3

a.

Paragraph 1	Paragraph 2
Mobile phones are very **useful** and a convenient way to contact **friends**. Also, mobile phones have become a lot cheaper in recent years. For example, some mobile phones have unlimited calls for $40 a month.	**Many men** and **women have** mobiles and **they think their phone** is good. **They can't sleep because phone** is fun to **check** email.

b. government, physical, pollution, spacious, connection, debatable, measure, believe, significant, abstract, frequent, demonstrate, skillful/skilful, appropriate, annual, argument

Unit 7: Grammatical Range and Accuracy

Activity 7.1

Secondly, the education in single-sex schools **helps** students **get** better results for their university entrance. Students can **concentrate** on the examination and not **worry** about **playing** with other boys and girls. **An** example of this **was in/at** my school. My friend always **thought** about **the** opinions of girls and he **did not study** hard then he **failed the** examination. After that he **studied** hard and **got** better results.

Activity 7.2

a. There are both positive and negative changes; **however**, the majority of these changes have negatively affected the way people communicate today.

b. **Because** we do not yet know the long-term effects of mobile phone use, the use of phones should be limited.

c. Childhood obesity is a problem **that** is difficult to solve **because** it affects both children and their parents. (Note: two dependent clauses)

d. **Even though** some languages are already dead, young people should be forced to learn some less common languages to keep them alive.

Activity 7.3

Nowadays, there is much controversy over regulating immunisations for children. Some people believe that vaccinations should be compulsory for all children, while others think that it should be the choice of parents. I believe that, whilst immunisations have many benefits, parents should be allowed to choose for themselves if they would like to give these vaccinations to their children.

On the one hand, vaccinations should be mandatory for all children as they help to prevent the spread of diseases and stop children from dying. Furthermore, there are many viruses that can modify very quickly in different forms. For this reason it is vitally important to give injections in childhood to strengthen children's immune systems. For example, many children in Africa die from diseases such as smallpox, although this could be avoided if children were vaccinated.

On the other hand, there is not enough knowledge and research about the side effects of some vaccines. Moreover, pharmaceutical companies are usually responsible for research but they also sell the vaccinations. This may be a conflict of interest as the pharmaceutical companies could change the research results to hide possible problems so that they could sell more medicines.

In conclusion, I am sure that it is important to immunise our children; however, I believe that parents should have a choice of whether or not to vaccinate their children as the consequences could be dangerous.

Activity 7.4

1. I agree with this point of view because childhood diseases can kill many children.

2. Although some people may agree that immunisations should be compulsory, I feel that parents should be allowed to decide what is best for their child.

3. Until immunisations are made compulsory, many children may die from contagious diseases that could be easily prevented.

4. In conclusion, I am certain that immunisations should be compulsory for all children.

Activity 7.5

Young people are an easy target for fast-food companies so parents have to check the quality of the food that their children are eating. Unfortunately, it is not easy to resist an advertising campaign. Moreover, children like toys and the atmosphere of fast-food restaurants is often fun and friendly. This gives a false idea about the quality of the food that the fast-food companies serve.

Unit 8: Editing

Activity 8.1

Task Response

Have you addressed the task?

Yes – this essay answers the question by discussing the reasons why governments should fund art galleries and museums; however, there is not a lot written about the other side of the argument (only in the conclusion). To improve this essay, add more information about the opposing argument. To do this quickly, whilst editing, add in a short, one- or two-sentence opposing body paragraph. Remember that it must be quick if you are making changes in the editing phase of the process – you should be aiming to spend only 3–4 minutes editing your work.

Have you supported your ideas?

Yes – there are two main arguments given and each is supported. For example, in the first body paragraph, the argument is supported by using an example of museum attendance in Russia.

Have you given your opinion?

Yes – with the statement 'I believe that goverments should invest in museums and galleries'. This opinion is reiterated in the conclusion.

Coherence and Cohesion

Have you used an Introduction/Body Paragraph/Conclusion structure?

Yes – we can see that this essay has an introduction that starts with a broad, general statement about the topic and then narrows down to the thesis statement, which also gives the writer's opinion. There are two body paragraphs that contain the main arguments and support, followed by a conclusion that restates the main opinion.

Have you used topic sentences for each paragraph?

Yes – each body paragraph starts with a topic sentence that contains the main idea for that paragraph.

Have you used linking words?

Yes – there are quite a few linking words and phrases used: the first and the most important reason / moreover / for example / furthermore / in conclusion / however.

Activity 8.2

Lexical Resource

Have you used a variety of academic vocabulary?

Yes – there is a good variety of academic vocabulary used in this essay, such as: cultural heritage, funding, unaffordable. However, the words 'museums and art galleries' are used quite a lot. In the conclusion, the use of 'public institutions' as a synonym for 'museums and art galleries' is well used.

The use of 'reasonable' in the first body paragraph is quite unusual but not wrong – if you have enough editing time, try to think of a better word. Also, the use of 'art organisations' in the same paragraph is awkward.

Is your spelling correct?

No – there are several spelling errors in this essay. The words 'government' and 'historical/ history' are spelt incorrectly each time they are used. It is important to check and correct any spelling errors whilst editing.

Grammatical Range and Accuracy

Have you used accurate grammar?

No – although the grammar is quite accurate, there are several basic errors, such as the use of 'is funded' rather than 'are funded' and 'have entertainment purpose' rather than 'have an entertainment purpose'. As these are basic errors, it is likely that they are errors the writer commonly makes and they should be corrected during editing time.

Have you used complex sentence structures?

Yes – there are no simple sentences used in this essay.

Is your punctuation correct?

Yes – there are no obvious errors with punctuation.

Unit 10: Practice Tests

Sample answer for Practice Test 1

The view that fast food companies have not to develop marketing strategy by toys to add sympathy of young people is gaining popularity. I agree this point of view because of damages for children to develop addiction to unhealthy alimentation.

Young people is an easy target for fast food company so parents have to check quality of the food. Unfortunately the pressure is too important and it is not easy to resist to advertisement campaign. Fore, children like toys and associated pleasure to play with toys, with a positive image of fast food, and atmosphere is fun and friendly and gives a false idea about the quality of service of the fast food campaign.

Fast food company produce a low level of quality for food. Too much fast food and sugar can be produce disease for young people and can be provoke addiction. The danger is big. We have to promote for young people a balance life because of the negative effect of fat food for young children.

On other hand toys can open the mind for young people and it is good for children to develop skill in playing with other children.

In my point of view, we have to banned marketing strategy of Fast Food Company when they manipulate children by toys. Young public has need to be protected to have an healthy life later.

(227 words)

Feedback

Task Response

This writer has addressed the task by discussing ideas that are related to the question. However, the main ideas become unclear at times and do need to be expanded. For example, the opposing argument (body paragraph 3) is only one sentence and should be further expanded. If this were a full paragraph the word count could have been reached. This sample answer is only 227 words and needs to be at least 250 words.

Coherence and Cohesion

The writer has a very good essay structure. The essay follows the pattern of:

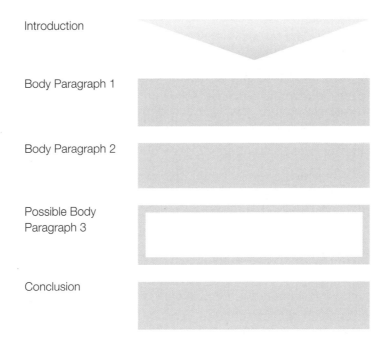

Introduction

Body Paragraph 1

Body Paragraph 2

Possible Body Paragraph 3

Conclusion

The introduction has a thesis statement containing the main idea of the essay, i.e. that the writer agrees with the point of view that fast-food companies should not be allowed to give away free toys with their food. Each body paragraph begins with a topic sentence, which is then supported, except in the opposing paragraph.

Although the writer has used some cohesive devices/linking words (e.g. *unfortunately*, *in my point of view*), there are some incorrect linking words (*fore*, *on other hand*) that could bring the band score down. Body paragraph 2 does not have any linking words.

Lexical Resource

The vocabulary used in this sample is good. There is a good variety of academic vocabulary, e.g. *manipulate*, *atmosphere*, *associated pleasure*. The writer has also used collocations and idioms well, e.g. *develop addiction*, *gaining popularity*, *open the mind*, *not easy to resist*. However, occasionally the wrong word is used (e.g. *sympathy*, *alimentation*).

Grammatical Range and Accuracy

There are a lot of complex sentences attempted in this essay; however, most of these sentences contain grammar errors. Also, the writer has some problems with verb choice, e.g. *'can be produce'*, *'can be provoke'*, *'have to banned'*, *'has need to be'*. Although there are a lot of errors in grammar, the writer does try to use higher-level sentence structures and communication is only slightly affected. The punctuation is accurate.

Overall, this essay would NOT reach a GOOD band score as it is under length and the grammar is not accurate enough.

Sample answer for Practice Test 2

Nowadays, learning a foreign language is a very popular phenomenon. The programmes of many school have a subject such as a foreign language. Learning a foreign language at school or university should be forced. I agree with this statement so I am going to tell my reasons.

First of all, learning a foreign language is much easier in young ages because the young brain can pick up every information much faster and without any problems. As we know an English language is the most popular language in the world as well as the most common, so people who learned this language can travel and work in most parts of our beautiful world. There are not dissadvantages to argue this point.

The second point is learning another language is a really important process of developing children's brain because they can improve their memory and it is a good skill to know how to think in a different language. For example, to speak in a foreign language fluently people have to think as a person who has this language as a native.

Finally, people (such as students) should be forced to learn a foreign language because they are generally very lazy. This situation is absolutely normal in a majority of people.

To sum up, learning a foreign language is a very difficult process so that is why teachers should force students especially at school to learn a different language. I think people who learned a foreign language in young ages make their life much easier in future.

(255 words)

Feedback

Task Response

The word count and format are both fine, the ideas are well developed and supported and the position of the writer is clear. However, unfortunately, this sample is off-topic. The writer has written about learning foreign languages at school or university rather than writing about lesser-known languages that need to be learnt to stop them from disappearing. If this was on the right topic, the writer could have achieved a GOOD band score; however, writing off-topic is penalised.

Coherence and Cohesion

Once again, this sample displays a clear structure with very good use of topic sentences and supporting ideas in each of the body paragraphs. The thesis statement is clear and acts as a signpost for the rest of the essay. The conclusion is good.

The writer uses linking words all the way through their essay, for example, *first of all, the second point, finally, to sum up*. Although there are not a lot of linking words within the paragraphs, the examples used are sufficient for a good band score.

Lexical Resource

This writer uses an adequate range of vocabulary throughout the essay. The language used is not highly sophisticated; however, it is suitable to express the ideas well. There is only one spelling error (*dissadvantages*), which has no impact at all on the communicative aspect of this essay.

Some errors with word choice are displayed, e.g. the use of *young ages* instead of *youth*, and the phrase *'has this language as a native'* is confusing to the reader.

Grammatical Range and Accuracy

The grammar in this sample essay is reasonably accurate, particularly in the simpler sentence structures. However, the range of sentence structures used is not highly sophisticated. Some minor grammar errors, such as articles (*an English language, a majority of people*) and tenses (*who learned*) exist. Some punctuation is missing. Overall, though, the grammar errors do not affect communication in this essay.

Overall this essay would NOT reach a GOOD band score as it is off-topic.

Sample answer for Practice Test 3

For the past decade, parents, students and psychologists have clashed over the issue where should children be educated in single-sex schools or in the same schools. I believe that education in single-sex schools is more efficient for boys and girls for two reasons.

First, boys and girls have the big difference in mental development. Some research shows that a girl's brain is different from a boy's brain. If you accept that premise, coeducation probably will not work satisfactorily for every child. For example, I studied with female and male and I remember that in primary school girls could perceive information more easily than boys; however, in high school boys was definitely more successful. Moreover, coeducation does have the advantage of being politically acceptable at the same time it has not anything with improvement of academic performance.

The second reason to support the education in single-sex schools is that it helps students to achieve good results and focus on study. It is fact that boys feel more comfortable and self-confident in single-sex schools, because they do not need to show off and worry about what the girls might think. For instance, it was really hard to concentrate on study in my class, because I always thought about opinions of others. Thus, male and female become more competitive in a single-sex setting.

In conclusion, children become more successful to be educated in separate classes, because it helps them break down gender stereotypes. Moreover, single-sex education is a good way to encourage children to be enthusiastic, to be curious and self-confident.

(263 words)

Feedback

Task Response

The writer has responded very well to this task. The essay presents the writer's position clearly and extends and supports the main ideas. However, the task requires both views to be discussed and this writer needs to extend their discussion on the opposing view. The word count is fine.

Coherence and Cohesion

The structure of this essay is good – it is logically organised and follows the standard layout of an essay with a strong thesis statement at the end of the Introduction, topic sentences followed by supporting statements and examples in each Body Paragraph, and a solid Conclusion, which gives the writer's opinion.

The writer has used a variety of linking words well, for example, *moreover*, *for instance*, *thus*, *in conclusion*.

Lexical Resource

The use of academic vocabulary in this essay is both varied and accurate. Some examples of high-level vocabulary include *psychologists*, *coeducation*, *academic performance*, *gender stereotypes, curious*. This writer has also used some less common phrases such as *'have clashed over'*, *'if you accept that premise'*, *'break down gender stereotypes'*. The use of *'it has not anything'* in the first Body Paragraph is confusing due to a wrong word choice; however, this seems to be the only problem with word choice. There are no spelling errors.

Grammatical Range and Accuracy

This essay has a variety of complex sentences and many of these have no errors. However, there are some errors, mostly with basic grammar items such as articles (*the education*) and singular/plural use (*female and male*). The grammar errors do not interfere with meaning in this essay and overall it displays a good use of grammar.

Overall this essay would achieve a GOOD band score and is very well written.

Sample answer for Practice Test 4

In today's busy world, the majority of people tend to work long hours, which can leave very little time to spend with friends and family or to pursue hobbies. Some people feel that making money and chasing career goals is more important than having sufficient leisure time; however, I feel that both work and leisure should be of equal value.

Work is of importance in our lives for two reasons: firstly, and most obviously, we need to work to earn an income, and secondly, work provides people with a sense of purpose. Earning an income is the main reason most people go to work, and as we all need money to eat, live and play, this does make work seem the higher priority. Furthermore, without a reason to get out of bed everyday, we can feel somewhat lost and goalless, which in turn can lead to emotional problems.

However, leisure is also of value in our lives. It is essential to have time to rest and recuperate from the stresses of work – this helps keep us mentally and physically healthy. Having free time to pursue hobbies or interests and to relax, laugh and play with our family and friends also gives our life some meaning. Without this, we would not be well-balanced people.

Overall, there is no doubt that work is important and without it we could not actually afford to undertake leisure activities, however, in my opinion, a balance between both work and leisure makes for a more contented and meaningful life.

(253 words)

Feedback

Task Response

This sample fully answers the question given in this task in that the writer has discussed both aspects (work and leisure) and given their opinion. The ideas presented are extended and supported.

Coherence and Cohesion

This sample flows well and the writer has successfully managed all aspects of coherence. The paragraphing is good and the essay is organised. There is an overuse of the linking word 'however' – it would be better with some synonyms to give some variety to the cohesive devices.

Lexical Resource

The vocabulary used in this essay is accurate and there are no spelling errors. There is a high level of academic vocabulary used and it is used well. Some phrases are a little informal, such as *'chasing career goals'* and *'get out of bed'*.

Grammatical Range and Accuracy

The grammar is accurate and a full range of structures typical of a native speaker are used.

Overall this essay would achieve an EXCELLENT band score and is extremely well written with no grammar errors.

READING ANSWER SHEET

1	
2	
3	
4	
5	
6	
7	
8	
9	
10	
11	
12	
13	
14	
15	
16	
17	
18	
19	
20	

21	
22	
23	
24	
25	
26	
27	
28	
29	
30	
31	
32	
33	
34	
35	
36	
37	
38	
39	
40	

Academic Writing Task 1 Self-study Checklist

Feature		Example
Task Achievement (Unit 2)		
Does it give an overview of main patterns?		
Does it talk about the most important details?		
Does it have any irrelevant information (for example, personal experience or opinions)?		
Does it quote numbers and other data accurately?		
Coherence and Cohesion (Unit 3)		
Is it well organised?		
It is easy to understand how one idea flows to the next one?		
Does it use a variety of linking words and linking structures?		
Lexical Resource (Unit 4)		
Does it use a wide variety of vocabulary, including phrasal verbs, academic words, and collocations?		
Are most words spelled correctly?		
Grammatical Range and Accuracy (Unit 5)		
Does it use a variety of grammatical structures?		
Are grammar and punctuation mostly correct?		

This page may be photocopied.

Editing Checklist for Task 2

1 Read the essay through the first time and check:

Task Response

Have you addressed the task?

Have you supported your ideas?

Have you given your opinion?

Coherence and Cohesion

Have you used an Introduction/Body Paragraphs/Conclusion structure?

Have you used topic sentences for each paragraph?

Have you used linking words?

2 Read the essay through again and check:

Lexical Resource

Have you used a variety of academic vocabulary?

Is your spelling correct?

Grammatical Range and Accuracy

Have you used accurate grammar?

Have you used complex sentence structures?

Is your punctuation correct?

ACKNOWLEDGMENTS

Louisa would like to dedicate her contribution to this book to her sisters Muriel and Naomi.

All the authors would like to thank Michael James of IDP for facilitating contact and providing meeting venues and all the IELTS centre staff at the centres we work at: IDP, UWA and PIBT as well as students and colleagues who have provided written and spoken samples and have trialled materials.